THE WORLDS OF
THE EARLY GREEK
PHILOSOPHERS

THE WORLDS OF
THE EARLY GREEK
PHILOSOPHERS

James B.
WILBUR
State University of New York
College at Geneseo

Harold J.
ALLEN
Adelphi University

Buffalo, New York 14215

Published 1979 by Prometheus Books
1203 Kensington Avenue, Buffalo, New York 14215

Library of Congress Catalog Number: 79-3089
ISBN 0-87975-115-0

Printed in the United States of America

PREFACE

The authors of this book have tried to do two things in presenting the written materials ascribed to the early Greek philosophers (c. 585 B.C.–400 B.C.) and the historical context in which those writings occurred. The first was to present a more fully fleshed out picture of the ideas of these men than has been given in the past. Perhaps under the influence of a narrow empiricism there has been a preference for letting the fragments speak for themselves. The trouble with this approach is that, even where there is a goodly number of fragments left, as, for instance, by Heraclitus, an adequate context for interpretation is not always evident from the fragments alone. And in the case of a thinker such as Anaximander, on the other hand, where there is so little firsthand evidence, what does remain is obscure taken solely on its own terms. Opposed to this Scylla of parsimony, there is, of course, the Charybdis of prodigal speculation. But we did not wish to hew a predetermined course equidistant from these two extremes. Rather the goal was to suit our passage to the winds and waters, sometimes nearer one than the other, as seemed best.

The second aim, also in the nature of a mean between extremes, was to find a happy balance between overwhelming the reader with all the scholarly paraphernalia of etymology and philology, and presenting a stripped-down version of the ideas that conveys no sense of the condition and source of our knowledge about them. While, for all but the specialist, the former detracts from the ideas presented, the latter fails to give a proper appreciation of the subject. In practice, this means that we tried to indicate, whenever possible, who attributed an idea to a given philosopher while at the same time providing the student with the relevant passage so he can read for himself what, for instance, Heraclitus said about Pythagoras. For this reason, the fragments themselves as well as essential interpretive passages are included in the text. Testimonials by other thinkers, which are of great importance to our knowledge of the earliest of these Greek philosophers, are either included in the body of the text or referred to at the bottom of the page, depending upon their relevance. A guide to these testimonial sources appears at the end of the book, along with a selected bibliography for the period as well as for the thinkers.

The overall objectives of the book have also shaped it in some unique ways. First, to supply as much hard evidence as possible about what the early Greek philosophers said, the book includes complete collections of the remaining fragments from each of these men except Democritus, Hippocrates, and the Sophists. In addition, a variety of contemporary interpretations is presented—points of view on general as well as specific aspects. Finally, where there are disagreements among authorities in the field that the authors felt are either particularly significant or unusually interesting, these have been reported.

In accord with our objectives and within present limitations of space, we have written what we hope will be a useful book about the Greek thinkers up to the time of Socrates. If we have succeeded, it will be because of the many fine scholars who have worked in this area and upon whom we have relied. Happily, the number of people so engaged seems to be increasing as the task of reexamining the intellectual foundations of our western civilization goes on. Any errors of omission as well as commission are, of course, our own. While it is true that we have collaborated throughout, Mr. Allen has been primarily concerned with Chapters 3, 5, 6, 8, 9, 10, and 11, and Mr. Wilbur, Chapters 1, 2, 4, 7, and 12.

We wish to thank Charlotte Farley, our Prometheus Books editor, for the care and concern with which she has cleaned and refurbished our manuscript. And we wish also to recognize the services and commend the efforts of Miss Freda Hark, Mrs. Annette Stewart and Miss Therese Ginty in the typing and preparation of the manuscript.

H.J.A.
J.B.W.

ACKNOWLEDGMENTS

We are grateful to the authors and publishers of the following previously published works for permission to quote passages from them:

Ancilla to the Pre-Socratic Philosophers by Kathleen Freeman, Basil
Blackwell & Mott Ltd. 1962;

Companion to the Pre-Socratic Philosophers by Kathleen Freeman,
Basil Blackwell & Mott Ltd.;

Euripides and His Age, by Gilbert Murray, by permission of Oxford
University Press;

The First Philosophers of Greece by Arthur Fairbanks, Routledge
and Kegan Paul Ltd.;

From Religion to Philosophy by F.M. Cornford, Harper and Row
Publishers, Inc.;

The Genesis of Plato's Thought by Alban Dewes Winspear, second
edition, revised, copyright 1956 A. D. Winspear, (New York: Russell &
Russell, 1956);

The Giants of Pre-Socratic Greek Philosophy by F. M. Cleve, Martinus Nijhoff, Publisher;

The Greek Experience by C. Maurice Bowra, World Publishing Co.,
Mentor Edition, pp. 23-24, copyright 1957 by C. Maurice Bowra,
reprinted by permission of Harper & Row Publishers, Inc., and George
Weidenfeld and Nicolson, Ltd.;

Greek Science by Benjamin Farrington, Penguin Books Ltd.;

The Greek Way by Edith Hamilton, W.W. Norton & Company, Inc.;

Heraclitus, by Philip Wheelwright, copyright 1959 by Princeton University Press. Reprinted by permission of Princeton University Press;

A History of Greek Philosophy by W. K. C. Guthrie, © Cambridge University Press. Reprinted by permission of Cambridge University Press;

Mainsprings of Civilization by Ellsworth Huntington, by permission of Mrs. Rachel B. Huntington and John Wiley & Sons, Inc.

Myth, Sacred History and Philosophy by Cornelius Loew, Harcourt Brace Jovanovich, Inc.;

The Oresteia of Aeschylus, trans. George Thompson, Cambridge University Press;

The Origins of Scientific Thought by Giorgio de Santillana. Copyright 1961 by Giorgio de Santillana. Reprinted by arrangement with The New American Library, Inc., New York;

Our Knowledge of the External World by Bertrand Russell, Mentor Books, London, 1960;

Oxford Translation of Aristotle, ed. W. D. Ross, by permission of Oxford University Press;

Paideia: The Ideals of Greek Culture by Werner Jaeger, by permission of Oxford University Press;

Plato: The Last Days of Socrates, trans. Hugh Tredennick, Penguin Classics, Revised Edition, 1969, pp. 155, 156, copyright Hugh Tredennick, 1954, 1959, 1969. Reprinted by permission of Penguin Books Ltd.;

Plato: Protagoras and Meno, trans. W. K. C. Guthrie, Penguin Classics 1956, pp. 47-48, 49-50, 71. Copyright W. K. C. Guthrie, 1956. Reprinted by permision of Penguin Books Ltd.;

Plato: Socratic Dialogues, trans. W. D. Woodhead, Thomas Nelson and Sons Ltd., Edinburgh & New York;

Plato and Parmenides by F. M. Cornford, Bobbs-Merrill Company, Inc.;

Plato's *Theaetetus*, trans. F.M. Cornford, by permission of Princeton University Press;

Plato's *Phaedrus*, trans. R. Hackforth, Cambridge University Press;

The Pre-Socratic Philosophers, 2nd ed. G. S. Kirk and J. E. Raven, © Cambridge University Press 1957. Reprinted by permission of Cambridge University Press;

The Theology of the Early Greek Philosophers by Werner Jaeger, trans. Edward S. Robinson, 1947, by permission of Oxford University Press;

Theophrastus & The Greek Physiological Psychology Before Aristotle by Malcolm Stratton, George Allen & Unwin, Ltd.;

Diodorus Siculus' *Library of History*, trans. C. H. Oldfather;
Diogenes Laertius' *Lives of the Philosophers*, trans. R.D. Hicks;
Herodotus' *The Persian Wars*, trans. A. D. Godley;
Hesiod's *Theogony*, trans. H. G. Evelyn White;
Hippocrates' *Ancient Medicine, Precepts, The Sacred Disease*, and
The Nature of Man, trans. W. H. S. Jones and E. T. Withington;
Plato's *Republic*, trans. Paul Shorey;
Strabo's *Geography*, trans. Horace L. Jones;
all by permission of The Harvard University Press and The Trustees of
the Loeb Classical Library.

KEY TO REFERENCES

1. Explanatory references, indicated by †, ‡, and §, appear at the bottom of each page.

2. Source references are separated by chapter and appear at the end of each chapter.

3. References marked by asterisks and appearing at the bottom of the page are part of the material being quoted.

4. Material in square brackets within quoted passages or text is supplied by the authors of this book.

5. "Frg." is an abbreviation for "Fragment" and indicates, along with its appropriate number, an existing portion of the work of the early Greek philosopher under discussion. Unless otherwise stated, all fragments and fragment numbers are taken from Kathleen Freeman's *Ancilla to the Pre-Socratic Philosophers,* Oxford, Basil Blackwell, 1962, being a translation of the fragments of the Pre-Socratic philosophers appearing in Diels' *Fragmente der Vorsokratiker*, 5th ed., Walter Kranz, ed., Berlin, 1934-38.

6. "T" stands for "Testimonium" and indicates a portion of the work of an ancient writer having direct reference to the life and thought of the early Greek philosopher under discussion. Unless otherwise stated, all those from Aristotle are from *The Oxford Translation of Aristotle* by W. D. Ross. Several other sources are abbreviated in square brackets, e.g., "[K&R]" for "Kirk and Raven."

7. In Chapter 11, the quoted passages from Hippocrates are marked "S1"-"S9" to indicate they are selections from whole works and not fragments. "[Loeb]" refers to the Loeb Classical Library.

8. Numbered footnote references to ancient commentators give only the ultimate source, except where a page number is included.

9. Complete bibliographical information for all references is listed under "Sources Cited."

TABLE OF CONTENTS

INTRODUCTION

WHO ARE THE EARLY GREEK PHILOSOPHERS?

The early Greek philosophers are often regarded as only forerunners of Socrates, Plato and Aristotle and their more highly developed philosophies. For this reason, they are often referred to as the Pre-Socratics, although, strictly speaking, the later members of this group were contemporaries of Socrates and Plato.

From a distance of twenty-five hundred to three thousand years, the Pre-Socratics are but a pinpoint on the horizon of philosophical thought—a pinpoint so far removed that it is easy either to ignore or to forget them. Yet it is from this pinpoint that Western thought developed. And if we should sometimes feel pangs of guilt for what might appear to be a chauvinistic concern with *Western* philosophy, the Greeks, who were, after all, Westerners, are the first men anywhere from whom we have any historical record of philosophical thought.

If it is true that before the Greeks there was no philosophy, the natural question is, "Why the Greeks?" There just isn't any satisfactory answer. It is, of course, important to consider the general conditions of Greek life, times, and thought, which supported the Greek contribution. But these factors remain only favorable conditions under which it flowered, when what is needed is an appreciation of how the Greek intellect expressed itself.

For more than two thousand years, the intellectual activity of succeeding generations in the Western world has continued to express wonder and admiration for the promethean creativity of these ancient Greeks. We are here concerned with a part of this creation, the part which is basic to the intellectual foundations of our civilization. If it is true that the child is father to the man, then seeing how our ideas arose, primitively and simply, will help us to know ourselves. And such a return to the *fons et origo* of our ideas might just possibly afford the windows of our philosophic perception a badly-needed cleaning. But first let us consider some of the conditions of Greek civilization in general, and Greek philosophy in particular, which encouraged this intellectual growth.

A. *The Greek Environment*

The mainland of Greater Greece is a rugged country of steep mountainsides and narrow valleys. The very irregularity of these features provides a material barrier to invasion by land from the north, and makes overland travel from one village to the next a difficult matter. The quickest and easiest way to travel is by boat—and indeed the three successive invasion-migrations into the Aegean area betweeen 3000 and 1000 B.C. by three differing but related peoples from the north and east were largely by way of the sea. Very early, control of the sea became of prime importance for the safety of commerce as well as of hearth and home.

From the end of the third wave of invasion by the Dorians in about 1000 B.C. until the Persian invasion of the Aegean area around 500 B.C., there were no serious threats from outside to the development of the civilization of mainland Greece. It took an active, industrious, ingenious people to work these lands successfully, and the results, if not bountiful, were at least adequate. The necessarily small population, scattered about in largely self-sustaining groups, farmed the scarce bottomlands and terraced the stony hillsides. They fished the sea, invaded and traded with one another, and, by establishing colonies just like themselves on the mainland of Asia Minor, on the many mountain-peak islands of the northeastern Mediterranean, and along the coasts of Italy and Sicily, they made the Aegean Sea both the avenue to and the center of the Greek community. Over the years, there developed that unity of culture, language, and spirit that allows us to speak of the Greeks as a people—a people who came to be known for self-reliance and that sense of individual independence which comes with living under harsh but surmountable conditions. This growth came to visible fruition in Athens under Solon about 560 B.C. with the establishment of a citizen's government based upon citizen-made law and with the defeat of the Persians at the hands of unified Greek forces during the period 490-479 B.C.

Despite the demands of this arduous existence, the Greeks possessed an interest in and devotion to another side of life, as Edith Hamilton points out:

> For somewhere among those steep stone mountains, in little sheltered valleys where the great hills were ramparts to defend and men could have security for peace and happy living, something quite new came into the world; the joy of life found expression...The Greeks were the first people in the world to play, and they played on a great scale. All over Greece there were games; all sorts of games...; games so many one grows weary with the list of them. If we had no other knowledge of what the Greeks were like, if nothing were left of Greek art and literature, the fact that they were in love with play and played magnificently would be proof enough of how they lived and how they looked at life. Wretched people, toiling people, do not play... 'Solon, Solon, you Greeks are all children,' said the Egyptian priest to the great Athenian. At any rate, children or not, they enjoyed themselves. They had physical vigor and high spirits and time, too, for fun. The witness of the games is conclusive.[1]

Whether or not the Greeks were, as Edith Hamilton maintains, the first people in the world to play, their involvement in play provides an important clue to the origin of their cultural achievement. The playing of games is an affair of the imagination and the mind, as well as the competitive spirit; it is an ordered activity, and the Greek genius may be looked upon as the fusing of order and action on one of the highest levels of excellence ever attained by man. This concern with games is of a piece with the imaginative attempts of the Greeks to understand phenomena through the application of ordered systems of rules. It is well exemplified by their development of geometry beyond the Egyptian rules of thumb for surveying the Nile delta. But what accounts for this extraordinary achievement? Or more generally: Whence this passion for order, clarity and intelligibility so evident in so many products of the Greek genius? C.M. Bowra makes a good beginning at an answer:

> No less powerful was the influence which the Greek scene had on the Greek eye and the Greek mind.... What matters above all is the quality of the light. Not only in the cloudless days of summer but even in winter the light is unlike that of any other European country, brighter, cleaner, and stronger. ...The beauty of the Greek landscape depends primarily on

the light, and this had a powerful influence on the Greek vision of the world....Such a landscape and such a light impose their secret discipline on the eye, and make it see things in contour and relief rather than in mysterious perspective or in flat spatial relations. They explain why the Greeks produced great sculptors and architects, and why even in their painting the foundation of any design is the exact and confident line.

Nor is it perhaps fanciful to think that the Greek light played a part in the formation of Greek thought....If the Greeks were the world's first true philosophers in that they formed a consistent and straightforward vocabulary for abstract ideas, it was largely because their minds, like their eyes, sought naturally what is lucid and well defined. Their senses were kept lively by the force of the light, and when the senses are keenly at work, the mind follows no less keenly and seeks to put in order what they give it. Just as Plato, in his search for transcendental principles behind the mass of phenomena, tended to see them as individual objects and compared his central principle to the sun which illuminates all things in the visible world and reveals their shapes and colours, so no Greek philosophy is happy until it can pin down an idea with limpid definition and make its outline firm and intelligible. That the Greeks were moved by some such consideration may be seen from their use of the words *eidos* and *ideâ* to mean 'notion' or 'idea.' Originally they meant no more than 'form' and were applied to such obvious forms as the human body. The transference of the word from concrete to abstract, from visible to invisible, shows how the Greek mind worked when it moved from the gifts of the senses to the principles behind them.[2]

B. *Economic Factors*

Economic factors undoubtedly encouraged the general upsurge of philosophical activity among the ancient Greeks, and also the differentiations in philosphical outlook. Huntington addresses himself to the general thrust of these forces:

Since the days of early Babylonia and Egypt two great inventions had been made. One was the art of fashioning iron into tools with a cutting edge. The other was the building of seagoing ships, which was presumably first accomplished by the Phoenicians. This art was not fully practicable until iron axes were available for hewing timber. In addition, man's ability to protect himself from the weather had increased somewhat through improvements in the arts of weaving, architecture, and, to a slight degree, heating. Hence man could now live quite comfortably in climates somewhat colder and more humid than those of Babylonia and Egypt. Other arts, especially pottery-making, had also made progress, and the number and quality of the materials that enter into trade had increased.

Early in the seventh century B.C. coined money, another great invention, also began to act as a stimulant to trade. Hence the need for travel and transportation increased still more, and good means of transportation became more important than ever before. . . .

After metal axes and wooden ships had added the sea to the natural conditions which man was able to control, there was a new and great need for safe harbors, many islands and calm seas. The Aegean Sea supplied this need. . . . As a place in which to use the power to build ships, control the sea, and employ coined money as a means to facilitate trade, it would be hard to find a better location.[3]

Greek geography dictated that Greek trade should be industrial rather than agricultural:

Even in the more rainy phases of ancient cycles agriculture in Attica was comparatively unprofitable, except on the best lands which belonged almost wholly to a relatively few powerful old families. Barley grew better than wheat. Exports of grain were prohibited much of the time. Hence the Athenians, like the early New Englanders, turned from agriculture to industry and commerce. This transition brought many foreign merchants and skilled artisans with new and sometimes valuable ideas. Industry was aided by the fact that Attica has an abundance of an unusually fine kind of clay, as well as excellent marble. The exceptional artistic skill of the people enabled them to make beautiful and widely sought urns for water, huge jars for grain, oil, and wine, and other ornamental wares. Sheep throve in all Greece, especially Attica. Their wool was another resource which the exceptional artistic ability of the Athenians converted into fine cloth that sold for a good price in coined money. In exchange for such products of human skill the Athenians imported grain, lumber, and other supplies.[4]

C. *Geography and Chronology*

The Western philosophical tradition began on the periphery of the Greek community in Asia Minor, in the southern part of what is now

Turkey, about 600 B.C., spread to the Italian and Sicilian coasts within a century, and finally centered on the mainland of Athens by the Age of Pericles, about 450 B.C.

The table on p. 7 lists the names of the philosophers with whom we will be concerned, the approximate dates at which they flourished†, and the geographic areas with which they were most closely associated. The name of Socrates with the appropriate dates has been included as a point of reference. Because of the importance of both Plato and Aristotle as sources for our information about these early thinkers, it is worth noting that in 399 B.C., when Socrates was executed in Athens, Plato was twenty-eight years old and Aristotle was not to be born for another fourteen years.

EARLY GREEK CONVICTIONS AND THEIR SYMBOLIC EXPRESSION‡

A.   *Cosmogonical and Cosmological Convictions*

The epic poetry of Homer and the didactic poetry of Tyrtaeus and Hesiod were primarily responsible for disseminating the conviction-bearing mythology of Greek culture up to the time of the Pre-Socratics, but the writings and activities of political reformers such as Solon were influential as well. Jaeger argues for the primacy of epic poetry on the ground that art is the best educator[5] and epic poetry the best conveyor of ideals.[6] According to him, history and philosophy both arose from the conflict of ideas in Greek poetry.[7] Whether the poet and philosopher were originally two different types or whether they are variants on a more basic type—the shaman, as maintained by Cornford,[8] the Greeks were unique among ancient civilizations in having no priestly class, a fact making it possible for poet and philosopher to assume their important roles. Some material in the Iliad and Odyssey goes back in the oral tradition perhaps as far as 1500 B.C., but the written version of the Iliad dates from about 750 B.C. and that of the Odyssey from about 50 years later. Hesiod also flourished during the Eighth Century B.C., and Tyrtaeus was active during the Seventh Century B.C.; Solon's dates are ca. 639-559 B.C.

---

†Because of the fragmentary nature of information on these thinkers, exact dates are not known. All dates supplied are those suggested by Kathleen Freeman in her *Ancilla to the Pre-Socratic Philosophers,* Basil Blackwell, Oxford, 1962.
‡See pp. 15-17 for a discussion of the nature of convictions.

The Early Greek Philosophers
Grouped by
Geographical Area of Closest
Association

Asia Minor (Ionia)	Italy & Sicily	Greek Mainland
The Milesians Thales of Miletus (ca. 585 B.C.)		
Anaximander of Miletus (ca. 560 B.C.)		
Anaximenes of Miletus (ca. 546 B.C.)		
Xenophanes of Colophon (ca. 530 B.C.)	Pythagoras of Samos (ca. 530 B.C.)	
Heraclitus of Ephesus (ca. 500 B.C.)		
	Alcmaeon of Croton (beginning of 5th Century B.C.)	
	The Eleatics Parmenides of Elea (ca. 475 B.C.)	Anaxagoras of Clazomenae (ca. 460 B.C.)
	Zeno of Elea (ca. 450 B.C.)	
	Melissus of Samos (ca. 440 B.C.)	
		The Atomists Leucippus of Abdera (ca. 430 B.C.)
		Democritus of Abdera (ca. 420 B.C.)
	Empedocles of Acragas (ca. 450 B.C.)	
Hippocrates of Cos (latter half of 5th Century B.C.)		Diogenes of Apollonia (latter half of 5th Century B.C.)
		Socrates (470–399 B.C.)
		The Sophists Protagoras of Abdera Gorgias of Leontini Thrasymachus of Chalcedon Hippias of Elis Antiphon (of Athens?) (All of the Sophists mentioned either lived or were active during the latter half of the 5th Cen- tury B.C.)

The Greeks knew the Olympian gods to be of late origin, knew that the legends about their ancestors had been given their present form by the poets, and identified Homer as the first to transpose their myths and legends into song.[9] The relative freedom with which this mythological material is manipulated and the broad limits of tolerance in these matters by the Greeks suggests that even the Greek gods were but expressions of still deeper convictions. This coincides with the view of Cornford that Greek polytheism, though older than Greek philosophy, must be related to the same underlying framework.[10] In Homer, Zeus is god of the heavens, Poseidon god of the sea, and Hades god of either the 'misty darkness' (i.e., air) or earth. Each god has his own proper domain which he guards jealously, punishing those who violate its limits. The view developed by the Pre-Socratic philosophers that there are four elements—fire, air, earth and water—as well as their ideas about the principles governing interaction among these four elements, bear a strong resemblance to the notions about the domains of the gods and the relations among them. Cornford maintains that these analogous characteristics as well as the grouping of the elements into pairs of contraries by the philosophers (hot vs. cold and moist vs. dry) can be understood as a projection of the structure of Greek society. Just as totemic Greek society may have been divided into four clans, so there are four domains of the gods and four elements; just as there are rigid rules separating the clans, so there are rigid boundaries between divine domains and between elements. Finally, the pairing of the elements as opposites can be regarded as a projection of the division of the tribe into two exogamous phratries, or clans.

As important as is the question of each god's domain and the analogy between the ordering of the human group and the ordering of the whole cosmos, there is yet a prior question, central to the whole of subsequent Greek thought, the answer to which is found in Hesiod's *Theogony*. In this work we have a genealogy of creation, an explanation of how, from the original condition of the universe things came to be as they are. This is linked theologically to Hesiod's account of the genealogy of the gods, and gives rise to the philosophical problem of the nature of change.

Unlike the Judeo-Christian tradition, there is no idea of creation from nothing; for the Greeks there was always something, and in the very beginning everything was One. Ancient myth has this One differentiate itself generally into two principles, Heaven and Earth, the former male and the latter female. This type of myth is common to early Chinese thought as well as to the Egyptian and Mesopotamian peoples. Hesiod's version of the myth begins

> Verily at the first Chaos came to be, but next wide-bosomed
> Earth, the ever-sure foundation of all the deathless ones who

hold the peaks of snowy Olympus, and dim Tartarus in the depth of the wide-pathed Earth, and Eros (Love), fairest among the deathless gods, who unnerves the limbs and overcomes the mind and wise counsels of all gods and all men within them. From Chaos came forth Erebus and black Night; but of Night were born Aether and Day, whom she conceived and bore from union in love with Erebus. And Earth first bare starry Heavens, equal to herself, to cover her on every side, and to be an ever-sure abiding-place for the blessed gods. And she brought forth long Hills, graceful haunts of the goddess-Nymphs, who dwell amongst the glens of the hills. She bare also the fruitless deep with his raging swell, Pontus, without sweet union of love. But afterwards she lay with Heaven and bare deep-swirling Oceanes, Coeus and Cruis and Hyperion and Iapetus.....[11]

Several points are to be noted here. First, the method of generation is biological. This is typical, and undoubtedly has much to do with the Greek view of the Cosmos as in some sense living: many of the early Greek cosmological modes of explanation and description are drawn from what, for us, has become a way of talking only of living things. Second, the primary figure is Gaia, Mother Earth, from whom all comes. This is indicative of a source far more antique than anything found in Homer. It may also indicate the order of conquest of the peoples in and around the Greek mainland. The Acheans and their close affiliates, the Mycenean peoples of Crete, worshipped the Earth Mother, Demeter, and developed practices having much in common with the fertility religions of Egypt and Babylonia. These seem to have been supplanted in Greece sometime around 1200 B.C. through an invasion from the north which brought the family of Olympus, with its male Zeus, into the picture. Hesiod's order of generation starts with basic cosmic principles and forces (i.e., Heaven, Ocean, Night) and continues through the castration of Ouranos by the eldest son Kronos and the era of the Titans, down to the capture and incarceration of Kronos by Zeus and the establishment of the Greek pantheon as we know it, a terminus heralding the rule of Justice and Law in the cosmos. A third and last point, also with some later philosophical significance, is that it is Eros, the god of Love or Desire, who brings all this about.

B. *Changing Moral Convictions*

The earlier suggestion that the order discovered in nature by the early Greek philosophers was a projection of the social order makes it easy to see how they came to regard it as a moral order. Let us now turn to an examination of the development of some key concepts and symbols defining the moral convictions of the ancient Greeks as they emerged and developed through three historical stages: the Archaic, the Classical, and the "Individualist-Intellectual."[12] In the Archaic stage, portrayed best in Homer, these concepts and symbols exhibit most clearly their tribal origins. Cornford suggests their primitive associations, with the morally compelling power of "convictions" constituting the "collective representation":†

> The negative aspect of this superindividual moral power—
> its aspect as repression, imposing an external constraint—
> will give rise to conceptions such as Avenging Anger
> (*Nemesis*), Justice (*Diké*) and Destiny (*Moira*), when these
> are conceived as keeping individuals in their places, and
> asserting against arrogant egoism the self-protective instinct
> of the social group.[13]

The original sense of *Moira* is evident in Homer where Poseidon is forced to retire to his legitimate domain:

> *Moira* simply means "part", "allotted portion", from that
> primary meaning it is agreed that the meaning "destiny" is
> derived. . . . Each god has his allotted portion or province—a
> certain department of nature or field of activity. . . . he must
> not transgress its frontiers, and he will feel resentment
> (*nemesis*) at any encroachment by another.[14]

The connection of law (*Nomos*) with *Moira* is evident from its association with the verb *nemein*, to "distribute" or "dispense."[15] *Moira* and *Nomos* are negative and positive sides, respectively, of one power or force: ". . .*Moira* stands for the limit of what you may do. . .*Nomos* rather means what you must do within your limits, . . ."[16] *Moira*, the supreme power of the universe, is allied to *Nomos* in the sense of constitutional order.[17] It is perhaps because they so valued the man of action that the Greeks were at the same time so aware of the danger of being "carried away" or blinded by infatuation (*Atè*), as were both Agamemnon and Archilles in the *Iliad*. Whoever is blinded by *Até* forsakes his duty (*Aidos*), is guilty of overbearing pride or arrogance (*Hybris*), and thereby subjects himself to *Nemesis*. Such behavior is contrary to virtue (*Areté*). For the Archaic Greek, *Areté* is honor thought of as public esteem (*Timé*): the culture of Archaic Greece was a "shame culture" (where the rightness or wrongness of actions is judged according to what others think) rather than a "guilt culture" (where right and wrong are judgments made by an individual conscience).[18]

The Classical stage of development in Greek culture is characterized by the growth of loyalty to the emerging city-state (*Polis*) rather than to

---

†See pp. 15-17 for a discussion of the nature of "convictions" and "collective representations."

the tribe. Hesiod, Tyrtaeus, and Solon all contributed to the new ideas associated with this shift. Jaeger maintains that it was Hesiod who first introduced the ideal of justice[19] in that, as spokesman for the discontented peasantry of his time, he was the first to distinguish *Diké* from right established by judicial decision (*Themis*). Initially *Diké* and *Themis* were so intimately associated as to be almost indistinguishable:

> Zeus gave to the Homeric kings "the sceptre and themis".
> Themis is the epitome of the judicial supremacy of the early
> kings and nobles. Etymologically, the word means "institu-
> tion". The feudal judge gives his decision in accordance with
> the institutions set up by Zeus, and derives their rules from
> his knowledge of customary law and from his own intuition.
> ...The parties to a dispute were said to "give and take diké,
> ...and the judge "allots diké." Hence the fundamental
> meaning of diké is much the same as "due share".[20]

The peasantry was unhappy with discrepancies between the decisions handed down by the aristocratic judges and what they regarded as their fair share. Hesiod's elevation of *Diké* as an ideal distinct from *Themis* became their rallying point and signaled the decline of the old tribal order.

Tyrtaeus, aristocratic spokesman for Sparta, was the first to preach a new loyalty—loyalty to the *Polis*. Though Tyrtaeus' definition of *Areté* as the "savage valor" of the citizen-soldier in defense of his *Polis* shows his ideal to be closely linked to the militarism of Sparta, the ideal of preservation of the *Polis* as the ultimate value captured the Greek spirit. The *Polis* thus became for the Classical Greek the center of all social and intellectual activity.

Solon's contribution to this classical development was to synthesize the ideal of the *Polis* with that of *Diké* by asserting the operation of *Diké* to be immanent in the *Polis* insofar as the effects of just and unjust acts made themselves felt in the social fabric of the *Polis* itself.[21] Also associated with Solon's view was a new emphasis on the importance of individual responsibility and good judgment.[22] The culture of the Athenian state founded by Solon carried forward the Ionian spirit of individual freedom along with the Spartan devotion to the *Polis* as a center of allegiance.[23]

Ionian thought spans the Archaic and Classical periods. Ionian thinkers include the Milesians (Thales, Anaximander and Anaximenes), Xenophanes, and Heraclitus. Although the Milesians were primarily concerned with nature, just to this very extent their thought expressed the Archaic stage of development of moral convictions. Xenophanes was critical of the moral convictions of his society in the name of reason, but unsystematically: his rational criticism heralded the arrival of the Classical stage. Finally, Heraclitus judged all moral as well as physical truth in the name of the *Logos*, a rational structure permeating the cosmos and finding its most complete embodiment in the *Polis*. Such a view fulfills the Classical ideal.

With the advent of the Individualist-Intellectual period of Greek cultural development (Greek Enlightenment), we come into the Age of Pericles. It is a time during which the Classical view continues to find its defenders, but one which saw the rise of the Sophists, the most vocal spokesmen for the Individualist-Intellectual criticism of that classical view. The cultural role of the Sophists is discussed in Chapter 12.

C.   *Gods, Nature and The Human Soul*

Cultural development in the post-Homeric period was not without its religious dimension.

In general it might be said that there were two religious traditions in ancient Greece. The Olympian religious tradition was associated with the gods who dwelt on Mount Olympus and who were worshipped in the Parthenon and immortalized by Homer: Zeus, Hera, Apollo, Athena, Aphrodite and their company—the gods of the ruling aristocracy. Because Apollo so typifies the Olympian gods, this tradition can also be called Apollonian. But alongside this religion of the dominant social order there likewise existed the mystery religions of the countryside closely tied to the soil and the seasons. Because of the importance of the Mystery Religion of Dionysus, this tradition is most often referred to as Dionysian or Dionysiac.

> The gods took on new functions—Apollo at Delphi becoming a god of the aristocrats; Athena symbolizing the state as an organ of reconciliation; Hermes, the god of the merchants and the patron of commerce.[24]

Another feature of the period was the rise of Orphism. Just how old Orphism is, as well as precisely what it is, is difficult to tell. There appears to be no specifically Orphic body of written materials until the fifth and sixth Centuries B.C., although the term Orphic seems to have been applied to diverse teachings earlier than that. The name itself derives from the mythical figure of Orpheus, master musician from Thrace, who is supposed to have lived several generations before Homer. Legend has it that he sailed with Jason and the Argonauts, and the story of his visit to the underworld to find his wife Eurydice is well-known but of late origin (A.D. 200). The body of belief that came to be associated with Orphism no doubt included the practices of the very early cult of Dionysus which came to Greece from Asia. Homer seems to have known of it, but regarded it as of little importance.

In Orphism we see a different version of the Theogony found in

Hesiod. The chief importance of this for us is that in the sixth generation, Zeus, having defeated the Titans and Kronos, fathers the god Dionysus, who is killed and then restored to his father. Like Persephone, who was abducted by Hades but returns every spring to her mother Demeter, Dionysus was associated with the creation of new life in the spring. He was also the giver of wine. The cult of Dionysus involved becoming one with the life-giving god through his representative. Originally this included human sacrifice in which the chosen one was torn apart and devoured by the members of the cult, but there is no record that the Greeks used human offerings.

Surrounding and deriving from their view of creation is the dualistic view of man as made up of a divine soul and an earthly body. The latter was, at best, the soul's prison. Not only did Orphism offer salvation through Dionysiac participation, but it also prescribed a strict regimen for the purification of the soul, which was necessary because of the belief in transmigration; only through purification could the soul be released from the weary wheel of reincarnation. Orphism attempted to contain and reconcile both ecstatic Dionysian elements and disciplined Apollonian elements. It was essentially a belief for individuals, and always remained outside the official, socially-oriented religions of Greece. Then, too, the implied disintegration of the body and the concentration on attaining a future state were notions that did not, in general, recommend themselves to the Greeks, who were more often than not of a this-worldly cast of mind.

From our point of view, Orphism and the Mystery Religion of Dionysus are of considerable interest because of their relevance to the basic problem of Sixth Century philosophic thought: how both men and the things of sense experience are related to nature (*Physis*).

Physis as the original philosophic datum is, according to Cornford, a projection of the positive dynamic power of the social group. It is regarded by the Pre-Socratics as the "substrate of all things and the source of their growth."[25] It is also alive and divine. Indeed, its relation to men and the objects of sense experience parallels the relation assumed by Greek religion to exist between God and men as well as between God and the world.[26] The relation of God to the world is further regarded by the early Greek philosophers as similar to the relation between soul and body.[27] The relevance of Orphism and Dionysiac religion to these considerations is twofold. First, Dionysiac notions of God, soul, and the relation between them differ fundamentally from those associated with the Olympian religious tradition. Second, Orphism as an Apollonian transmutation of Dionysiac material is marred by the contradiction of attempting simultaneously to incorporate both sets of notions. We follow Cornford's account:

> Man in Homer has two souls. His *eidolon* or *psyche* escapes
> from his mouth at the moment of death; it is his recognizable
> shape, which may, for a time, revisit his survivors in dreams.
> It does not exist until the moment of death; and it does not
> carry with it to the world of shades any of his vital force. This
> resides in the other soul ($\theta\upsilon\mu\acute{o}\varsigma$)† whose visible vehicle is the
> blood; . . .As contrasted with the individual and recogniza-
> ble *eidolon*, it is less personal—the same in all men alike—
> and thus bears the mark of its original collective charac-
> ter. . . .The *eidolon* soul, the recognizable shape or image, is
> the soul as object (and later as subject) of *knowledge*; the
> blood-soul is the soul as the principle of force and *motion*.[28]

Insofar as the *Thymos* soul retains the vital force of the social group and
is in fact a projection of the felt, morally persuasive force of the group
onto the group, it is what Cornford calls a group soul.[29] In this respect,
the *Thymos* soul is akin to the Dionysiac notion of soul. The Dionysiac
god also has the group soul as a prototype,[30] a fact making possible
communion and reunion between god and man either through *enthusiasm*, whereby the god enters into his group, or through *ecstasy*, whereby
man steps out of the limitations of his individuality to lose himself in the
divine.[31]

> Orgiastic ritual ensures that the passage from the human
> plane to the divine remains open, and is continually trav-
> ersed. God can enter into man, and man can become God.[32]

The *Eidolon* soul, the notion of soul associated with Olympian
religion, is an intellectual object rather than something emotionally felt.
As an object it is similar to what Cornford refers to as a "nature-
daemon", i.e., a projection of human will power onto a species of
natural phenomena.[33] Because it is individual, it is deprived of the
power associated with a nature-daemon and is necessarily shadowy and
insubstantial.[34] The Olympian god also has the nature-daemon as a
prototype. The Olympian god differs from the *Eidolon* soul in retaining
the species character of the nature-daemon, and therefore lacks genuine
individuality. But though his purely formal nature bestows on him an
immortal immutability, it also deprives him of the vital force associated
with a nature-daemon.[35] A consequence of depriving both the *Eidolon*
soul and Olympian god of any emotional ties is that no commerce
between them is possible:

> For lack of the mystical link of communion, the Olympian
> recedes from man, as well as from Nature. A cardinal princi-
> ple of Olympian theology is that man cannot become a God
> or "immortal", neither can God become man. Each is con-

---

†Thymos

fined to his own region, and the boundary of *Moira* set
between them cannot, and must not, be passed.[36]

The nature of philosophical currents associated with Dionysiac *Thymos* soul and Olympian *Eidolon* soul will be suggested in the next section. The cross-currents and eddys stirred up in the Pythagorean attempt to reconcile these conflicting symbolisms are dealt with in the last section of Chapter 4 on Pythagoras and the Pythagoreans.[†]

THE TASK OF INTERPRETATION: SOME PROBLEMS AND ALTERNATIVES

The material to be considered in this section might equally well be read after the rest of the book because it is concerned with what to make out of the whole early Greek development and presupposes some knowledge of it. But it does seem necessary to suggest some of the problems of interpretation at this point, and several important interpretive issues will be discussed by way of establishing our orientation towards our materials.

A.   *From Cultural Myth to Rational Theory*

Myths as distinct from legend, saga, fable, and fairy tale are "nothing less than a carefully chosen cloak for abstract thought."[37] They are vehicles for what Cornford, borrowing from the sociologist L. Lévy-Bruhl, calls "collective representations" and what Cornelius Loew refers to as "convictions". Concerning the nature of "collective representations", Cornford quotes Bruhl:

> They are common to the members of a given social group
> within which they are transmitted from generation to
> generation; they are imposed upon the individuals, and
> awaken in them, as the case may be, feelings of respect, fear,
> adoration, etc. towards their objects.[38]

And Loew, characterizing "convictions" as persuasions of a religious nature about good and bad, gods and devils, representations of the ideal man, state, and society, the meaning of history, nature and God, goes on to say that they are regarded by those convinced by them as having final authority, as valid, binding, permanent and sacred.[39]

It is Cornford's contention that, through totemism, primitive man came to think of the structure and operation of the world as similar to the structure and operation of human society.[40] Then, when the early Greek philosophers began to speculate freely about nature, they were led to make hypotheses structurally similar to the collective representations on which they were nurtured and to read into nature the structure and ways of operation of Greek society. If the question is raised why

---

†See pp. 94 ff.

Greek speculation about nature preceded speculation about man and
society, as in fact it did, one answer might be that this seems a
psychologically natural course of development. As Cornford suggests,
the Pre-Socratic philosophy of nature may be thought of as analogous
to the outward-looking curiosity of childhood, and the Sophists'
concern for man as comparable to the rebellious thirst for self-
knowledge that accompanies the adolescent search for independence.[41]
On this view, Heraclitus' conception of man and society as fitting into
the order of nature, as expressing and manifesting that order, is perhaps
comparable to pre-adolescent acceptance of parental order and discipline.

The historical fact that man began to theorize about nature before he
began to theorize about himself and society, as well as Heraclitus'
interpretation of man and society as manifestations of the order of
nature, both stand in rather interesting juxtaposition to Cornford's
view that the order man found in nature when he began to speculate
about it was really his own and society's image. Thus the early Greek
philosophers sometimes thought of nature as a living organism and
sometimes as a Cosmos, i.e., as a society of interacting individuals, in
both cases guided by a purpose and a will. In this view, Heraclitus, for
example, would be understood as having first unconsciously projected a
cosmic order into nature and then taken man and society as exemplifications of this very same cosmic order. If one is inclined to reject such a
procedure out of hand, consider first the development of the Old
Testament conception of the character of God as both a projection of
the gradually dawning conception of man's self as well as a standard for
the guidance of human behavior. Consider also the growing importance
of the machine to society in the eighteenth and nineteenth centuries as
well as the increasingly mechanical nature of society in that period,
along with the concomitant rise of the view of both man and nature as
themselves machines. Consider, finally, the ever increasing distance of
the individual in contemporary society from the sources of social control and the consequent necessary reliance on symbolism of every sort,
in conjunction with our present view of both nature and man as subject
to manipulation and control through the application of abstract
mathematical laws.

In this connection, it is Stephen Pepper's thesis that differing metaphysical views of the world are grounded in, built upon, and clarify
certain "root metaphors." He speaks of four major "world hypotheses"
for contemporary thought, each grounded in its own root metaphor:
formism, mechanism, contextualism and organicism.[42] Comparing
the almost biological way in which the earliest of our thinkers viewed
reality with the mechanical explanations of Democritus, one of the

latest, it is tempting to see the Greek philosophical development as a steady progression toward a root metaphor of the world as a machine and the world hypothesis of mechanism. One perfectly acceptable motive for such an interpretation lies in the importance of Democritean atomism for our own understanding of science. But it should be remembered that, whatever its later historical importance, the atomism of Democritus is the quick-dying branch of Greek philosophy and that it is in the "formism" of Plato and the "contextualism" or "organicism" of Aristotle that Greek philosophy reaches its highest expression. It could be argued with equal plausibility that, even though Greek thought produced the atomism of Democritus, there was something about it not in keeping with the Greek viewpoint, and so it dropped from sight. But which of these interpretations recommends itself will in large part depend upon one's view of the nature of science and of the relation of these Greek thinkers to the development of science.

B. *In What Sense Scientific?*

Reliance on rational rather than mythological explanation is a marked characteristic of the early Greek philosophers. It is perhaps this trait more than any other which distinguishes them as philosophers, and the nature, meaning, and implications of the shift from myth to reason have therefore given rise to much controversy regarding the relation of early Greek philosophy to religion and to what we later came to know as science. One question central to the controversy is the relation of science to theory and practice. Farrington quotes with approval J. G. Crowther's definition of science as "the system of behavior by which man acquires mastery of his environment",[43] relating science closely to the practical techniques of production. But it is Malinowski's view that science defined in such a fashion is common to all primitive cultures insofar as it then becomes indistinguishable from art and craft.[44] And even if science is defined as a theoretical enterprise, Malinowski suggests that no primitive culture may be said to be entirely without science any more than it is without religion.[45] A question thus arises concerning the originality of the Pre-Socratics. To what extent did their philosophizing represent a departure from the theological or religious mythologizing of their predecessors, and in what sense is it legitimate to speak of them as contributing to the emergence of scientific method? Malinowski's observations suggest that the matter is not cut and dried: in some ways the Pre-Socratics are scientific in the modern sense; in some ways they are not. As we shall see, their "rational explanations" are not entirely devoid of mythological content.

Though it might well be granted that science is at least partially rooted in practice, certainly it also involves the reasoned ordering of practice, i.e., a theoretical component. The same might be said of theology as distinct from religion. Aristotle takes account of this similarity between "theologians" such as Hesiod and the early Greek philosphers; but he also points out an important difference. The Pre-Socratic philosophers resemble "theologians" like Hesiod insofar as they proclaim certain doctrines, but they differ in their employment of reasoned literalness rather than myth as justification.[46] On the other hand, with the exception of Hippocrates, the early Greek philosphers do not limit their proclaimed doctrines to what can be tested by observation; they are all prone to *a priori* theorizing to a greater or lesser degree, which leads them to conclusions reminiscent, at least in structure, of the myths of the theologians. This is not to say that the strict empiricism of Hippocrates is to be preferred to the hypothetical reasoning of the other Pre-Socratics. One is as necessary to modern scientific method as the other, and it might be argued that the theorizers were performing the essentially philosophical task even in a modern sense. That the results of philosophical theorizing in a culture turn out to be structurally similar to the religious myths of that culture should not be too surprising either, if both are assumed to be free expressions of the same cultural outlook. A case in point would be Deism considered in relation to the Newtonian scientific world view.

Cornford voices a common criticism of philosophy:

> Almost all philosophic arguments are invented afterwards, to recommend, or defend from attack, conclusions which the philospher was from the outset bent upon believing, before he could think of any arguments at all. This is why philosophical reasonings are so bad, so artificial, and so unconvincing.[47]

Rigidity in adhering to a single belief or narrow set of beliefs out of all regard for their logical relations to the larger context of other beliefs also adhered to is indeed open to criticism. Yet it is well worth keeping in mind Kenneth Burke's thought that the terms "reasoning" and "rationalizing" are question-begging words inasmuch as, while the former is applied to explanations of which we approve, the latter is used to characterize explanations of which we disapprove.[48] But it is not easy to say in what way any hypothesis lacking in deductive support differs from a "rationalization" in the pejorative sense. Therefore, we should not be critical of the early Greek philosophers for their theorizing; indeed, Cornford himself regards the unrestricted character of this theorizing, i.e., unrestricted by supposed supernatural boundaries, as the beginning of science.[49] It should be remembered that the system of ideas we know as Euclidean geometry was the model of science for nearly twenty-five hundred years, and even though we now view its applicability in more restricted terms, it still remains as a model for scientific theory. If we speak of science in the sense of ordered explanation or rational demonstration, then surely the early Greek philosophers invented science; but of science as experimental verification they had but a limited notion. They observed their world, but reason was their canon, not experience.

C. *Limitations of Available Source Materials.*

The problem of understanding the early Greek thinkers is made more difficult by the fragmentary state of our direct knowledge of their writings. Of the very early ones such as Thales and Phythagoras, nothing survives, of several others only a few bits, and even where the bits and pieces add up to considerable information, as in the case of Heraclitus and Democritus, the problem remains of relating them to one another to form an intelligible and plausible picture. We are, of course, aided in this by a wealth of secondary materials, but problems arise here too. For instance, important as Aristotle is as a source of information, comments he makes often reflect his own point of view and problems rather than those of the person he is talking about. Likewise, in the case of Heraclitus, whose conception of the Logos was made central to post-Aristotelean Stoicism, it is not clear when the commentators, many of whom are Stoics, are reading their own Stoic conceptions back into Heraclitus or when they are conveying information about the Heraclitean ideas. Undoubtedly there is a middle ground to be found here. But what such middle ground may be often depends upon current fashion in ideas. This can be illustrated from our recent past and is worth considering at some length just because of the immensity of the problem of interpretation.

One of the chief strains of modern Anglo-Saxon thought has been empiricism, and we are quite likely to speak of "empirical science," emphasizing the experimental approach and the appeal to experience in scientific endeavor. This produces a tendency, in the name of truth, science and adherence to fact, to let the fragments from the early Greek thinkers speak for themselves, unencumbered by the conceptual paraphernalia of interpretation. There is value in this view, of course; but the fragments taken as they are don't tell us very much at all, and there are several such treatments in print to prove it. It is this same emphasis that gave rise to the question, considered in the preceding section, of whether the early Greek philosophers can be called "scientists" and whether they can be said to have been "doing" science.

On a more general and metaphysical level, the overriding dichotomy of the early Twentieth Century was between materialism (usually in the company of empirical science), on the one hand, and idealism, on the other. As a way of classifying these early materials, there is something too procrustean about the approach to be acceptable; but as indicative

of different kinds of emphasis, they often turn up relationships important in the treatment of specific ideas and thinkers which enrich our
total perspective. Let us look at two versions of the materialism-
idealism type of thinking. The first is somewhat heavy-handed in application, but enlightening, nonetheless, in certain narrowly defined areas;
the second, though still procrustean, is successful and illuminating
because of the variation and depth with which it is applied across the
whole range of this early Greek period.

D.   A Marxist View

Illustrative of the first sort of approach just mentioned, two Marxist
thinkers, Benjamin Farrington and Alban Winspear, explore the effect
of class interests in determining the range of early Greek philosophical
opinion. Farrington points out that the positive content of the sorts of
explanation used by the earliest Pre-Socratics, i.e., the Ionians, was
conditioned by their familiarity with certain industrial techniques, such
as the domestication of animals, agriculture, horticulture, pottery,
brick-making, spinning, weaving, and metallurgy.[50] He cites their use of
such examples as the phenomenon of raised beaches, the silting up of
river mouths, felting,[†] the occurrence of such allusions as the oven, the
soldering iron, the bellows, and the potter's wheel, and the invocation of
such explanatory principles as condensation and rarefaction and tension, as evidence for his view.[51] From Winspear's perspective, the
earliest impulse of Greek philosophy was in this fashion materialistic
(which he regards as "progressive"), and for him materialism is one pole
of the Greek philosophical spectrum. The other pole is idealism (which
he regards as "conservative"), a perspective that, according to him, had
its roots in the development of class antagonisms, and in the attempt of
the landed aristocracy, wherever it was dominant, to defend its position
by an appeal to the transcendant authority of "eternal principles."[52]

Winspear links differences in the development of class antagonisms
(and consequently of philosphical outlook) to differences in geographical regions.[53] In Sparta, and to a lesser extent in Italy and Sicily, the
landed aristrocracy was powerful. Philosophy never developed in
Sparta at all because all of its energies were devoted to conquest. In Italy
and Sicily, philosophy was primarily idealistic. In Ionia, where tribal
chieftains evolved directly into a class of wealthy merchants, philosophy was basically materialistic and "dialectical". Finally, in Athens,
where there was a greater degree of conflict between landed aristocracy
and wealthy merchants, the result was philosophical compromise.
Relating any of the major thinkers considered in this volume to the
geographical region with which he is most closely associated,[‡] will

---

†To cause to adhere or mat together (as in the process of making felt).
‡See p. 7.

make evident Winspear's overall evaluation of that thinker. The only exceptions are Alcmaeon of Croton and Empedocles of Acragas (both of the latter from the Italian-Sicilian area), whom Winspear regards as progressive and materialistic rather than conservative and idealistic.[54] Neither Winspear nor Farrington mentions Diogenes of Apollonia, but he appears to fit without too much difficulty into the materialist mold.

While the ideas of Farrington and Winspear are helpful, several cautions are in order. With the exception of the Atomists, none of the Pre-Socratics can be properly classified as materialists in the modern sense of the term; nor should any of them be regarded as modern idealists. The distinctions between animate and inanimate, formal and material, abstract and concrete, all essential to the modern distinction between idealism and materialism, had not yet been clearly made. Another caution: though Farrington and Winspear would undoubtedly regard "progressive" and "conservative" as value terms, it would seem an error to conclude that positive contributions to the development of philosophic and scientific thought came only from those early Greek philosophers of a predominantly progressive cast. Surely the Italian school, for the most part conservative and idealist, according to Farrington and Winspear, also contributed heavily. Lastly, though the facts of the early Greek experience tend to support the association of progressive ideology with the materialist outlook, and of conservative ideology with the idealist outlook, it would appear unwarranted on the face of it to regard these associations as universally necessary, an assumption which would unquestionably be made by Farrington and Winspear.

E. F. M. Cornford's View

Making use of a dominant cultural motif as a principle of classification rather than using an economic or ideological orientation, Cornford divides the Pre-Socratics into two categories: those in the "mystical tradition" and those in the "scientific tradition", a classification that corresponds roughly with that of Farrington and Winspear. He traces the mystical tradition to Dionysiac religious influences, and the scientific tradition in philosophy to the Olympian tradition in religion. Cornford describes the relation between the Olympian religious tradition and the scientific tradition in philosophy as follows:

> The type of philosophy to which an Olympian theology will give rise will be dominated by the conception of spatial externality, as *Moira* had dominated the Gods; and it will tend towards discontinuity and discreteness. Originating in an essentially polytheistic scheme, it will be pluralistic. It

will also move steadily towards materialism, because, having no hold upon the notion of life as an inward and spontaneous principle, it will reduce life to mechanical motion,
communicated by external shock from one body to another.
It will level down the organic to the inorganic, and pulverize
God and the Soul into material atoms.[55]

Thinkers classified by Cornford as definitely belonging to the scientific
tradition include the Milesians, Anaxagoras, and the Atomists.[56] A few
of the philosophers we will consider are not considered by Cornford.
These are Alcmaeon of Croton (assuming his status as a Pythagorean is
in doubt), Diogenes of Apollonia, Hippocrates of Cos, and the
Sophists.

Speaking of the religion of Dionysus, Cornford says:

It is the parent of mystical philosophies, of monistic and
pantheistic systems, which hold that the One can pass into
the Many and yet remain One. It is also idealistic in tendency, in the sense that it is other-worldly: the One is not
only within, but beyond and above, the Many, and more
real, because more powerful, than they. Accordingly, the
Many, as such, are condemned to unreality, to mere "seeming" or appearance—half-false representations of the One
reality.[57]

Philosophers of the mystical tradition would include Xenophanes,
Heraclitus, Pythagoras, the Pythagoreans, Parmenides and Empedocles. [58]

Insofar as the Mystical tradition focuses on the importance of the
One, it exhibits a kinship with the Dionysiac concept of Thymos-Soul.
This is why individuals are regarded as mere appearances in relation to
the one reality. But inasmuch as the world of appearing individuals is
constantly changing, time and number (the measure of time in the sense
of counting rhythmical repetitions of the same occurrence) guided by
the vision of *Diké* take the place of necessity guided by the image of
Moira (the dominant factor in the scientific tradition) in governing the
universe.[59]

F.   *The Viewpoint of a Primitive Phenomenology*

Still another attractive approach to the early Greek philosophers is
that of H. and H. A. Frankfort—an approach that might be said to rely
on a "primitive phenomenology" because of its attempt to get beneath
the traditional encrustations of Western thought down to something
like what must have been the early Greek thinkers' own experience of
their world.

Philosophical speculation is probably never entirely self-conscious, and the closeness of the early Greeks to primitive modes of thought implies that they failed to make or were unclear about some distinctions which for us are commonsense and commonplace. One major such distinction not made by the primitive thinker is that between subject and object. The Frankforts characterize the attitude of ancient man toward nature as hovering between the nonemotional and articulate state appropriate to a relation between subject and object, and the emotional and inarticulate state associated with understanding another person. Paralleling Buber's idea, they refer to the relation of ancient man to nature as an "I-Thou" relation, and further point out its personal character and inescapable particularity.[60] The latter characteristic goes a long way toward explaining the difficulties encountered by early Greek thinkers in their attempt to deal with generalizations and the closely associated notions of thought and abstraction. (For example, Heraclitus' *Logos*, Parmenides' Being, Empedocles' Love and Hate, and Anaxagoras' Mind, all to some degree mental in character, are also regarded by the thinkers concerned as in some sense concrete.) According to the Frankforts, blurring of the distinction between subject and object also implies blurring of distinctions between dream and reality, hallucination and reality, living and dead, symbol and symbolized, concept and instance.[61] The Frankforts also maintain that causality, space, and time are other concepts conceived differently by primitive thinkers, than by ourselves. For the primitive thinker, causality is interpreted particularly and in terms of personal will rather than as impersonal, mechanical and law-like[62]; space[63] and time[64] are concrete and emotionally colored rather than part of an infinite, continuous and homogeneous matrix. These attitudes, together with the prominence of the I-Thou relation, characterize what the Frankforts call "mythopoeic thought"[65]—the kind of thinking from which the Pre-Socratics may have tried to free themselves, but which nevertheless accounts for much of the content of their thought.

In what follows, we will assume something like a primitive phenomenological orientation from which the thought of these early philosophers started and out of which it grew. And we will couple this with a broad interpretation of the nature of science as well as an appreciation of the function of reason in the transition from myth to theory. Finally, we will avail ourselves of the insights of Farrington, Winspear, Cornford, the Frankforts, and many others in trying to construct a general framework for understanding.

NOTES

1. Edith Hamilton, *The Greek Way* (New York: W.W. Norton & Co., 1942), p. 30ff.

2. C. M. Bowra, *The Greek Experience* (New York: World Publishing Co., 1959), pp. 23-4.

3. Ellsworth Huntington, *Mainsprings of Civilization* (New York: John Wiley & Sons, Inc., 1945, Mentor Books, 1959), pp. 590-1.

4. *Ibid.*, p. 592.

5. Werner Jaeger, *Paideia: The Ideals of Greek Culture* 2nd ed. (Oxford: Oxford University Press, Galaxy Books, 1965), pp. 36-7.

6. *Ibid.*, p. 42.

7. *Ibid.*, p. 43.

8. F. M. Cornford, *Principium Sapientiae* (New York: Harper & Row Torchbooks, 1965), p. 43.

9. Cornelius Loew, *Myth, Sacred History and Philosophy* (New York: Harcourt Brace and World, Inc., 1967), p. 186.

10. F. M. Cornford, *From Religion to Philosophy* (New York: Harper and Row Torchbooks, 1957), pp. 38-9.

11. Hesiod, *Theogony*, trans. H. G. Evelyn White (Cambridge: Harvard University Press, Loeb Classical Library), 116. Hereafter cited as [Loeb].

12. See Jaeger, *Paideia*, vol.1, p. ix. The first two periods are clearly distinguished by Jaeger; the third, though not so clearly, is yet suggested by him.

13. Cornford, *From Religion to Philosophy*, p. 82.

14. *Ibid.*, p. 16.

15. *Ibid.*, p. 29.

16. *Ibid.*, p. 34.

17. *Ibid.*, p. 54.

18. E. R. Dodds, *The Greeks and the Irrational* (Boston: Beacon Press, 1957), pp. 17-8.

19. Jaeger, *Paideia*, p. 62.

20. *Ibid.*, p. 103.

21. *Ibid.*, p. 141.

22. *Ibid.*, p. 148-9.

23. *Ibid.*, p. 137.

24. Alban D. Winspear, *The Genesis of Plato's Thought*, 2nd. ed. rev. (New York: Russell and Russell, 1956), p. 62.

25. Cornford, *From Religion to Philosophy*, p. 123.

26. *Ibid.*, p. 135.

27. *Ibid.*, p. 129.

28. Cornford, *From Religion to Philosophy*, pp. 109-10.

29. *Ibid.*, pp. 94-95.

30. *Ibid.*, p. 111.

31. *Ibid.*, p. 112.

32. *Ibid.*

33. *Ibid.*, p. 97.

34. *Ibid.*, p. 110.

35. *Ibid.*, p. 115.

36. *Ibid.*, p. 118.

37. *Ibid.*, p. 15.

38. L. Lévy-Bruhl, *Fonctions mentales dans les sociétés inférieures*, 1910, p. 1, quoted in Cornford, *From Religion to Philosophy*, p. 44.

39. Loew, p. 3.

40. Cornford, *From Religion to Philosophy*, pp. 59–60.

41. F. M. Cornford, *Before and After Socrates* (Cambridge: At the University Press, 1965), pp. 38–9.

42. Stephen C. Pepper, *World Hypotheses* (Berkeley: University of California Press, 1966), p. 141.

43. Benjamin Farrington, *Greek Science* (New York: Penguin Books, 1953), p. 18.

44. Bronislaw Malinowski, *Magic, Science and Religion and Other Essays* (New York: Doubleday Anchor Books, 1955), p. 34.

45. *Ibid.*, pp. 34–5.

46. Aristotle *Meta.* 100a4, 18.

47. Cornford, *From Religion to Philosophy*, p. 138.

48. Kenneth Burke, *Permanence and Change*, 2nd ed., rev., (Indianapolis: Bobbs-Merrill Co., Inc., Library of Liberal Arts, 1965), p. 11.

49. Cornford, *From Religion to Philosophy*, pp. 7–8.

50. Farrington, pp. 22 and 41.

51. *Ibid.*, pp. 48–9.

52. Winspear, p. 77.

53. *Ibid.*, pp. 76–7.

54. *Ibid.*, p. 114.

55. Cornford, *From Religion to Philosophy*, p. 123.

56. *Ibid.*, p. 144.

57. *Ibid.*, p. 114.

58. *Ibid.*, pp. 143n and 194.

59. *Ibid.*, p. 160 and note.

60. H. & H. A. Frankfort, John A. Wilson, Thorkild Jacobsen, *Before Philosophy*, reprint (New York: Penguin Books, 1954), pp. 13–14.

61. *Ibid.*, pp. 20–23.

62. *Ibid.*, p. 24.

63. *Ibid.*, p. 30.

64. *Ibid.*, pp. 32–3.

65. *Ibid.*, p. 19ff.

PART I

THE IONIANS

The Milesians
    —Thales
    —Anaximander
    —Anaximenes
Xenophanes of Colophon
Heraclitus of Ephesus

CHAPTER 1
The Milesians

Philosophy (if we take the first known historical records as indicative) began in the sixth century B.C. at the southeastern corner of the Aegean community on the Ionian coast, specifically at Miletus, Colophon and Ephesus, three cities within fifty miles of each other as the crow flies (This fifty mile stretch also includes the island of Samos, Pythagoras' birthplace, where he spent the first forty years of his life before migrating to Italy.[1]) There is at least one compelling reason why philosophy could not very well have begun in any other quarter of the Greek world. The last of the three invasion-migrations into the area from the north, the Dorian, between 1200 and 1000 B.C., ushered in a period very much like our own Dark Ages, the darkness having been thickest in the north near the source and becoming less and less Stygian towards the south as the effects became less and less. This left these southern cities relatively undisturbed, and they were well within the orbit of the Phoenician sea trade and at the Mediterranean end of the overland traffic with the Orient. Babylonian astronomy, Egyptian surveying techniques, Phoenician navigational lore, and the cultural products of the Orient and Near East were all available.

Though the modern political terminology he uses borders on the inappropriate, Winspear supplies an excellent reconstruction of the conditions which led in Ionia to the growth of a wealthy and enterprising merchant class unhampered by conflicts with an aristocracy and free to devote its energies to creative cultural activities including the pursuit of wisdom:

29

The geographical position of the Ionian cities, clinging, as it were, to the coastal fringe of Asia Minor, forced their peoples into the position of middlemen. There was less land to be had. The possession of landed estates was relatively unimportant. The men of Ionia were caught in historical times between the great empires of the interior, Lydia first and then Persia, and the world of the Aegean. Moreover, founded as they originally must have been as agricultural extensions of the mainland, the tribal structure was relatively weak in the islands. There was, therefore, no social bulwark behind which landed proprietors could have defended their pre-eminence and developed a landed aristocracy. They were forced to develop into another, i.e., a mercantile development [sic] with an interesting consequence: in several Ionian cities, and particularly, we may conjecture, in Miletus and Ephesus, the mercantile oligarchy had only one opponent, the lower classes. They were not forced, as were the Pericleans at Athens, to fight on two fronts, i.e., against aristocrats and left-wing democrats. ...And so, the break-up of the tribal structure in Ionia fostered a class of wealthy merchants. In Attica, the same social movements gave power at first to the great landholders. The struggle, therefore, between the wealthy landholders and the merchant and financial classes, a struggle which was so conspicuous a feature of Athenian history in the fifth century B.C., took quite different forms in a city like Miletus or Ephesus.[2]

Miletus was the home of the first three philosophers of which we have any knowledge.† Thales, Anaximander and Anaximenes seem to have been colleagues, with Thales the oldest and the others perhaps his pupils. The two other Ionian philosophers of consequence—Xenophanes of Colophon and Heraclitus of Ephesus— will be considered in separate chapters to follow.

† Not only did Miletus produce the first philosophers but also the first historian, Hecataeus (c. 500 B.C.). The word ἱστορίν according to Jaeger, is Ionian in origin and orginally applied to physical inquiry too (Jaeger, *Paideia*, p. 382). The ideas of history and science both presuppose the idea of a cosmos or natural order of events—an idea originating, as we shall see, with Anaximander. And the Milesian Hecataeus was the first historian, as we use the term, insofar as he "was the first to transfer his 'investigation' from the whole of nature to one special field, the inhabited earth—which had hitherto been considered simply as a part of the cosmos...." (*Ibid.*) Hecataeus preceded even Herodotus in application of a scientific and rational approach to human events. (*Ibid.,* p. 484 note).

The contributions of the Milesians to philosophic thought center on the notion of *Physis*. It is at once both an ultimate "stuff" and an ultimate principle of explanation. It is also at the same time alive and divine. Jaeger points out that in its early usage, *Physis* was also synonomous with "genesis," meaning not only growth and development but origin as well.[3] That *Physis* was assumed by these earliest of philosophers to possess this constellation of conflicting qualities should not dismay us: it is to be remembered that they had not yet arrived at the stage where distinctions now obvious to us had been made explicit. While they were the first to ask questions about this primordial stuff, and to attempt answers within the frame of a natural order, it should not be forgotten that the Milesians were functioning within the context of a far more ancient belief in a single source of all things. This fact helps explain how their achievement was possible and at the same time highlights the originality of that achievement. Cornelius Loew calls it "one of the great differentiating insights in human history."[4]

With the proviso, then, that what the Milesians are seeking is also a principle of explanation, Aristotle's report that Thales was the first to ask questions about the ultimate "stuff" from which everything proceeds can be properly interpreted to characterize the whole Milesian school. Use of the term "stuff" here rather than some possible alternative such as "matter", "element" or "substance" on the one hand avoids the fixedness of type or kind they convey, and at the same time makes it possible to understand that we are concerned with something ultimate in nature from which everything can be derived and in terms of which everything can be explained. It has been suggested that the Milesians be called "Hylozoists", combining the Greek words *hylē*, most often rendered "matter," with *zoé* meaning, "life". To the extent that the philosophic datum they postulate is thought of in these terms, their view is rooted in the Dionysiac notion of *Thymos-soul*, understood as a life-principle common to a community of individuals. Another term often applied to the Ionians in general and to the Milesians in particular, and appropriate enough in a general way, is "Nature Philosophers," "nature" being a rendition of the Greek work *Physis*. Unfortunately, *Physis* is at the same time the root of our modern term "physics", a coincidence which, in view of the foregoing, surely has misleading associations.

The Milesians sought for unity amidst diversity in the guise of a principle of explanation such as we have been discussing, and they each made a singular contribution to this quest. As far as we know, Thales was the first to seek such a principle; Anaximander was the first to interpret it nonsensuously; and Anaximenes was the first to suggest a mechanism whereby qualitative differences could be explained. For our immediate predecessors, happily convinced of the truth of the Newtonian world view, the attempts of these earliest of Greek philosophers to understand nature were little more than childishly inadequate. But in our own time when all of the foundations of our immediate past are being called into question, the intimations of the Milesians are highly suggestive and significant. A natural history of the meaning of *Physis* would probably show the meaning given to the idea of nature by the later ancients and, to a degree, by all of Western Civilization, to be rooted in the "naive" questioning of the Milesians.

THALES

Thales of Miletus, called the father of philosophy, flourished about 585 B.C.†While some commentators attribute a book to him, there are no extant fragments in Thales' own words, and indeed, since no one of the ancients, even among his immediate successors, seems to be aware of such writing, it is generally held that he wrote nothing. Certainly nothing survives, and all we know of his teachings comes from indirect sources.

From the commentators, however, it is clear that Thales was a man of wide activities, famous in his own time for his works in mathematics (a theorem of geometry still bears his name) as well as in the practical areas of navigation (he is credited with books on *Nautical Astronomy, On the Solstice,* and *On the Equinox,*‡ but while indicative of his interests their authorship is doubtful), meteorology, astronomy, politics, and commerce. From Herodotus, the great fifth century B.C. historian, we learn that he foretold an eclipse of the sun, which could well have been done on the basis of existing Babylonian tables and charts. He is also said to have studied the Hyades,§ stars famous for their association with rainy weather.

T1 Herodotus *The Persian Wars* 1. 74 [Loeb]
They (Medes and Lydians) were still warring with equal success, when it chanced, at an encounter which happened in the sixth year, that during the battle the day was suddenly

---

†As a rule of thumb ancient chronologists considered a man to "flourish" at forty years of age, and as Thales is reported to have attained the age of seventy-eight, this would place his life span between 625 and 542 B.C.
‡Freeman's presumably doubtful Fragments 1 and 4-
    1. (*Title*: 'Nautical Astronomy'),
    4. (*Titles*: '*On the Solstice*', '*On the Equinox*').
§Freeman's Fragment 2-
    2. (*There are two Hyades, one north and one south*).

turned to night. Thales of Miletus had foretold this loss of
daylight to the Ionians, fixing it within the year in which the
change did indeed happen.

With our dating system this eclipse would have occurred on the 28th of
May, 585 B.C., and is usually taken as indicating the central period of
Thales' career. From the same source we learn that he advised the
Ionians to federate with a joint council at Teos in the face of the Persian
threat[5], and that he explained the periodic flooding of the Nile in terms
of the Etesian winds which blew the water back up the river from its
mouth.[6] Tradition held that Thales diverted the river Halys so that King
Croesus might cross his army, but Herodotus didn't believe it.[7] In
another anecdote, Plato tells how Thales fell down a well while star-
gazing.

T2 Plato *Theaetetus* 174a[8]
The same thing as the story about the Thracian maidservant
who exercised her wit at the expense of Thales, when he was
looking up to study the stars and tumbled down a well. She
scoffed at him for being so eager to know what was happen-
ing in the sky that he could not see what lay at his feet.

And in Aristotle's *Politics* we hear the story of how and why he cornered
the olive market one year:

T3 Aristotle *Politics* 1259a9–18[9]
He was reproached for his poverty, which was supposed to
show that philosphy was of no use. According to the story,
he knew by his skill in the stars while it was yet winter that
there would be a great harvest of olives in the coming year;
so, having little money, he gave deposits for the use of all the
olive-presses in Chios and Miletus, which he hired at a low
price because no one bid against him. When the harvest-time
came, and many were wanted all at once and of a sudden, he
let them out at any rate which he pleased, and made a
quantity of money. Thus he showed the world that philosophers can easily be rich if they like, but that their ambition
is of another sort.

In a wide scattering of other sources†, we learn that Thales was famous
as an astronomer and mathematician: the discovery of the constellation
called the Little Bear is attributed to him as well as the bringing of
geometry from Egypt to Greece, along with such practical knowledge as

---

†The *Lives of the Philosophers* by Diogenes Laertius of the second century B.C.; the *On
Euclid* by Proclus, fifth century A.D. Neo-platonic commentator; the *Commentaria* of
Simplicius, a sixth century A.D. commentator; the *Physical Opinions* of Theophrastus,
friend of Aristotle and his successor as head of the Lyceum; the *De Natura Deorum* of
Cicero; and the *Civitatis Dei* of Saint Augustine.

measuring the height of something by the length of its shadow and the distance of a ship at sea by the height of its mast.† Whether all this is factual or not is unimportant, but it clearly shows him to be a man of broad interests and widely differing activities. Antiquity counts him among the Seven Sages of Ancient Greece.‡ As such, he appears to us as a symbol as well as a source of the new attitudes and new knowledge, of which the Milesian School is the beginning and Thales the founder.

PHYSIS AS WATER

But Thales' practical activities are not what make Aristotle call him the founder of philosphy, and it is from Aristotle that we learn of his most important doctrines: his theory that the primordial stuff is Water (T4) and that the earth floats on Water (T5), that all things are full of gods (T6) and that the magnet has a "living power" to move iron (T7):

T4 Aristotle *Meta*. 983b6–13, 17–27
Of the first philosophers, then, most thought the principles which were of the nature of matter were the only principles of all things. That of which all things that are consist, the first from which they come to be, the last into which they are resolved (the substance remaining, but changing in its modifications), this they say is the element and this the principle of things, and therefore they think nothing is either generated or destroyed, since this sort of entity is always conserved, . . . for there must be some entity—either one or more than one—from which all other things come to be, it being conserved. Yet they do not all agree as to the number and the nature of these principles. Thales, the founder of this type of philosophy, says the principle is water (for which reason he declared that the earth rests on water), getting the notion perhaps from seeing that the nutriment of all things is moist, and that heat itself is generated from the moist and kept alive by it (and that from which they come to be is a principle of all things). He got his notion from this fact, and from the fact that the seeds of all things have a moist nature, and that water is the origin of the nature of moist things.

T5 Aristotle *De Caelo* 294a28–34
Others say the earth rests on water. This, indeed, is the oldest theory that has been preserved, and is attributed to Thales of

---

†The instrument used for this measurement was called a *gnomon*. For full description see p. 36 and note.
‡The names of this list of seven vary, with only four agreed upon by all; Bias of Priênê, Pittacus the tyrant of Mytelene, Solon the Athenian law-giver, and Thales of Miletus. All lived within fifty years of 600 B.C.

Miletus. It was supposed to stay still because it floated like wood and other similar substances, which are so constituted as to rest upon water but not upon air. As if the same account had not to be given of the water which carries the earth as of the earth itself!

T6 Aristotle *De Anima* 411a7–9
Certain thinkers say that soul is intermingled in the whole universe, and it is perhaps for that reason that Thales came to the opinion that all things are full of gods.

T7 Aristotle *De Anima* 405a20–22
Thales, too, to judge from what is recorded about him, seems to have held soul to be a motive force, since he said that the magnet has a soul in it because it moves the iron.

Even though "all things are full of gods" is a statement about things, coupled with the observation of the power of the magnet, it is clear that Thales was not thinking of a God in our traditional sense, or even the polytheism of the Greek religion, but instead about the *power* in things, which he held to be divine. Although the word "soul" appearing in T6 is not to be understood as anything more than a life principle, conceived in the broadest possible sense and belonging to everything, it, along with T5, constitutes our evidence for regarding Thales as a hylozoist.

At first glance, the statement that Water is the basic world stuff does not seem very satisfactory, and just what recommended this view to Thales can only be conjectured. But simple observation gives much evidence that water is ubiquitous. Besides the obvious changes of water itself into ice and vapor, life requires water and the seed of everything is wet. Just how Water becomes the things of the world for Thales is not known at all, but the condensation-rarefaction phenomenon so obvious with water itself is very suggestive and, in fact, becomes explicit in the thought of Anaximenes. Not only does observation suggest a basis for his view of water as primal, but it also carries overtones of the ancient myth that in the order of things Okeanos came first.†

ANAXIMANDER

There is very little information about the teachings of Thales; indeed, it is even possible to raise reasonable doubts as to whether Thales himself ever existed. But when we come to Anaximander we have evidence not only of a philospher-scientist reputed to be the younger colleague and successor of Thales in the development of that line of

†Kirk & Raven suggest a connection between the importance of water in Thales and "near eastern, and possible Egyptian, mythological accounts." G.S. Kirk & J.E. Raven, *The Presocratic Philosophers*, Cambridge University Press, 1957, pp. 77, 89, 90-91. Hereinafter cited as Kirk & Raven.

thought which is so characteristic of the Milesian school, but also of one of the great speculative minds in the western tradition.

Our chief sources of information about Anaximander are the writings of Aristotle and the Aristotelean school, referred to as the Peripatetics after Aristotle's habit of walking about while lecturing. Besides these accounts, we have what purports to be a direct quotation from the writings of Anaximander.

Diogenes Laertius gives us an insight into Anaximander's background and beliefs.

> **T8** Diogenes Laertius 2. 1-2 [Loeb]
> Anaximander, the son of Praxiades, was a native of Miletus. He laid down as his principle and element that which is unlimited without defining it as air or water or anything else.... He was the first inventor of the gnomon and set it for a sundial in Lacedaemon, as is stated by Favorinus in his *Miscellaneous History*, in order to mark the solstices and equinoxes; he also constructed clocks to tell the time. He was the first to draw on a map the outline of land and sea, and he constructed a globe as well.
>
> His exposition of his doctrines took the form of a summary which no doubt came into the hands, among others, of Apollodorus of Athens. He says in his *Chronology* that in the second year of the 58th Olympiad Anaximander was sixty-four, and that he died not long afterwards. Thus he flourished almost at the same time as Polycrates the tyrant of Samos.

From this account we can infer that he lived from 610/9–547/6 B.C. He is credited with being the first Greek to write his views on nature in prose, and is the first person about whom it can be said that he tried to give a complete and detailed account of the totality of man's experiences of the world. It is more probable that he introduced into Greece the *gnomon*† for telling time and date than that he discovered it,[10] and there is good reason to accept him as the first map-maker, although no copy of any of his maps survives. ‡

---

†Thales as well as Anaximander is said to have made use of the *gnomon*. It is defined as "an early astronomical instrument consisting of a vertical shaft, column, or the like, for determining the altitude of the sun or the latitude of a position by measuring the length of its shadow." (Random House Dictionary of the English Language, 1967)

‡For interesting research and reconstruction of what this map may have looked like, *see* C.H. Kahn, *Anaximander and the Origins of Greek Cosmology*, Columbia University Press, New York and London, 1960.

PHYSIS AS THE APEIRON

As an alternative to the Water of Thales, Anaximander posited an ultimate stuff which he called the *Apeiron*. His reasons for being dissatisfied with explaining everything in terms of a visible pheno-menon such as water are not known. Perhaps he reasoned that if everything is Water, then, since water is finite, it would be all used up in creation through time; perhaps he realized that this same result would be true for the stuff of experience in general; and perhaps he wondered how and why, if Water is ultimate, there was anything else to be experienced at all. But whatever his reasons, the fact that he used a concept rather than an item of experience like water as his principle of explanation sets Anaximander apart immediately. As we consider the meaning of *Apeiron* we must realize that, in attempting to find a principle which is first, ultimate, and the source of everything else, the most important considerations are derived not directly from experience but from the idea of what such a principle would have to be like in order to be first, ultimate, and the source of everything else. This appeal to concepts, and to the indirect mode of argument required to frame such principles of explanation is in a general way distinctive of both meta-physics and science according to our contemporary understanding of these terms.

> **T9** Simplicius *Phys.* 24. 13 [K&R105-7]
> Of those who say that it is one, moving, and infinite, Anaxi-mander, son of Praxiades, a Milesian, the successor and pupil of Thales, said that the principle and element of exist-ing things was the *apeiron*, being the first to introduce this name of the material principle. He says that it is neither water nor any other of the so-called elements, but some other *apeiron* nature, from which come into being all the heavens and the worlds in them.

The following quotation from Aristotle suggests how Anaximander may have thought the *Apeiron* to be related to the four elements, earth, air, fire and water:

> **T10** Aristotle *Physics* 204b22-29
> Nor...can the infinite body be one and simple, whether it is, as some hold*, a thing over and above the elements (from which they generate the elements) or is not thus qualified....
> We must consider the former alternatives; for there *are* some

---

*probably Anaximander

people who make this the infinite, and not air or water, in
order that the other elements may not be annihilated by the
element which is infinite. They have contrariety with each
other—air is cold, water moist, fire hot; if one were infinite,
the others by now would have ceased to be. As it is, they say,
the infinite is different from them and is their source.

There is a good deal of difference of opinion in the tradition as to just
how to translate *Apeiron*. It is generally agreed that to call it "infinite",
even though that is the name given to it by Aristotle and his followers, is
a mistake. The idea of the infinite with its mathematical implications is
much too complicated to be used here. One of the things that must be
resisted is to suppose that Aristotle's use of "infinite" reflects the original meaning rather than the language of the Peripatetic school. There
are, however, two alternative ways of rendering it, both of which are
helpful. It may be called "indefinite"[11] and this makes clear the idea that
out of this indefinite stuff comes all the qualitative variety of the world;
the *Apeiron* is indefinite as to qualitative determination. But to call it
merely "the indefinite" is to characterize it only from a qualitative point
of view. While such an interpretation of the *Apeiron* would make it
appear more conceptual than concrete, it would be a mistake to conceive of it in completely abstract terms. To do so would be to vitiate
Anaximander's claim to be a member of the Milesian school. It is
reasonable to believe that Anaximander thought of the *Apeiron* in
physical or quasi-physical terms. It takes nothing away from his
achievements as a philosopher, and to do so is entirely in keeping with
his time. For this reason, Jaeger's translation as the "boundless", which
retains the indefiniteness of qualitative determination and adds the idea
of an unlimited source, is appropriate. It also seems best to render
"*Apeiron*" in two words as "Boundless Stuff" in order to retain that
sense of the concrete which is so characteristic of the early Ionians. For
Anaximander, then, *Physis* is a Boundless Stuff out of which the
opposites hot-cold, wet-dry, are separated. It is the beginning of all
things but has no beginning itself; it is both divine and immortal, and
surrounds and steers all things.

T11   Aristotle *Physics* 203b7-9, 11-14
But there cannot be a source of the infinite or limitless, for
that would be a limit of it. Further, as it is a beginning, it is
both uncreatable and indestructible..., but it is this which is
held to be the principle of other things, and to encompass all
and to steer all, as those assert who do not recognize, alongside the infinite, other causes, such as Mind or Friendship.
Further they identify it with the Divine, for it is "deathless

and imperishable"† as Anaximander says, with the majority
of the physicists.

ANAXIMANDER'S BEST KNOWN FRAGMENT

It is when we ask what is the manner in which the Boundless Stuff is
related to the opposites which separate from it—how does the Boundless Stuff "surround all things and steer all"—that we come to the sole
existing fragment of consequence from Anaximander. The original
context is the account of Anaximander given by Theophrastus, but it
comes to us through a version by Simplicius:

> (Frg.1)...some other *apeiron* nature, from which come into
> being all the heavens and the worlds in them. And the source
> of coming-to-be for existing things is that into which de-
> struction, too, happens, ACCORDING TO NECESSITY:
> FOR THEY PAY PENALTY AND RETRIBUTION TO
> EACH OTHER FOR THEIR INJUSTICE ACCORDING
> TO THE ASSESSMENT OF TIME, as he describes it in
> these rather poetical terms.‡ [K&R105-7]

This fragment is both striking and far-reaching in its import. Essentially
what we have here is the birth of an explicit idea of a cosmos, as well as
certain claims about its manner of operation. Although there is no
evidence that Anaximander himself used the term "cosmos", he does
regard all coming into being and passing away as part of a cosmos (the
term originally signified "right order" in a state or other community)[12],
and this cosmos as well as the domain of human affairs is under the
governance of Justice, or to use Anaximander's own term, *Dike*. Despite the fact that all change is supposed by Anaximander to take place
"according to necessity," it should not be assumed that he had already
developed the concept of a law of nature in the modern sense. *Dike* was
orginally a moral notion, and a clear distinction between moral and
physical law is as yet beyond the ken of these early thinkers. It must not
be forgotten that, as Jaeger puts it, we are but at "the first [though most

---

†Compare Freeman's Frg.3, "(*The Non-Limited*) [i.e., the *Apeiron*] is immortal and
indestructible," and Freeman's Frg. 2, "This (essential nature, whatever it is, of the Non-
Limited) [i.e. the *Apeiron*] is everlasting and ageless."
‡Freeman's version of Frg. 1:
  1. The Non-Limited is the original material of existing things; further, the source from
     which existing things derive their existence is also that to which they return at their
     destruction, according to necessity; for they give justice and make reparation to one
     another for their injustice, according to the arrangement of Time.

important] stage in the projection of the life of the city-state upon the life of the universe."[13] However,

> it is not a compendious description of events, but a justification of the nature of the universe: Anaximander shows creation to be a cosmos "writ large"—namely a community of things under law.[14]

Nor should mention of necessity lead one to think of Anaximander's cosmos as a purposeless mechanism; it will be recalled that the *Apeiron* or "boundless" steers all. Not that steering is incompatible with mechanism as such—the word *kybernon* used by Anaximander for "steering" is the root of "cybernetics", our word for the study of controlling mechanisms. Though it would be misleading to attribute to Anaximander the notion that the *Apeiron* is a controlling mechanism, yet surely his cosmos is a purposeful one.

The experience of such opposing qualities as hot and cold, wet and dry, as well as the oscillations and rhythms of day and night and the seasons, must have been regarded as of key significance by Anaximander as they were by his contemporaries. Qualities such as these are surely among the "they" that Anaximander conceives of as paying "penalty and retribution to each other." But though the qualities hot and cold, wet and dry, which were regarded as polar opposites (i.e., contradictories)† took on even greater importance in the later evolution of Greek philosophy and science, the conflict and struggle characterizing Anaximander's cosmos may have applied equally to qualities that we regard as merely different from each other (i.e., contraries)‡ inasmuch as they are understood as strung together as developmental stages, one supplanting another. Indeed, they too may have been conceived as in opposition, the distinction between contradictories and contraries not yet having been clearly formulated. Both contraries and contradictories then may have been governed by "necessity" and the "assessment" or "allotment of time," the idea being that each determinate thing or stage has its own time in the sun, that everything comes to be by overcoming another and finishes insofar as it is overcome by another. And as Wheelwright suggests:

> The meaning can best be understood by looking at it in two perspectives successively. In biological perspective we can— on the analogy of an organism that grows, reproduces, and

---

†Contradictory qualities are negations of one another, e.g., black and non-black.
‡Contrary qualities are such that, though different, they are not negations of one another. For example, black and white are contraries because, though different, the existence of shades of gray is evidence that non-black is not the same as white and that non-white is not the same as black.

dies—regard a quality, such as summer heat, as coming into being, achieving full growth, and then, after a suitable time, making way for the opposite quality—in this case winter cold—which is to be conceived as going in its turn through the same life-cycle. In ethico-religious perspective the situation can be conceived through the typically Greek idea of *hybris*, which can be roughly translated *flagrant self-assertion*. Now what Anaximander's metaphysical imagination has done is to envisage the process of flagrant self-assertion together with its self-terminating outcome as applying not only to human life but to all entities whatsoever.[15]

Although Anaximander's conception of changes in the finite world of becoming as the result of opposites in strife with each other certainly is his own explanation and goes far beyond anything previous to it, still it is continous with that old Greek conception of reality as being originally parceled out into realms† and of the individual being fated to transgress these natural limits just by being an individual. Anaximander would seem to occupy a middle ground between this older view and the view of Heraclitus that the individual occurs within the tension created and maintained by the opposites.

SCIENTIFIC IDEAS

From the Boundless Stuff the opposites hot-dry and cold-wet are separated "out", as Aristotle sees it[16], or separated "off", as Simplicius reports.[17] It is not clear which, if either, of these should be attributed to Anaximander or even if he had as clear an idea of the opposites as is assumed by Aristotle; "out" suggests that the hot and cold are contained in the Boundless Stuff and separated out, "off" suggests that hot and cold are somehow a piece of the Boundless Stuff which gets separated off. It may equally well be that Anaximander never asked himself that question because when he calls the Boundless Stuff "divine" (*tò thèon*) it has exactly this power to produce the opposites and that is sufficient[18].

We learn from a work erroneously attributed to Plutarch that from the opposites comes a sphere of flame surrounding moist air with a condensation of earth at the center, and this encompassing flame fits the air like the bark on a tree.[19] Finally the sphere of flame bursts, forming circular tubes of fire enclosed by the moist air, and the heavens are formed of three of these fire tubes, the sun being the outer, then the moon, and then the fixed stars, the inner circle. The sun and moon are

†See pp. 8, 10.

glimpses of the celestial fire allowed by a hole in the moist air of the two outer circles, and the fixed stars of the fire of the inner circle as seen through a multiplicity of such holes:

> **T12**   Hippolytus *Ref.* 1. 6. 4–5. [K&R135]
> The heavenly bodies come into being as a circle of fire separating off from the fire in the world and enclosed by air. There are breathing-holes, certain pipe-like passages, at which the heavenly bodies show themselves; accordingly eclipses occur when the breathing holes are blocked up. The moon is seen now waxing, now waning according to the blocking or opening of the channels. The circle of the sun is 27 times the size of (the earth, that of) the moon (18 times); the sun is highest and the circle of the fixed stars lowest.

> **T13**   Aetius 2. 20. 1. [K&R135]
> Anaximander says the sun is a circle 28 times the size of the earth, like a chariot wheel, with its felloe hollow and full of fire, and showing the fire at a certain point through an aperture as though through the nozzle of a bellows.†

These passages constitute a good part of the evidence relied upon by Farrington to illustrate the close association of Ionian thought with a knowledge of technique.[20] And it is interesting to note in passing the geometrical proportions used to describe the relation between heavens and earth. Presumably the circle of the fixed stars is nine times the size of the earth. The earth itself is built like a drum, and its width is three times its depth, a proportion analogous to the ratios of the heavenly bodies. If there is anything to the tradition that Pythagoras was a pupil of Anaximander, this interest in number relations as descriptive of the cosmos which is central to Pythagoreanism could well be rooted in the Milesian school.

The earth is like a stone column‡ and rests at the center of the *Cosmos*, and Anaximander is supposed to have taught that it is kept where it is at the center because of its balance and harmony within the whole system:

> **T14**   Aristotle *De Caelo* 295b10–16
> ...there are some, Anaximander, for instance, among the ancients, who say that the earth keeps its place because of its indifference. Motion upward and downward and sideways

---

†Freeman's Frg. 4:
   Nozzle of the bellows.
‡Freeman's Frg. 5:
   (*The Earth is like*) a stone column.

were all, they thought, equally inappropriate to that which is
set at the centre and indifferently related to every extreme
point; and to move in contrary directions at the same time
was impossible: so it must needs remain still.

This is a startling explanation, when you come to think of it, and is based
neither upon common sense nor any kind of observation. On the
strength of it, de Santillana attributes to Anaximander the first use of an
aspect of a way of thinking that has since become "a pillar of scientific
thought", i.e., the principle of sufficient reason."[21] In his terms: "It states
that causes which are undistinguishable intrinsically, when considered
by themselves, cannot produce distinguishable effects."[22]

It is perhaps also of interest that the readily observable meteorological phenomena of experience were explained by Anaximander in terms
of various conditions and movement of wind:

> **T15** Aetius 3. 3. 1–2 [K&R138]
> (On thunder, lightening, thunder bolts, whirlwinds and
> typhoons.) Anaximander says that all these things occur as a
> result of wind: for whenever it is shut up in a thick cloud and
> then bursts out forcibly, through its fineness and lightness,
> then the bursting makes the noise, while the rift against the
> blackness of the cloud makes the flash.

In conclusion, we note that Anaximander held all life to have started
in mud and slime through action of the sun.[23] Perhaps he was building
upon the generalization of Thales about water being the basis of things,
perhaps he was formalizing traditional beliefs and perhaps he was
explaining his direct experience—very likely all three. He must have
observed that man needs a long period of gestation before birth as well
as a long period of nurture afterwards and he seems to have held that,
developmentally, man first came from the fish.

> **T16** Aetius 5. 19. 4 [K&R141]
> Anaximander said that the first living creatures were born in
> moisture, enclosed in thorny barks; and that as their age
> increased they came forth on to the drier part, and when the
> bark had broken off, they lived a different kind of life for a
> short time.

Of the Milesians, Anaximander seems to have been the most widely
known among the early Pre-Socratic philosophers. It is reasonable to
assume that it is Anaximander who set the general shape of Ionian
cosmology. The differing way of characterizing the ultimate stuff
employed by his colleague Anaximenes and the latter's development of
the principle of condensation and rarefaction need not be thought of as

changing the basic cosmological outlines—outlines which would not be hostile to the views of Xenophanes and Heraclitus and certainly formed part of the ground and basis for Pythagorean thought.

ANAXIMENES

The very best estimates make Anaximenes about twenty-five years junior to Anaximander, and he is reported to have flourished about 546–5 B.C., the year in which Sardis was captured by Cyrus, the Persian king.[24] Nothing is known of the details of his life and activities. The reference in Diogenes Laertius to his use of language, coupled with what purports to be a quotation, makes it fairly certain that he wrote a book.[25]

PHYSIS AS AIR

Philosophically, Anaximenes represents a return to the general position of Thales regarding the Ultimate Stuff, for he chose one of the traditional elements, Air, to be primary.

> **T17** Theophrastus *ap.* Simplicium *Phy.* 24, 26 [K&R 144]
> Anaximenes son of Eurystrathus, of Miletus, a companion of Anaximander, also says that the underlying nature is one and infinite like him, but not undefined as Anaximander said but definite, for he identifies it as air; and it differs in its substantial nature by rarity and density. Being made finer it becomes fire, being made thicker it becomes wind, then cloud, then (when thickened still more) water, then earth, then stones: And the rest come into being from these. He, too, makes motion eternal, and says that change, also, comes about through it.

Anaximenes certainly thought that Air was quantitatively unlimited and probably considered that the qualitative limitation of any single element such as Air posed no problem because of his explanation of change. This he did in terms of the condensation and rarefaction of Air in which the opposites, hot and cold, play a basic part. These come to exist directly from Air, and they in turn give rise to the other things of experience. Wheelwright points out that the innovation in this conception lies in placing all of the elements along a condensation-rarefaction continuum and conceiving of all change as a serial progression along that continuum, and avers that this conception is not so far from Heraclitean "upward and downward ways."[26]

Just how explicitly Anaximenes conceived of his one principle of explanation is not known, but implicitly it means that differences in kind are ultimately a matter of quantity of Air. The meteorology and cosmology of Anaximenes involve the application of the condensation-rarefaction principle to every conceivable kind of phenomenon.

T18 Aetius 3. 3. 2. [K&R 157-8]
Anaximenes said the same as he (Anaximander), adding what happens in the case of sea, which flashes when cleft by oars. Anaximenes said that clouds occur when the air is further thickened; when it is compressed further rain is squeezed out, and hail occurs where the descending water coalesces, snow when some windy portion is included together with the moisture.

There is more than a hint here of Pythagoreanism, in which everything is explained in terms of number, as well as of the idea of reduction of quality to quantity, which becomes explicit in the work of the Fourth Century B.C. pluralists, Empedocles, Anaxagoras, and Democritus. The idea that qualitative difference can be ranged along a continuum of quantitative relatedness is, of course, also of first importance for the development of science.

If we ask ourselves what could have recommended Air as the ultimate stuff to Anaximenes, he may have seen Air as the only really unlimited element and therefore sufficient for creation. It is also reasonable to assume that the close parallel between "breath", which was one of the traditional sources of life for the Greeks, and "air" was a major consideration. Certainly the one fragment of any consequence which survives would suggest exactly this connection. It is found in the writings of Aetius:

(Frg.2) As our soul, being air, holds us together, so do breath and air surround the whole universe.

As the self-moving source of all motion, Air is thought of as divine, and it is more than likely that Anaximenes thought of the whole world as living and permeated with life and soul in much the same way that the other members of his school did. This idea was later to be revived in the fifth century thought of Diogenes of Apollonia.†

The only other known fragments of Anaximenes are the following two, neither of which is particularly helpful:

(Frg.1) (*Paraphrase containing the word*) Loose (= rare).
(Frg.2a) (*The sun is broad*) like a leaf.

---

†See Chapter 10.

NOTES

1. Porphyrius, *Vita Pythagorae* 9; Kirk & Raven, p. 217.

2. Winspear, pp. 126-7.

3. Werner Jaeger, *Theology of the Early Greek Philosophers* (Oxford: Clarendon Press, 1947), p. 20.

4. Loew, pp. 216-7.

5. Herodotus 1. 170.

6. Herodotus 2. 20.

7. Herodotus 1. 75.

8. Edith Hamilton and Huntington Cairns, eds., trans. F. M. Cornford, *Plato: The Collected Dialogues*, Bollingen Series 71, (Princeton: Princeton University Press, 1961), p. 879.

9. All testimonia from Aristotle are from *The Oxford Translation of Aristotle,* ed. W. D. Ross (Oxford: Oxford University Press n.d.) unless otherwise stated.

10. Herodotus 2. 109.

11. As do Kirk & Raven, p. 104ff.

12. Jaeger, *Paideia,*vol. 1, p. 110.

13. *Ibid.*, p. 161.

14. *Ibid.*, p. 160.

15. Philip Wheelwright, *Heraclitus* (New York: Atheneum, 1964), p. 5.

16. Aristotle *Phys.* 187a12.

17. Simplicius *Phys.* 24. 21; Kirk & Raven, p. 129.

18. Kirk & Raven, p. 130.

19. [Plutarch] *Stromateis 2*; Kirk & Raven, p. 131 (brackets indicate erroneous ascription of authorship).

20. Farrington, p. 38. See also p. 20ff of present volume.

21. Giorgio de Santillana, *The Origins of Scientific Thought* (New York: Mentor Books, New American Library, 1961) pp. 34-5.

22. *Ibid.*

23. Hippolytus *Ref.* 1. 6. 6; Kirk & Raven, p. 141.

24. Diogenes Laertius 2. 3.

25. Kirk & Raven, p. 143.

26. Wheelwright, p. 6.

CHAPTER 2
Xenophanes

From the fragments left by the early Greek thinkers, Xenophanes is the only one who comes through to us as a person. This is partly due, undoubtedly, to the lack of any systematic philosophical structure like that of the Milesians. There would seem to be no system ot Xenophanes. Although he is Ionian by birth and heritage, he did not share that interest in physical nature which characterizes the Milesian school. His approach is a much more personal and religious one, and even though based upon Ionian conceptions, his views exhibit more of the human and mystical aspects which to some degree are part and parcel of the later, more completely developed philosophies of thinkers such as Heraclitus, Pythagoras, Parmenides, Empedocles and Plato. While his insight and conviction led him to ideas which are of first importance not only to subsequent Greek philosophy but to the whole Western tradition, there are many who consider him more seer than philosopher. But surely, while he has a religious relationship to the ultimately real, his attempts to think clearly and correctly about *tò Thèon* are as important to science in the sense of rational explanation and the development of theory as they are for religion, unless indeed science is to be understood in a narrowly empirical way. To carry the point further, the Milesian nature philosophers were primarily concerned with problems of change and the Many. The concern of Xenophanes is with the nature of the One from which all proceeds, and his concern for the One takes a form which the Milesians, except for the imaginative *Apeiron* of Anaximander, never consider. But, as Windelband points out,[1] insofar as his One is eternal and changeless it can no longer be used to explain the Many of experience.

T19   Diogenes Laertius 9. 18 [Loeb]

Xenophanes, a native of Colophon, the son of Dexius or, according to Apollodorus, of Orthomenes....He was banished from his native city and lived at Zancle in Sicily...also ...in Catana.... His writings are in epic metre, as well as elegiacs and iambics attacking Hesiod and Homer and denouncing what they said about the Gods. Furthermore he used to recite his own poems. It is stated that he opposed the views of Thales and Pythagoras and attacked Epimenides also. He lived to a very great age, as his own words somewhere testify: "Seven and sixty are now the years that have been tossing my cares up and down the land of Greece; and there were then twenty and five years more from my birth up, if I know how to speak truly about these things...." [Frg.8.]† He flourished about the 60th Olympiad [540-537 B.C.].

On the basis of this, and assuming that the occasion of his leaving Colophon was the fall of his native city to the Medes *circa* 546 B.C., Xenophanes would have been born about 570 B.C. and would have written the above passage around 478 B.C. Generally, however, the years 570-475 are given for him. One reason for taking the year of the fall of Colophon as pivotal lies in a fragment in which Xenophanes recalls the character of life in pre-Medean Colophon:

(Frg.3) (The men of Colophon), having learnt useless forms of luxury from the Lydians, as long as they were free from hateful tyranny, used to go to the place of assembly wearing all-purple robes, not less than a thousand of them in all: haughty, adorned with well-dressed hair, steeped in the scent of skilfully-prepared unguents.

It is reasonable to suppose that, after leaving his native city, he spent the rest of his life wandering about, largely in Sicily.

POETIC STYLE AND MORAL CAST OF THOUGHT

All of Xenophanes' writings were in verse and he created the satirical verse form called "silloi," which was much used and admired by later poets. It seems he recited these poems himself, and while some ancient

---

†Freeman's rendition of Frg. 8: "By now, seven and sixty years have been tossing my care-filled heart over the land of Hellas. From my birth till then (*that is, till his exile*), there were twenty-five years to be added to these, if indeed I am able to tell correctly of these matters."

sources, on the basis of this, considered him to be an Homeric rhapsode, it is not likely.

The following fragments exemplify his poetic style, and even though of little relevance philosophically, they convey something of the style of his thought and the moral cast of the man.

(Frg. 1) For now, behold, the floor is clean, and so too the hands of all, and the cups. One (*attendant*) places woven garlands round our heads, another proffers sweet-scented myrrh in a saucer. The mixing bowl stands there full of good cheer, and another wine is ready in the jar, a wine that promises never to betray us, honeyed, smelling of flowers. In our midst the frankincense gives forth its sacred perfume; and there is cold water, sweet and pure. Golden loaves lie to hand, and the lordly table is laden with cheese and with honey. The alter in the centre is decked with flowers all over, and song and revelry fill the mansion.

It is proper for men who are enjoying themselves first of all to praise God with decent stories and pure words. But when they have poured a libation and prayed for the power to do what is just—for thus to pray is our foremost need—it is no outrage to drink as much as will enable you to reach home without a guide, unless you are very old. But the man whom one must praise is he who after drinking expresses thoughts that are noble, as well as his memory (*and his endeavor*) concerning virtue allows, not treating of the battles of the Titans or of the Giants, figments of our predecessors, nor of violent civil war, in which tales there is nothing useful; but always to have respect for the gods, *that* is good.

(Frg. 22) One should hold such converse by the fire-side in the winter season, lying on a soft couch, well-fed, drinking sweet wine, nibbling peas: "Who are you among men, and where from? How old are you, my good friend? What age were you when the Mede came?"

(Frg. 2) But if anyone were to win a victory with fleetness of foot, or fighting in the Pentathlon, where the precinct of Zeus lies between the springs of Pisa at Olympia, or in wrestling, or in virtue of the painful science of boxing, or in the dread kind of contest called Pancration†: to the citizens he would be more glorious to look upon, and he would acquire a conspicuous seat of honour at competitions, and

---

†Combining wrestling and boxing.

his maintenance would be provided out of the public stores by the City-State, as well as a gift for him to lay aside as treasure.

So too if he won a prize with his horses, he would obtain all these rewards, though not deserving of them as *I* am; for my craft (wisdom) is better than the strength of men or of horses. Yet opinion is altogether confused on this matter, and it is not right to prefer physical strength to noble Wisdom. For it is not the presence of a good boxer in the community, nor of one good at the Pentathlon or at wrestling, nor even of one who excels in fleetness of foot—which is the highest in honour of all the feats of strength seen in men's athletic contests—it is not these that will give a City-State a better constitution. Small would be the enjoyment that a City-State would reap over the athletic victory of a citizen beside the banks of Pisa! These things do not enrich the treasure-chambers of the State.

These fragments have something in common; they oppose the common practices of the day. What is more common among men at drink and leisure than talk of heroes and violence and yet there "is nothing useful" in this. Talk should be of what is "noble." Here we have the moral mind at work. Further, he opposes the popular cult of athletic excellence as not being worthy of the high honors given it. If we ask what is to be cultivated in the City, the answer is Wisdom. But the wisdom of Xenophanes is of an intellectual kind. We have no description of this intellectual wisdom, but his criticisms of traditional religion show what he is against, and his statements about the true nature of the divine give some positive indications.

CRITICISM OF RELIGION

(Frg.10) Since from the beginning all have learnt in accordance with Homer....

(Frg.11) Both Homer and Hesiod have attributed to the gods all things that are shameful and a reproach among mankind: theft, adultery, and mutual deception.

(Frg.12) They have narrated every possible wicked story of the gods: theft, adultery, and mutual deception.

Exactly who "they" are in Frg. 12 is unclear, but presumably the religious teachers of Greece, including, of course, Homer and Hesiod. It is wrong to picture the gods in immoral actions. But the root of the matter goes much deeper than this, and constitutes one of the major contributions of Xenophanes. The problem is not merely that immoral actions are assigned to the gods, but that actions typical only of humans are attributed to the gods. Xenophanes is the first to level the charge of anthropomorphism—the attribution of human characteristics to the nonhuman (in this case, gods). The implication that such anthropomorphism is common among men and that all finite kinds of creatures would act in the same way by virtue of their limitations is made very clear by the next two fragments.

> (Frg.15) But if oxen (and horses) and lions had hands or could draw with hands and create works of art like those of men, horses would draw pictures of gods like horses, and oxen of gods like oxen, and they would make the bodies (of their gods) in accordance with the form that each species itself possesses.

> (Frg.16) Aethiopians have gods with snub noses and black hair, Thracians have gods with grey eyes and red hair.

Not only is it "unseemly" so to characterize the gods; but of equal importance, it is also untrue.

The background against which Xenophanes makes his criticism of the traditional religion seems to be the new cosmological ideas of the Ionian thinkers. Their systematic attempts to find the ultimate stuff force a reappraisal of the divine nature as it had been perceived. But it is not as a philosopher and cosmologist that Xenophanes carries out the implications of the new thought. His pronouncements are those of a profoundly religious man whose criticisms come not as the conclusion of a cosmological inference, but rather flow from a personal insight into the nature of the divine itself. There is general agreement that these attempts to define the divine nature, taken together, are a major contribution to Western thought; and there is something very real about the image of this outspoken old poet, "tossing around" Hellas, astounding and disturbing people with his exalted and brand new ideas about *tò Theòn*, the divine. Jaeger attributes to Xenophanes the first statement of that theological universalism which is so characteristic of Greek thought and which forms one of its contributions to Christianity.[2] On the basis of this insight, the anthropomorphism of the tradition is for him "unseemly". He also regards it as untrue, and in the first recorded expression of philosophical theology in the West, Xenophanes turns his attention to the question of the nature of the divine considered from a strictly intellectual point of view.

THE DIVINE: TÒ THEÒN

Christian believers have more often than not taken Xenophanes to be a monotheist on the basis of the following, but there is no reason to ignore the phrase that it contains: "among gods."

> (Frg.23) There is one god, among gods and men the greatest,
> not at all like mortals in body or in mind.

As will be seen in the next fragment (Frg.14), the references are to the "gods." There may very well be individual gods—the Ionian thinkers made no attempt to deny them—but there is also one supreme divinity, and it is radically different from the lower and individual gods.

> (Frg.14) But mortals believe the gods to be created by birth,
> and to have their own (mortals') raiment, voice and body.

That his disagreement with this way of thinking has an intellectual ground also seems to be indicated by Aristotle in the *Rhetoric*, where the non sequitur of attributing birth or death to a universal and infinite deity is said to have been declared by Xenophanes.[3] But he is far from denying to the One the characteristics of a personal deity to whom he most certainly had a religious relationship. He merely denies that the divine has eyes to see, or ears to hear, or a mind to think, and ingeniously asserts that

> (Frg.24) He sees as a whole, thinks as a whole, and hears as a whole.

Nor does he think that all the activity and running about of the Olympian gods is appropriate; and therefore the divine is motionless, at rest, as befits his state, and everything that is follows effortlessly from his thought.

> (Frg.26) And he always remains in the same place, not moving at all, nor is it fitting for him to change his position at different times.

> (Frg.25) But without toil he sets everything in motion, by the thought of his mind.

It may not be too presumptuous to conclude from these passages that the divine is transcendent as well as immanent for Xenophanes, as indeed it comes to be in the later tradition.

XENOPHANES AND THE ELEATICS

There is a tradition connecting Xenophanes with the Eleatics. Perhaps this was inevitable since, like Parmenides, he spoke of the divine One. This connection expresses itself in Diongenes Laertius (9. 20) where Xenophanes is said to have written 2000 lines on the founding of his native city of Colophon as well as on the founding of Elea. Also there is the report set down by Aristotle[4] that Parmenides was the pupil of Xenophanes, coupled with the spurious Aristotelean treatise, *de Melliso Xenophane Gorgia*, in which Xenophanes' divinity is given a full interpretation in terms of Parmenidean being. Plato refers to him as a founder, or at least an early member, of the Eleatic school.[5] There is nothing known to deny the possibility of his visiting Elea, but there is also no reason to connect the Xenophanean One with Parmenidean Being. There is nothing at all to show that Xenophanes was concerned with the metaphysics of being, and as evidence against such an assumption there is Aristotle's statement that Xenophanes, although the first to "postulate a unity," did not touch on the metaphysical aspects of it.[6]

XENOPHANES ON NATURAL PHENOMENA

What we have of Xenophanes' ideas on scientific matters is a collection of miscellaneous utterances upon natural phenomena, some directly contrary to the Ionian thinkers, and some founded upon what appear to be quite penetrating observations.

(Frg.29) All things that come into being and grow are earth and water.

(Frg.33) We all have our origin from earth and water.

By themselves these express a rather common and naive opinion, but read in conjunction with a testimonium from Hippolytus and Frg. 27 to follow, they suggest a cyclical view of history.

T20 Hippolytus *Ref.*, 1. 14. 3. [K&R172–3]

The sun comes into being each day from little pieces of fire that are collected, and the earth is infinite and enclosed neither by air nor by the heaven. There are innumerable suns and moons, and all things are made of earth.

However, Frg. 27 conflicts with Frgs. 29 and 33 above in that it makes earth primary, and, if accepted, it would require the denial of truth to Aristotle's statement that none of the ancient thinkers who believed in one ultimate stuff—which is somehow transformed into everything else—none of them held the ultimate to be earth.[7]

(Frg.27) For everything comes from earth and everything goes back to earth at last.

While Aristotle's own philosophical interests and ideas color his ability to understand his predecessors on some topics, there is no reason to doubt his report here, especially in the presence of Frgs. 29 and 33, and Frg.27 is now generally considered to be spurious.

There is some controversy over how to understand Xenophanes' view of the way the major elements are arranged to form the shape and content of the cosmos. Ultimately this depends upon the translation from the Greek of the following fragment.†

---

†Problems of translation are not uncommon. Not only is this particular instance of some interest in itself, but it also serves to remind us that below the level of philosophical interpretation lies the philological level.

(Frg.28) This is the upper limit of the earth that we see at our
feet, in contact with the air; but the part beneath goes down
to infinity.

There is no problem with the first phrase, but in the second the translation of Kirk & Raven differs from Freeman's rendering (as given) of
Diels' German in the handling of the *Apeiron*: "But its underneath
continues indefinitely."[8] We have already pointed out the difficulties
with the use of "infinite" to convey the meaning of the *Apeiron*†. In any
case, both Freeman and Kirk & Raven intend it to mean that the earth
extends downwards without end. Cleve takes issue with this interpretation. His reading of the second phrase of Frg.28 is based upon a parallel
construction with the first part: "But the lower (end) comes to the
infinite."[9] He interprets this to mean that the earth extends downwards
to the surrounding indefinite stuff. In Cleve's words:

> Instead of understanding *'to kato'* in the second verse as
> parallel to *'tóde peĩras' 'áno'* in the first and meaning "the
> lower end," he obviously mistook it for "the part below (our
> feet)." "And *'és ápeiron' 'iknễitai'* he paraphrased as if the
> meaning were "it stretches into infinity,". . .[10]

The "he" in the above refers to Empedocles, who is supposed to have
made the mistake in the first place. It was taken up, says Cleve, by
Aristotle and becomes the basis for the traditional interpretation, i.e.,
that of Freeman and Kirk & Raven. In interpreting their own translation, Kirk & Raven say that Xenophanes

> gives an extreme kind of common sense account, based
> upon the Hesiodic description of Tartarus as being as far
> below the earth as sky is above it (Theog. 720, cf. 11. 8, 16
> and see p. 11). At Theogony 726f. (2) the roots of earth and
> unharvested sea are above Tartarus. Thus in the Hesiodic
> picture the earth stretches a defined distance downwards,
> but in reality this distance was obviously thought of as
> indefinitely vast—the height of the sky in fact. Xenophanes
> was not seriously emending it in calling it 'indefinite'. That
> the earth does stretch downwards indefinitely is a naive but
> understandable view which Xenophanes probably intended
> as an implied criticism of the dogmatic theories of the Mile-
> sians on this subject.[11]

Cleve's understanding of the matter in contrast—with earth below,
water in the middle, and air above, the whole enclosed by the *Apeiron*—
is designed to describe a world-sphere consistent with reports by
Cicero,[12] Sextus Empiricus,[13] Simplicius,[14] and Hippolytus[15] of the
divine of Xenophanes as ball-shaped and perhaps not vastly different
from that of Anaximander.

---

†See pp. 37-8.

In a sense, both points of view are correct. To suppose that Xenophanes is cosmologically naive and yet that his conception of the divine stems from the new thought of the Milesians is somewhat difficult but not impossible. As was suggested with the thought of Anaximander, the old and new lie very close together, with the new being an extension and specification of the old. Certainly Xenophanes' primary interest is religious rather than philosophical, but it is reasonable to consider him as knowledgeable regarding the new thought as well as aware of the old traditions.

We learned from Hippolytus (T20) that Xenophanes held a new sun was created every day from collected fire, and we learn from Aetius that he explained eclipses as the withdrawal of the particular sun involved from our region to another region:

T21 Aetius 2. 24. 9 [K&R173]

Xenophanes said there are many suns and moons according to regions, sections and zones of the earth, and that a certain time and disc is banished into some section of the earth not inhabited by us, and so treading on nothing, as it were, produces the phenomenon of an eclipse. The same man says that the sun goes onwards *ad infinitum*, but seems to move in a circle because of the distance.

And Frg.31 speaks of "the sun rushing on its way above the earth and giving it warmth."

(Frg.30) The sea is the source of water, and the source of wind. For neither could (the force of the wind blowing outwards from within come into being) without the great main (sea), nor the streams of rivers, nor the showery water of the sky; but the mighty main is the begetter of clouds and winds and rivers.

(Frg.32) And she whom they call Iris [rainbow], she too is actually a cloud, purple and flame-red and yellow to behold.

(Frg.37) Also, in (certain) caves, water drips down.

The traditional and common sense view of the primacy of water is expressed in these fragments along with the ultimate explanation of meteorological phenomena in these terms. In another passage from Hippolytus, and perhaps Frg.37 is an echo in particular application, we have a truly remarkable report giving evidence once again for a cyclical theory of history, change, and human existence. Xenophanes may not have made the observations of fossils in question, but the fact that he recognized them as relevant in support of his theory shows a high degree of that same scientific spirit that characterizes the Ionian thinkers.

T22   Hippolytus *Ref.* 1. 14. 5. [K&R177]
Xenophanes thinks that a mixture of earth with sea is going
on, and that in time the earth is dissolved by the moist. He
says that he has demonstrations of the following kind: shells
are found inland, and in the mountains, and in the quarries
in Syracuse he says that an impression of a fish and of
seaweed has been found, while an impression of a bayleaf
was found in Paros in the depth of the rock, and in Malta flat
shapes of all marine objects. These, he says, were produced
when everything was long covered with mud. All mankind is
destroyed whenever the earth is carried down into the sea
and becomes mud; then there is another beginning of
coming-to-be, and this foundation happens for all the
worlds.

THE LIMITS OF HUMAN KNOWLEDGE

Along with his universalization of the divine, the views of Xenophanes on the nature and limits of human knowledge form his most
influential contributions to the physical tradition. The following five
fragments are relevant to this latter point:

(Frg.18) Truly the gods have not revealed to mortals all
things from the beginning; but mortals by long seeking
discover what is better.

(Frg.34) And as for certain truth, no man has seen it, nor will
there ever be a man who knows about the gods and about all
the things I mention. For if he succeeds to the full in saying
what is completely true, he himself is nevertheless unaware
of it; and Opinion (seeming) is fixed by fate upon all things.

(Frg.35) Let these things be stated as conjectural only, similar to the reality.

(Frg.36) All appearances which exist for mortals to look at.
. . .

(Frg.38) If God had not created yellow honey, they would
say that figs were far sweeter.

Certainly Frgs. 18 and 34 can be understood as a direct result of his view
of the extreme difference between man and the divine. This is not to be
taken as indicating skepticism, even though the skeptical tradition has
always regarded Xenophanes with particular affection. Although Xenophanes does not believe it possible for the finite to encompass the
infinite, man may yet acquire some understanding through experience

and "long seeking." In the light of this, Frg.35 takes on the form of an admonition against all dogmatism. It is this mixture of knowledge and doubt first found in the fragments of Xenophanes that characterizes the Socratic attitude in the Platonic dialogues. This, coupled with his first flights in rational and natural theology, gives Xenophanes an important place in Greek and hence Western thought.

REMAINING FRAGMENTS

The following fragments, the significance of which is either unclear or, for our purpose, unimportant, are presented for the sake of completeness:

(Frg.4) (*The Lydians first struck coinage*).

(Frg.5) Nor would anyone first pour the wine into the cup when mixing it, but rather the water, and on to that the pure wine.

(Frg.6) For, having sent a kid's ham, you received in return the fat leg of a bull, a precious prize for a man whose fame shall reach all over Hellas, and shall not cease so long as the race of Hellenic bards exists.

(Frg.7 [1st part] Now again I shall pass to another Theme, and shall show the way....†

(Frg.9) Much feebler than an aged man.

(Frg.13) (*Homer was earlier than Hesiod*).

(Frg.17) (*The Bacchic branches*) of fir-wood stand round the firm-built dwelling.

(Frg.19) (*Xenophanes admired Thales for having predicted solar eclipses*).

(Frg.20) (*Xenophanes said that he had heard that Epimenides lived to the age of 154*).

(Frg.21) (*Of Simonides*). Skinflint.

(Frg.21a) Erykos (*Eryx, in Sicily*).

(Frg.39) Cherry-tree

(Frg.40) (*Ionian dialect-word for a frog*).

(Frg.41 (*Word for*) A pit.

---

†This fragment has been broken into two parts. The second part, because it refers to Pythagoras, appears in Chapter 4 as T28 on p. 84. (See Kathleen Freeman, *Companion to the Pre-Socratic Philosophers,* Harvard University Press, Cambridge, Mass., 1966, p. 99. Hereafter cited as Freeman, *Companion.*)

NOTES

1. Wilhelm Windelband, *History of Ancient Philosophy* (New York: Dover Books, 1956), p. 49.

2. Jaeger, *Theology of the Early Greek Philosophers*, p. 48.

3. Aristotle *Rhet.* 1399b6.

4. Aristotle *Meta.* 986b18.

5. Plato *Sophist* 242d.

6. Aristotle *Meta.* 986b23. See Jaeger, *Theology of the Early Greek Philosophers*, p. 51ff.

7. Aristotle *Meta.* 989a5.

8. Kirk & Raven, p. 175.

9. Felix M. Cleve, *The Giants of Pre-Socratic Greek Philosophy*, 2 vols. (The Hague: Martinus Nijhoff, 1965) vol. 1, p. 11.

10. *Ibid.*

11. Kirk & Raven, p. 175-6.

12. Cicero *Academica* 2. 118. A34; Cleve, p. 10.

13. Sextus Empiricus *Pyrr. Hypot.* 1, 224. A35; ibid.

14. Simplicius *Phys.* 22. 22. A31; ibid.

15. Hippolytus *Ref.* 1. 14. A23; ibid.

CHAPTER 3
Heraclitus

Heraclitus was in his middle years around 500 B.C. We know little of the externals of his life, and about the only details beyond the above date of which we may be reasonably certain are that he lived in Ephesus; came from an aristocratic family, the Basalidae, descendants of the Athenian king Codrus, which, according to legend, migrated to Ephesus around 1100 B.C.; and was on bad terms with the Ephesians. For some reason, perhaps arrogance, he resigned the hereditary kingship, a largely religious office, in favor of his brother.[1] It is worth noting, however, that his life span coincides with the Persian conquest of Asia Minor completed about 515 B.C. His adult life was lived largely in an occupied city. The Persian state religion was Zoroastrianism, with its dual principles of Good and Evil and reality seen as the struggle between the two. Undoubtedly, as Guthrie says, the wealth of anecdote surrounding him must be considered apocryphal, arising from his sayings.[2] Here is a sample of such anecdotal material:

T23 Diogenes Laertius 9. 1. 3. [Loeb]
Heraclitus, son of Bloson or, according to some, of Heracon, was a native of Ephesus. He flourished in the 69th Olympiad (504–500 B.C.). He was lofty-minded beyond all other men and over-weening, as is clear from his book in which he says:[Frg. 40] "Much learning does not teach understanding; else would it have taught Hesiod and Pythagoras, or, again, Xenophanes and Hecataeus...." Finally, he became a hater of his kind and wandered on the moun-

59

tains, and there he continued to live, making his diet of grass and herbs. However, when this gave him dropsy, he made his way back to the city and put this riddle to the physicians, whether they were competent to create a draught after heavy rain. They could make nothing of this, whereupon he buried himself in a cowshed, expecting that the noxious damp humour would be drawn out of him by the warmth of the manure. But, as even this was of no avail, he died at the age of sixty.

It is not certain whether or not Heraclitus wrote a book. Kirk & Raven are extremely skeptical, basing their skepticism primarily on the disjointedness of Heraclitus' available fragments;[3] Guthrie, on the other hand, feels that Aristotle's reference[4] to a book by Heraclitus in a manner indicative of considerable familiarity is strong evidence that Heraclitus was in fact the author of such a book.[5]

One of the most significant and interesting ideas developed by Heraclitus is his notion that man is subject to the same law as the cosmos. If, as Jaeger suggests, the cosmos of Anaximander is the completion of the projection of the human community upon the world at large, then in Heraclitus we have this same notion of cosmic law applied back to man and his institutions. This idea is fundamental to Heraclitus' whole position. The same *Logos*-Fire that directs the cosmic course of events also operates in individual human souls as reason. Reason is at least a potential endowment of all men if they would but listen, and is the source of the law which guides the city-state—an assumption which provides an ontological ground for the social bond. Heraclitean thought is the intellectual fulfillment of what is widely regarded as the Classical stage in the Greek conception of the world and the moral development of man. At the end of the third play of the Aeschylean Oresteia Trilogy, the *Eumenides*, the same conception is set forth as a solution to the problems of the house of Atreus. At the termination of a time of blood and fury, Athena (Reason), the daughter of Zeus, says:

Citizens of Athens, hear my declaration
At the first trial in the history of man.
This great tribunal shall remain in power
Meeting in solemn session on this hill,
Where long ago the Amazons encamped
When they made war on Theseus, and sacrificed
To Ares—hence its name. Here reverence
For law and inbred fear among my people
Shall hold their hands from evil night and day,
Only let them not tamper with the laws,
But keep the fountain pure and sweet to drink.

I warn you not to banish from your lives
All terror but to seek the mean between
Autocracy and anarchy; and in this way
You shall possess in ages yet unborn
An impregnable fortress of liberty
Such as no people has throughout the world.
With these words I establish this tribunal
Grave, quick to anger, incorruptible,
And always vigilant over those that sleep....[6]

The Heraclitean expression of this view in terms of the Logos is taken up by and becomes central to Stoicism, and is the original source of the natural law tradition. Heraclitus is noted for his obscure style, as will become evident when we get down to an analysis of his fragments, which are studded with paradox, aphorism, metaphor and symbolism. Guthrie suggests several reasons for this, among them Heraclitus' contempt for his readers, his preference for a prophetic rather than a dialectical mode of expression, and the fact that the subtlety of his thought exceeded that of his contemporaries as well as that of the language at his disposal.[7] One consequence of Heraclitus' obscurity is that the commentators are quite unreliable in interpreting him. For this reason we will rely most heavily on his fragments in attempting to reconstruct his thought. Fortunately there are a good many of them.

OPINION VERSUS WISDOM

Heraclitus makes a sharp distinction between conjectural opinions and genuine wisdom. He has a low estimate of the former, regarding them as out of place in philosophy.

(Frg.70) Children's toys (*i.e. men's conjectures*).

(Frg.46) Conceit: the sacred disease (*i.e. epilepsy*).†

(Frg.47) Let us not conjecture at random about the greatest things.

Unfortunately, no one seems to be aware of the unique nature of philosophy, says Heraclitus, and even the most reputable simply accept common opinion.

(Frg.108) Of all those whose discourse I have heard, none arrives at the realization that that which is wise is set apart from all things.

---

†The word "conceit" may here be interpreted to mean opinion as well as self-deceit. Despite the fact that the Greeks referred to epilepsy as the "sacred disease," Heraclitus' assimilation of conceit to epilepsy in the present instance is assumed to have a derogatory connotation.

(Frg.28, 1st part) The most wise-seeming man knows, (*that is*), preserves, only what seems; ...†

This includes not only those who were concerned with the amassing of factual knowledge, such as Pythagoras and Hecataeus, but also poets such as Homer, Hesiod, and Archilochus, and the poet-philosopher Xenophanes. In Heraclitus' view, they confuse mere surface knowledge with true understanding.

(Frg.40) Much learning does not teach one to have intelligence; for it would have taught Hesiod and Pythagoras, and again, Xenophanes and Hecataeus.

(Frg.42) Homer deserves to be flung out of the contests and given a beating; and also Archilochus.

Pythagoras is singled out for special scorn in two fragments.

(Frg.81) (*On Pythagoras*), Original chief of wranglers.

(Frg.129) Pythagoras, son of Mnêsarchus, practised research most of all men, and making extracts from these treatises he compiled a wisdom of his own, an accumulation of learning, a harmful craft.‡

Not that Heraclitus underestimates the value of a first-hand acquaintance with particulars: as a matter of fact, he considers such first-hand experience essential to the acquisition of wisdom. To see for oneself is far preferable to hearsay. But just as the miner must sift through much ore to find his precious metal, so must the philosopher realize that wisdom is a rare thing which only comes through much experience.

(Frg.35) Men who love wisdom must be inquirers into very many things indeed.

(Frg.101a) The eyes are more exact witnesses than the ears.

(Frg.55) Those things of which there is sight, hearing, knowledge: these are what I honour most.

(Frg.22) Those who seek gold dig much earth and find little.

The trouble is that men do not grasp the significance of particular experiences even when they take note of them. This applies not only to sense experience but also to understanding of the spoken word. One must know *how* to listen: it is the meaning of the words—not the words themselves—that are important.

(Frg.17)For many men—those who encounter such things—do not understand them, and do not grasp them

---

†This fragment has been broken into two parts. The second part appears on p. 00.
‡This fragment, though rejected as spurious by Diels, is accepted as genuine by Kranz, Burnet, Kirk and Guthrie. See Freeman, *Companion*, p. 75, n.; also W.K.C Guthrie (*A History of Greek Philosophy,* Cambridge University Press, 1962), vol. 1, p. 157, n.

after they have learnt; but to themselves they seem (*to understand*).

(Frg.34) Not understanding, although they have heard, they are like the deaf. The proverb bears witness to them: 'Present yet absent.'

(Frg.87) A foolish man is apt to be in a flutter at every word (*or, 'theory': Logos*)

(Frg.19) Men who do not know how to listen or how to speak.

THE LOGOS

What Heraclitus calls the *Logos* is, for him, the key to genuine wisdom. It is the key to his philosophy as well because it serves to relate so many of the implications of his thought under one unifying concept. Though the unification achieved is misleading insofar as it is dependent on the then-primitive state of development of Greek thought and a consequent failure to make certain elementary distinctions, it is at the same time insightful and suggestive because it reveals connections which we, with greater analytical sophistication, tend to overlook.

The doctrine of the *Logos* depends on an assimilation to one another of words, the thoughts to which words give rise, the physical entities to which words refer, and the meaning of words considered in a purely logical sense, as well as the values that lead us to think and use words in a certain fashion. For Heraclitus, the *Logos*, though (1) both spoken and listened to, is at once also to be identified with (2) thought itself and, as such, an intelligent moving and directing force, (3) physical fire, smoke or a kind of hot exhalation, and, as such, a physical, moving force, (4) the one unchanging logical principle in terms of which the plurality of changing things becomes intelligible, and (5) the divine source of ethical, political and religious value.

Knowledge of the *Logos* requires a kind of intuitive insight to which the knower must be appropriately receptive. Heraclitus' reference to the limitations of barbarian souls in the first of the following fragments (Frg.107) is particularly suggestive in this connection because, from the Greek point of view, the barbarian is regarded as the antithesis of the virtuous man: one must be virtuous in order to be receptive to theoretical knowledge of the *Logos*. Even more interesting is the double reading that may be given Frg.2 in this context. It can be interpreted to mean that theoretical knowledge is only attainable through intellectual apprehension of the *Logos* which is common to all men; but it can also be read as implying that the *Logos* is a guide to action and the moral life. The theme of the *Logos* as an ethical standard will be developed subsequently. The point here is that if the virtuous man can have theoretical knowledge of the *Logos*, then only the man who follows the *Logos* in himself can know the *Logos* in other things. This brings out another point, viz., Heraclitus' view that knowledge of the *Logos* is *both* introspective *and* intersubjective. While it can only be intuitively grasped through a kind of self-search, it is common to all men as well as to all things. Though Heraclitus makes claim to a unique kind of wisdom, he feels that others cannot make the same claim for their incredulity and obstinacy. In any event, he regards the *Logos* rather than himself as the source of his knowledge, and claims that each man can confirm it by appealing to the *Logos* within himself. The last fragment of the group (Frg.1) is an excellent summary statement.

(Frg.107) The eyes and ears are bad witnesses for men if they have barbarian souls.

(Frg.78) Human nature has no power of understanding; but the divine nature has it.

(Frg.32) That which alone is wise is one; it is willing and unwilling to be called by the name of Zeus.†

(Frg.86) (*Most of what is divine*)‡ escapes recognition through unbelief.

(Frg.41) That which is wise is one: to understand the purpose which steers all things through all things.

(Frg.64) The thunder-bolt§ (*i.e. Fire*) steers the universe.

(Frg.2) Therefore one must follow. . .that which is common (*to all*). But although the. . .[*Logos*] is universal, the majority live as if they had understanding peculiar to themselves.§§

(Frg.72) The. . .[*Logos*]: though men associate with it most closely, yet they are separated from it, and those things which they encounter daily seem to them strange.

(Frg.101) I searched into myself.

(Frg.50) When you have listened, not to me but to the [*Logos*], it is wise to agree that all things are one.

---

†Suggesting the divine character of the *Logos*.
‡Presumably, manifestations of the *Logos*.
§The thunder-bolt is associated with Zeus, again suggesting the divine character of the *Logos*.
§§In this fragment and in a good number of others, Freeman uses the English word "Law" to translate the Greek word "*Logos*". Though the meaning of "*Logos*" is thereby partially conveyed, no one English word can do justice to its multi-dimensional significance in these instances. For this reason it would seem preferable to have simply used the word "*Logos*." The word "Law" has therefore been deleted from Freeman's translation, and the word "*Logos*" either retained or substituted in its place in each such case.

(Frg.1) The . . .[*Logos*] (*of the universe*) is as here explained; but men are always incapable of understanding it, both before they hear it, and when they have heard it for the first time. For though all things come into being in accordance with this *Logos*, men seem as if they had never met with it, when they meet with words (*theories*) and actions (*processes*) such as I expound, separating each thing according to its nature and explaining how it is made. As for the rest of mankind, they are unaware of what they are doing after they wake, just as they forget what they did while asleep.

The distinction between understanding through the *Logos* and reliance on mere conjectural opinion is compared by Heraclitus to the distinction between wakefulness and sleep. Just as the *Logos* is common to all, so those who are awake live in a public world. In contrast, conjectural opinion is analogous to the fantasy and dreams of sleep. Frg. 21 (below) introduces the theme that the world understood by those who have wisdom through the *Logos*, i.e., those who are awake, is a world of change and flux, a world where things perish and die. Of course, even those who adhere only to common opinion, i.e., even those who are asleep, act under the governance of the *Logos* whether they are aware of it or not.

(Frg.89) To those who are awake, there is one ordered universe common (*to all*), whereas in sleep each man turns away (*from this world*) to one of his own.

(Frg.21) All that we see when we have wakened is death; all that we see while slumbering is sleep.

(Frg.73) We must not act and speak like men asleep.

(Frg.75) Those who sleep are workers and share in the activities going on in the universe.

THE HIDDEN CHARACTER OF TRUTH

Though the truth is accessible to all if they will only take the trouble to seek it out, the hidden character of truth makes this difficult. For Heraclitus, the nature of the truth is not obvious; indeed, it can only be expressed in terms of metaphor, paradox, and riddle. The oracular style of the Sibyl† and the oracle at Delphi are referred to with approval. Though the language of the Delphic oracle, for example, may appear to conceal deliberately, Heraclitus maintains that this is not so. Rather,

---

†A prophetic woman.

the nature of truth is such that language cannot express it directly, but only by "giving a sign". Such would also undoubtedly be Heraclitus' explanation of the "dark" character of many of his own pronouncements.

> (Frg.18) If one does not hope, one will not find the unhoped-for, since there is no trail leading to it and no path.

> (Frg.123) Nature likes to hide.

> (Frg.56) Men are deceived over the recognition of visible things, in the same way as Homer, who was the wisest of all the Hellenes; for he too was deceived by boys killing lice, who said: 'What we saw and grasped, that we leave behind; but what we did not see and did not grasp, that we bring.'

> (Frg.92) The Sibyl with raving mouth uttering her unlaughing, unadorned, unincensed words reaches out over a thousand years with her voice, through the (*inspiration of the*) god.

> (Frg.93) The lord whose oracle is that at Delphi neither speaks nor conceals, but indicates.

THE PERVASIVENESS OF CHANGE

Fundamental to Heraclitus' ontology is his notion of the pervasiveness of change. Though particulars seem to come into being and perish in chaotic fashion, yet there is a cyclic order in all.

> (Frg.52) Time is a child playing a game of draughts; the kingship is in the hands of a child.

> (Frg.124) The fairest universe is but a dust-heap piled up at random.

> (Frg.126) Cold things grow hot, hot things grow cold, the wet dries, the parched is moistened.

> (Frg.100) (*The sun*† is in charge of the seasonal changes, and) the Hours (Seasons) that bring all things.

THE IDENTITY AND CONFLICT OF OPPOSITES

For Heraclitus conflict between opposites is the answer to a problem a step beyond that of the Milesians—and even the Pythagoreans. The Milesians sought a unifying principle of change—a stuff in terms of which change would become intelligible. Anaximenes, foreshadowing

---

†Associated with Fire and the *Logos* by Heraclitus. See pp. 68ff.

the Pythagoreans, offered condensation and rarefaction as a principle of why different kinds of things behave differently. But Heraclitus' conflict of opposites is an explanation of why things change at all. Conflict is written into the very nature of the cosmos: the *Logos* or cosmic order is in fact the measure of conflict. By way of contrast, the Pythagoreans think of order as possible only with the elimination of conflict.

The theme of the flowing river epitomizes Heraclitus' approach to change—so much so that he has been called "the river philosopher."

> (Frg.91, 1st part) It is not possible to step twice into the same river. (It is impossible to touch the same mortal substance twice,...)...†

> (Frg.12, 1st part) Those who step into the same river have different waters flowing ever upon them....‡

> (Frg.49a) In the same river, we both step and do not step, we are and we are not.

This last fragment introduces another characteristic Heraclitean idea, viz., the identity of opposites. Whether or not violation of the logical law of contradiction is implicit in Heraclitus' view, his statements in this connection are intelligible on a variety of other grounds, and his penchant for paradox is a sufficient explanation of why he may have been led to make them. In the case of Frg. 49a, for example, his intention may have been to contrast the usual meaning of stepping twice into the same river with the unusual meaning he has introduced in Frg. 91 and perhaps amplified in Frg. 12 in terms of the usual meaning. In ordinary language, i.e., in the language of Frg. 12 and Frg. 49a, we *can* step twice into the same river; it is only in the language of Frg. 91 that we cannot.

Though the theme of the identity of opposites recurs again and again in Heraclitus, the following cosmological fragments are illustrative. The thought that change is cyclical is also central in this group. Opposite directions at points diametrically opposed on the circumference of a circle are really the same direction: the opposed directions at different parts of a cycle are equally essential to its nature. The plurality of particulars emergent from the cyclical processes of nature are at the same time manifestations of the unity of these very cyclical processes. Insofar as they move in opposition, just like bones connected by joints, they are both unified and separate: their opposed movement is the essence of their harmonious interaction. But Heraclitus regards the oppositions of his cosmological cycles as more obvious than their unities, which are hidden.

---

†This fragment has been broken into two parts. The second part appears on p. 70.
‡This fragment has been broken into two parts. The second part appears on p. 72.

(Frg.57) Hesiod is the teacher of very many, he who did not understand day and night: for they are one.

(Frg.59) For the fuller's screw, the way, straight and crooked, is one and the same.

(Frg.60) The way up and down is one and the same.

(Frg.10) Joints: whole and not whole, connected-separate, consonant-dissonant.

(Frg.8) That which is in opposition is in concert, and from things that differ comes the most beautiful harmony.

(Frg.54) The hidden harmony is stronger (*or* 'better') than the visible.

Not only does change involve opposites and oppositions operating as part of a unity so as to produce harmony, but opposition or conflict between opposites, i.e., strife or "war" is essential to the unity and harmony of the changing process, the existence of particulars involved in the process, and even change itself. The unity and harmony of which Heraclitus speaks are in this respect quite different from that of the Pythagoreans, for whom conflict is the anthithesis of unity and harmony, and for whom unity and harmony can only be achieved with the removal of conflict.

(Frg.80) One should know that war is general (*universal*) and jurisdiction is strife, and everything comes about by way of strife and necessity.

(Frg.84a) It rests from change. (*Elemental Fire in the human body*).†

(Frg.51) They do not understand how that which differs with itself is in agreement: harmony consists of opposing tension, like that of the bow and lyre.

(Frg.48) The bow is called Life,* but its work is death.‡

(Frg.125) The 'mixed drink' (*Kykeôn: mixture of wine, grated cheese and barley-meal*) also separates if not stirred.

THE ROLE OF FIRE

Heraclitus' connection with the Ionian tradition is evident in his contention that the universe is "an ever-living fire." Though, like Thales

---

†As here translated by Freeman, this fragment makes little sense in association with other fragments of the group. It has been included here because of the alternative translations provided by Wheelwright and Guthrie. Wheelwright: "It is in changing that things find repose" (Wheelwright, Philip, *Heraclitus*, Atheneum, New York, 1964, p. 29). Guthrie: "In changing it is at rest" (vol. 1, p. 44).

*Pun on Bios, 'Life' and Biós, 'bow.'

‡i.e., to perish or change.

and Anaximenes, he thereby chooses a new element as the nature of things, his Fire bears some resemblance to the Air of Anaximenes. In the first place, it is not flame, but "a hot dry vapour,"[8] or smoke—something more akin to air than what we call fire. Heraclitus also identifies it with *psyche* or soul as Anaximenes had done with his Air. And finally, Heraclitus'[9] claim that Fire is transformed into all things "by regular measures" has some similarity with the operation of Anaximenes' principle of condensation and rarefaction.

> (Frg.30) This ordered universe (*cosmos*), which is the same for all, was not created by any one of the gods or of mankind, but it was ever and is and shall be ever-living Fire, kindled in measure and quenched in measure.

Logically speaking, perhaps the most difficult point about Heraclitus' identification of Fire with the ultimate nature of things is his conception of its relation to the *Logos*. As inconsistent as it may seem to equate something "spiritual" with something "physical," Heraclitus' Fire was regarded by him as identical with the *Logos*. True, *Physis* for the Milesians had been both a principle and something material; yet with Heraclitus, the contrast between stuff and principle, concrete and abstract, matter and power became more acute. Still, despite its intuitive strength, his thought had simply not yet developed to the point where any inconsistency was evident.

The sun is a good symbol for Fire. The following fragments make sense of this interpretation, and Frg. 3 and Frg. 99, Frg. 6 and Frg. 16 also fall into the usual paradoxical pattern of Heraclitean statement when regarded as juxtaposed pairs.

> (Frg. 94) The sun will not transgress his measures; otherwise the Furies, ministers of Justice, will find him out.

> (Frg.120) The limits of morning and evening are the Bear and, opposite the Bear, the boundary-mark of Zeus god of the clear sky.

> (Frg.3) (*On the size of the sun*): the breadth of a man's foot.

> (Frg.99) If there were no sun, so far as depended on the other stars it would be night.

> (Frg.6) The sun is new each day.

> (Frg.16) How could anyone hide from that which never sets?

Fire is not only a transcendent principle; it is immanent in all earthly processes. It exercises its control over them as a medium of exchange "by regular measures," and characteristically advances out of craving and retires when sated. Ordered cycles of transformation into the various other elements are the result. The "way down" is from Fire to air to water to earth; the "way up" the reverse. Frg. 31 suggests that the entire cycle is under the governance of a conservation law.

(Frg.90) There is an exchange: all things for Fire and Fire for all things, like goods for gold and gold for goods.

(Frg.66) Fire, having come upon them, will judge and seize upon (condemn) all things.

(Frg.91, 2nd part) (. . . *but through the rapidity of change*) they scatter and again combine (*or rather, not even 'again' or 'later', but the combination and separation are simultaneous*) and approach and separate.†

(Frg.65) Need and satiety.‡

(Frg.76) Fire lives the death of earth, and air lives the death of fire; water lives the death of air, earth that of water.

(Frg.31) The changes of fire: first, sea; and of sea, half is earth and half firey water-spout. . . . Earth is liquefied into sea, and retains its measure according to the same . . . [Logos] as existed before it became earth.

Diogenes Laertius gives the following account of some of Heraclitus' cosmogonical, cosmological and astrological ideas:

T24   Diogenes Laertius 9. 1. 8-11. [Loeb]
. . . .fire is the element, all things are exchanged for fire and come into being by rarefaction and condensation; but of this he gives no clear explanation. All things come into being by conflict of opposites, and the sum of things flows like a stream. Further, all that is is limited and forms one world. And it is alternately born from fire and again resolved into fire in fixed cycles to all eternity, and this is determined by destiny. Of the opposites that which tends to birth or creation is called war and strife, and that which tends to destruction by fire is called concord and peace.

Change he called a pathway up and down, and this determines the birth of the world. For fire by contracting turns into moisture, and this condensing turns into water; water again when congealed turns into earth. This process he calls the downward path. Then again earth is liquefied, and thus gives rise to water, and from water the rest of the series is derived. He reduces nearly everything to exhalation from the sea. This process is the upward path.

Exhalations arise from earth as well as from sea; those from sea are bright and pure, those from earth dark. Fire is fed by the bright exhalations, the moist element by the others.

---

†This fragment has been broken into two parts. The first part appears on p. 67.
‡The phases of fire.

He does not make clear the nature of the surrounding element. He says, however, that there are in it bowls with the concavities turned toward us, in which the bright exhalations collect and produce flames. These are the heavenly bodies.

The flame of the sun is the brightest and hottest; and other stars are further from the earth and for that reason give it less light and heat. The moon, which is nearer to the earth, traverses a region which is not pure. The sun, however, moves in a clear and untroubled region, and keeps a proportionate distance from us. That is why it gives us more heat and light. Eclipses of the sun and moon occur when the bowls are turned upwards; the monthly phases of the moon are due to the bowl turning round in its place little by little.

Day and night, months, seasons and years, rains and winds and other similar phenomena are accounted for by the various exhalations. Thus the bright exhalation produces summer, whereas the preponderance of moisture due to the dark exhalation, set aflame in the hollow orb of the sun produces day, the opposite exhalation when it has got the mastery causes night; the increase of warmth due to the bright exhalation brings about winter. His explanations of other phenomena are in harmony with this....

VARIETIES OF SOUL AND THE NATURE OF DEATH

The term "soul" is used by Heraclitus to refer not only to human souls, but also to a "cosmic" soul which he regarded as divine, and to the souls of the gods. In all of its manifestations, soul is the same as fire and undergoes the same cyclical transformations as fire. Insofar as it is a directive force, it is also regarded as intelligent. "Cosmic" soul is the source of individual differentiated souls.

(Frg.45) You could not in your going find the ends of the soul, though you travelled the whole way: so deep is its... (*Logos*).

On the "cosmic" soul:

(Frg. 67) God is day-night, winter-summer, war-peace, satiety-famine. But he changes like (fire) which when it mingles with the smoke of incense, is named according to each man's pleasure.

(Frg.115) The soul has its own... (*Logos*), which increases itself (*i.e. grows according to its needs*).

On the gods:

> (Frg.82) (*The most handsome ape is ugly compared with the human race.*)
>
> (Frg.83) (*The wisest man will appear an ape in relation to God, both in wisdom and beauty and everything else.*)
>
> (Frg.79) Man is called childish compared with divinity, just as a boy compared with a man.

The discussion of human souls involves the problem of death. In conformity with their fiery nature, the death of souls is regarded as a transformation—one that is but part of a cycle—and reversible. In this respect it is like sleep. Corpses, once discarded, are worthless, however.

> (Frg.36) To souls, it is death to become water, to water it is death to become earth. From earth comes water, and from water, soul.
>
> (Frg.12, [2nd part] Anhalation (*vaporisation*).... (Souls also are vaporised from what is wet).†
>
> (Frg. 62) Immortals are mortal, mortals are immortal: (*each*) lives the death of the other, and dies their life.
>
> (Frg.88) And what is in us is the same thing: living and dead, awake and sleeping, as well as young and old; for the latter (*of each pair of opposites*) having changed becomes the former, and this again having changed becomes the latter.
>
> (Frg.103) Beginning and end are general in the circumference of the circle.
>
> (Frg.26) In the night, a man kindles* a light because his sight is quenched; while living, he approximates to* a dead man during sleep; while awake, he approximates to one who sleeps.
>
> (Frg.96) Corpses are more worthy to be thrown out than dung.

The following fragment suggests that then, as now, the medical profession had not yet achieved universal popularity:

> (Frg.58) For instance, physicians, who cut and burn, demand payment of a fee, though undeserving, since they produce the same (*pains as the disease*).

What we know of Heraclitus' views concerning the state of the soul after death is limited. One usual claim: that souls in Hades (the nether world) perceive with the sense of smell is perhaps accounted for by the

---

†This fragment has been broken into two parts. The first part appears on p. 67.
*Pun on ἅπτεται, 'kindles,' and 'touches upon' (approximates to).

fiery nature of souls and Heraclitus' equation of fire with a hot, dry vapor, or smoke.

(Frg.27) There await men after they are dead things which they do not expect or imagine.

(Frg.63) When he (God?) is there, they (*the souls in Hades*) arise and become watchful guardians of the living and the dead.

(Frg.7) If all existing things turned to smoke, the nose would be the discriminating organ.

(Frg.98) Souls have the sense of smell in Hades.

ATTITUDE TOWARD DIONYSIAC RELIGIOUS PRACTICES

Heraclitus' attitude toward the contemporary mystery rituals of the cult of Dionysus as practiced by the vulgar is one of disdain. At the same time, he has a respect for what he regards as their deeper significance, and differentiates the performance of rituals by those who have been "purified" from those who have not. Characteristically, the deeper insight involves the identity of opposites—this time, the equating of Dionysus, the god of life, with Hades, the god of death. Rightly understood and practiced, the rites of the mysteries have therapeutic value: they are "remedies."

(Frg.14) Night-ramblers, magicians, Bacchants, Maenads, Mystics: the rites accepted by mankind in the Mysteries are an unholy performance.

(Frg.5) They purify themselves by staining themselves with other blood, as if one were to step into mud in order to wash off mud. But a man would be thought mad if any of his fellow-men should perceive him acting thus. Moreover, they talk to these statues (*of theirs*) as if one were to hold conversation with houses, in his ignorance of the nature of both gods and heroes.

(Frg.69) (*There are two sorts of sacrifice: one kind offered by men entirely purified, as sometimes occurs, though rarely, in an individual, or a few easy to number; the other kind material*).

(Frg.15) If it were not in honour of Dionysus that they conducted the procession and sang the hymn to the male organ (*the phallic hymn*), their activity would be completely shameless. But Hades is the same as Dionysus, in whose honour they rave and perform the Bacchic revels.

(Frg.68) (*Heraclitus called the shameful rites of the Mysteries*) Remedies.

THE GOOD SOUL

For Heraclitus, good and evil are human distinctions: to God all things are good. The conflict between good and evil is nonetheless essential to human existence, for not only would men be ignorant of good if there were no evil, but they would be without motivation. Frg.11, below, might be interpreted to make this last point.

(Frg.102) To God, all things are beautiful, good and just; but men have assumed some things to be unjust, others just.

(Frg.106) (*Heraclitus reproached Hesiod for regarding some days as bad and others as good*). Hesiod was unaware that the nature of every day is one.

(Frg.110) It is not better for men to obtain all that they wish.

(Frg.111) Disease makes health pleasant and good, hunger satisfaction, weariness rest.

(Frg.23) They would not know the name of Right, if these things (*i.e. the opposite*) did not exist.

(Frg.11) Every creature is driven to pasture with a blow.

The implication of Heraclitus' view is, of course, that human goods are such only in relation to man. The following fragments appear to bear this out.

(Frg.61) Sea water is the purest and most polluted: for fish, it is drinkable and life-giving; for men, not drinkable and destructive.

(Frg.37) Pigs wash themselves in mud, birds in dust or ashes.

(Frg.9) Donkeys prefer chaff to gold.

(Frg.13) Do not revel in mud. (*Swine enjoy mud rather than pure water*).

Yet Heraclitus is not a relativist in any pejorative sense. The good man, in contrast with the mass of men, is above all a man of character who knows his place in the universe and is not guilty of *hybris* or unwonted pride. Temperance and wisdom are his chief virtues. Frg.117, Frg.77, and Frg.118, which follow, reveal the cosmological underpinning of Heraclitus' ethics. The fiery nature of the soul makes it inimical to the element water, and so, in the interests of self-preservation, the good soul must strive to remain dry.

(Frg.119) Character for man is destiny.

(Frg.43) One should quench arrogance rather than a conflagration.

(Frg.112) Moderation is the greatest virtue, and wisdom is to speak the truth and to act according to nature, paying heed (*thereto*).

(Frg.28, 2nd part)... furthermore, retribution will seize the fabricators of lies and the (false) witnesses.†

(Frg.116) All men have the capacity of knowing themselves and acting with moderation.

(Frg.29) The best men choose one thing rather than all else: everlasting fame among mortal men.* The majority are satisfied, like well-fed cattle.

(Frg.4) If happiness lay in bodily pleasures, we would call oxen happy when they find vetch to eat.

(Frg.85) It is hard to fight against impulse; whatever it wishes, it buys at the expense of the soul.

(Frg.95) It is better to hide ignorance (*though this is hard in relaxation and over wine*).

(Frg.117) A man, when he gets drunk, is led stumbing along by an immature boy, not knowing where he is going, having his soul wet.

(Frg.77) It is delight, or rather death, to souls to become wet.... We live their (*the souls'*) death and they (*the souls*) live our death.

(Frg.118) A dry (desiccated) soul is the wisest and best.

Despite his concern for virtue, Heraclitus is not insensitive to the dangers of too great a rigidity in moral matters. Such a situation is as much a loss of sense of direction as intemperance. Endless repetition is deadening, and children should strike out on their own instead of blindly accepting rules laid down by their parents. Achievement is important.

(Frg.71) (*One must remember also*) the man who forgets which way the road leads.

(Frg.84b) It is a weariness to the same (*elements forming the human body*) to toil and to obey.

(Frg.20) When they are born, they are willing to live and accept their fate (*death*); and they leave behind children to become victims of fate.

---

†This fragment has been broken into two parts. The first part appears on p. 62.
*Or: 'rather than things mortal'.

(Frg.74) (*We must not act like*) children of our parents.

(Frg.25) The greater the fate (*death*), the greater the reward.

THE LOGOS AND THE CITY-STATE

Loyalty to the *Logos* is for Heraclitus the foundation of man's loyalty to the *Polis* and law (*Nomos*)—a loyalty for which he must be ready to do battle. On his courage in war depend both man's freedom and the freedom of his state. (Frg.53, below, which serves as the basis of this last conclusion, might be applied equally to the moral struggle carried on within the soul of each individual.) Yet Frg.33 suggests that Heraclitus was no democrat.

(Frg.114) If we speak with intelligence, we must base our strength on that which is common to all, as the city on the Law (*Nomos*) and even more strongly. For all human laws are nourished by one, which is divine. For it governs as far as it will, and is sufficient for all, and more than enough.

(Frg.113) The thinking faculty is common to all.

(Frg.33) To obey the will of one man is also Law (*political law, Nomos*).

(Frg.44) The people should fight for the Law (Nomos) as if for their city-wall.

(Frg.24) Gods and men honour those slain in war.

(Frg.53) War is both king of all and father of all, and it has revealed some as gods, others as men; some it has made slaves, others free.

True to his aristocratic temper, Heraclitus valued the superior individual over the vulgar. He was scornful of the money-oriented citizens of Ephesus, his native city, for their banishment of a man named Hermodôrus, about whom we know little else but that Heraclitus had a high opinion of his worth.

(Frg.49) One man to me is (*worth*) ten thousand, if he is the best.

(Frg.121) The Ephesians would do well to hang themselves, every adult man, and bequeath their City-State to adolescents, since they have expelled Hermodôrus, the most valuable man among them, saying: 'Let us not have even one valuable man; but if we do, let him go elsewhere and live among others.'

(Frg.125a) May wealth not fail you, men of Ephesus, so that you may be convicted of your wickedness!

In the first of the next three fragments (Frg.104), Heraclitus supplies a possible explanation for the behavior of his countrymen. The second, in the context of the badness of the many and the goodness of the few, places Bias of Priênê† among those few but does not explain. Frg. 97, which refers to dogs who bark at what they do not understand, also suggests what Heraclitus would undoubtedly regard as an apt comparison.

> (Frg.104) What intelligence or understanding have they? They believe the people's bards, and use as their teacher the populace, not knowing that 'the majority are bad, and the good are few'.*

> (Frg.39) In Priênê was born Bias son of Teutamos, whose fame (*or*, 'worth') is greater than that of the rest.

> (Frg.97) Dogs bark at those whom they do not recognize.

By way of summing up the overall political cast of Ionian thought in general and Heraclitus' thought in particular, Winspear addresses himself to what, from a Marxist point of view, is a paradoxical combination of a scornful attitude toward the people with an attitude of acceptance toward change and process. As he sees it, the weak tribal structure in Ionia and strong stimulus to mercantile development stemming from geographical location led to a situation in which a mercantile oligarchy was opposed only by the lower classes rather than having to deal with a landed aristocracy as well.‡

> ....This is the fundamental reason why they [the mercantile class] were able to face directly *their* problem, that of trade expansion, with its philosophical counterpart—motion, directly without finding a final static equilibrium lurking in the universe....This difference helps to explain why philosophy developed first in Ionia and why a theory of dialectics— although in a most primitive form—should develop in a thinker like Heraclitus. ....Nor, in view of the peculiar social development of Ionia, is it surprising that a thinker like Heraclitus should combine two qualities of thought which at first sight, and to a modern, may seem clearly incompatible— an aloof, scornful, even patronizing attitude toward the "people" with a profound interest in the laws of change and process.[10]

---

†Bias of Priênê in Ionia was one of the Seven Sages of Greece. See p. 34, note §.
*Saying attributed to Bias of Priênê.
‡See pp. 29-30.

REMAINING GENUINE FRAGMENTS

The following three fragments, the significance of which is either unclear or unimportant, are presented for the sake of completeness:

(Frg.105) Homer was an astrologer.

(Frg.38) (Thales was the first to study astronomy).

(Frg.122) (*Word for*) Approximation.

NOTES

1. Diogenes Laertius 9. 5.
2. W. K. C. Guthrie, *A History of Greek Philosphy*, 3 vols. (Cambridge: Cambridge University Press, 1962-9). Hereafter cited as Guthrie. Vol. 1, p. 408.
3. Kirk & Raven, p. 185.
4. Aristotle *Rhet.* 1407b11.
5. Guthrie, vol. 1, p. 408.
6. *Aeschylus*, Robert W. Corrigan, ed., trans. George Thomson (New York: Dell Publishing Co., 1965), p. 118-9.
7. Guthrie, vol. 1, pp. 413-4.
8. Ibid. p. 466.
9. *Ibid.*
10. Winspear, p. 127.

PART II

THE ITALIAN SCHOOL

Pythagoras and
    the Pythagoreans
The Eleatics
    Parmenides
    Melissus
    Zeno

CHAPTER 4
Pythagoras and the
Pythagoreans

With the advent of Pythagoras and his school, we have the first of the
two great Italian-based streams of thought—the other being the Eleatic
school of Parmenides—which together constitute the second phase in
the development of Pre-Socratic ideas. But, as we shall have occasion to
see, there is ample evidence of the dependence of both of these schools
upon the ideas of the Ionian mainland with which we have been
concerned.

THE PYTHAGOREAN TRADITION

There is little doubt about the importance of the ideas associated with
the name of Pythagoras and the Pythagoreanism which sprang from
them. But there is much doubt about the life and specific teachings of
Pythagoras himself, and there is no reliable way to separate the thought
of the founder from that of his disciples. The facts about the man are
shrouded in legend, and it is not impossible that the discoveries of his
disciples during his lifetime in the last three-quarters of the sixth century
B.C. have been attributed to Pythagoras himself. The records are just
not clear on these matters, and we shall follow the accepted procedure
of treating the ideas of the early Pythagoreans as related to the historic
personage of Pythagoras. The later Pythagoreanism of the fifth century
B.C. is often considered separately because of the criticisms of Parmenides and the Pythagorean attempts to answer them. According to
Cornford:

We can, in a word, distinguish between (1) the original sixth century system of Pythagoras, criticized by Parmenides— the mystical system—and (2) the fifth century pluralism constructed to meet Parmenides' objections, and criticized in turn by Zeno—the scientific system, which may be called 'Number-atomism'. There is also (3) the system of Philolaus, which belongs to the mystical side of the tradition and seeks to accommodate the Empedoclean theory of elements.[1]

The following diagram is used by Cornford to illustrate the development:[2]

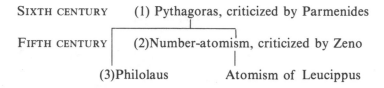

SIXTH CENTURY   (1) Pythagoras, criticized by Parmenides

FIFTH CENTURY   (2)Number-atomism, criticized by Zeno

       (3)Philolaus   Atomism of Leucippus

While these are technical matters of importance that may prove useful in our treatment of Parmenides and Zeno, they are not as important for our purpose here as presenting an overview of the entire Pythagorean tradition. In addition, very nearly all we know about this later period is to be found in the works of Aristotle, and very nearly all his references are to the school in general and not to separate thinkers. All considered, it seems best to treat Pythagoreanism as a whole in a single chapter and begin with the scant information we have of its founder.

Like Xenophanes, Pythagoras was educated and reached manhood in Asia Minor, specifically the island of Samos,[3] and he emigrated to Italy for political reasons. There is general agreement that he studied those ideas in mathematics and the Greek theory of numbers which we know today as the foundations of geometry,[4] and that at the age of about forty, at the height of his powers, he emigrated to the city of Croton in Italy, during the reign of the tyrant Polycrates.[5] There he and his followers met with such political success that they virtually ruled the city.[6] And the reputation of Pythagoras for wisdom grew and spread throughout Hellas. A fragment from Empedocles attests to this reputation.† And the dim view of it which Heraclitus took survives in two of his (Heraclitus') existing fragments.‡ Plutarch records that Pythagoras wrote nothing,[7] but Iamblicius attributes the lack of direct sources to the Pythagorean penchant for secrecy.[8]

That there was a brotherhood sworn to secrecy and to common practices is evident from the partial list of rules which has come down to

†See Empedocles, Frg. 129, p. 164 of this book.
‡See Heraclitus, Frg. 40 and Frg. 129, p. 62 of this book.

us, from which some appreciation of the flavor of the particular beliefs and practices may be gained.

T25 Iamblichus *Protr.* 21 [K&R226-7]

Let the rules to be pondered be these:

1. When you are going out to a temple, worship first, and on your way neither say nor do anything else connected with your daily life.
2. On a journey neither enter a temple nor worship at all, not even if you are passing the very doors.
3. Sacrifice and worship without shoes on.
4. Turn aside from highways and walk by footpaths.
6. Follow the gods and restrain your tongue above all else....
8. Stir not the fire with iron....
10. Help a man who is loading freight, but not one who is unloading.
11. Putting on your shoes, start with the right foot; washing your feet, with the left.
12. Speak not of Pythagorean matters without light.
13. Never step over a cross-bar.
14. When you are out from home look not back, for the Furies come after you....
17. Rear a cock, but do not sacrifice it; for it is dedicated to Moon and Sun.
18. Do not sit on a quart measure.
21. Let not a swallow nest under your roof.
22. Do not wear a ring....
24. Do not look in a mirror beside a lamp.
25. Disbelieve nothing strange about the gods or about religious beliefs.
26. Be not possessed by irrepressible mirth.
27. Cut not your finger-nails at a sacrifice....
29. When you rise from bed roll the bed-clothes together and smooth out the place where you lay.
30. Eat not the heart.
32. Spit upon the trimmings of your hair and finger-nails....
34. Leave not the mark of the pot in the ashes.
37. Abstain from beans....
39. Abstain from living things.

Some further insight into the thought of Pythagoras and the way in which the practices of the brotherhood and their mathematical and scientific investigations were related appears in the following two references:

> **T26** Proclus *in Eucl.* p. 65 Friedl. [K&R228]
> So Pythagoras turned geometrical philosophy into a form of liberal education by seeking its first principles in a higher realm of reality....

> **T27** Diogenes Laertius 8. 8. [Loeb]
> ....he compared life to the Great Games, when some went to compete for the prize and others went with wares to sell, but the best as spectators; for similarly, in life, some grow up with servile natures, greedy for fame and gain, but the philosopher seeks for truth.

In the latter passage an exalted view of the life of philosophy is evident and one tradition has it that it was Pythagoras who first coined the word "philosophy"—love of wisdom, *philo-sophia.*

THE SOUL

Though it will not prove difficult to understand the mathematical cosmology of the Pythagoreans in relation to the mathematical science and nature philosophy of the Ionians, the connection is not as clear with the Pythagorean doctrine of the soul because of its roots in the Dionysian religious tradition.† It is not unreasonable, however, to suppose some connection between the finer, purer, more active and higher element of the cosmos (the Air of Anaximenes, the Fire of Heraclitus) and the soul element in man which we find in the Ionian tradition. It is also reasonable to suppose that the discipline practiced by the Pythagorean brotherhood had as its aim the purification of the soul of man (from its contact with the grosser elements of creation), and its proper attunement with the ultimately real. Pythagoras became known for holding that the soul is immortal, that it takes on different forms of living things and that all living things are akin to each other.

> **T28** Diogenes Laertius 8. 8. (Xenophanes Frg.7, 2nd part) [Loeb]
> ....They say that, passing a belaboured whelp, he, full of pity, spake these words of dole: "Stay, smite not! 'Tis a friend, a human soul; I knew him straight whenas I heard

---

†See pp. 13ff. and 21ff.

him yelp!" Thus Xenophanes.†

In the *Phaedo* (86B–C) Plato sets forth the Pythagorean doctrine that the soul is an attunement of the opposite elements of the body, and Aristotle gives this same view.

T29 Aristotle *De Anima* 407b31–33
Its supporters say that the soul is a kind of harmony, for
(a) harmony is a blend or composition of contraries, and
(b) the body is compounded out of contraries.

That this understanding of the soul is grounded in a wider reality is further attested to by the same author, who reports a connection between the soul and the elements causing constant motion in the air.

T30 Aristotle *De Anima* 404a16–19
The doctrine of the Pythagoreans seems to rest upon the same ideas; some of them declared the motes in air, others what moved them, to be soul. These motes were referred to because they are seen always in the movement, even in a complete calm.

There would seem to be a relationship between this view and the older view associated with Homer of the Psyche as breath.‡

ALL IS NUMBER

Equally important and even perhaps more striking than his ideas about the soul is Pythagoras' belief that at the base of the whole cosmic structure and all the things that exist is number.

T31 Aristotle *Met.* 985b23–986a12, 15—b8
Contemporaneously with these philosophers, and before them, the Pythagoreans, as they are called, devoted themselves to mathematics; they were the first to advance this study, and having been brought up in it they thought its principles were the principles of all things. Since of these principles numbers are by nature the first, and in numbers they seemed to see many resemblances to the things that exist and come into being—more than in fire and earth and water (such and such a modification of numbers being justice, another being soul and reason, another being oppor—tunity—and similarly almost all other things being numerically expressible); since, again, they saw that the attributes and ratios of the musical scales were expressible in numbers;

---

†This fragment of Xenophanes has been broken into two parts. That this part refers to Pythagoras is testified to by Freeman on p. 99 of her *Companion*. The first part appears on p. 57 of the present volume.
‡See pp. 13-5.

since, then, all other things seemed in their whole nature to be modelled after numbers, and numbers seem to be the first things in the whole of nature, they supposed the elements of numbers to be the elements of all things, and the whole heaven to be a musical scale and a number. And all the properties of numbers and scales which they could show to agree with the attributes and parts and the whole arrangement of the heavens, they collected and fitted into their scheme; and if there was a gap anywhere, they readily made additions so as to make their theory coherent, e.g., as the number ten is thought to be perfect and to comprise the whole nature of numbers, they say that the bodies which move through the heavens are ten, but as the visible bodies are only nine, to meet this they invent a tenth—the 'counter-earth'. . . . .Evidently, then, these thinkers also consider that number is the principle both as matter for things and as forming their modifications and their permanent states, and hold that the elements of number are the even and the odd, and of these the former is unlimited, and the latter limited; and the one proceeds from both of these (for it is both even and odd), and number from the one; and the whole heaven, as has been said, is numbers.

Other members of this same school say there are ten principles, which they arrange in two columns of cognates—limit and unlimited, odd and even, one and plurality, right and left, male and female, resting and moving, straight and curved, light and darkness, good and bad, square and oblong. . . .[†]

From both these schools, then, we can learn this much, that the contraries are the principles of things; and how many these principles are and which they are, we can learn from one of the two schools. But how these principles can be brought together under the causes we have named has not been clearly and articulately stated by them; they seem, however, to range the elements under the head of matter; for out of these as immanent parts they say substance is composed and moulded.

The importance of these ideas for Western Civilization cannot be exaggerated. Just what led Pythagoras to them we cannot be sure; but two considerations about which we do know, when taken together,

---

†The passage omitted here is found on p. 227, T 131.

undoubtedly point in the right direction. The first is the nature of Greek mathematics and the second is the discovery by Pythagoras of musical proportion. We will consider them separately.

MATHEMATICAL IDEAS

Aristotle tells us that the Pythagoreans were the first to advance the study of mathematics, and the name of Pythagoras is still associated with the theorem in Euclidean geometry which applies the equation to the right triangle.

T32   Proclus *in Eucl.* p. 426 Friedl. [K&R231]
(The square on the hypotenuse of the right-angled triangle is equal to the sum of the squares on the sides enclosing the right angle.) (Corrupted, but the sense)—If we pay any attention to those who like to recount ancient history, we may find some of them referring this theorem to Pythagoras, and saying that he sacrificed an ox in honour of his discovery.

According to Porphyry, the followers of Pythagoras were divided into two groups, the Mathematicians, who were in possession of the most detailed aspects of his doctrines, and the Acousmatics, who were acquainted only with the general outlines.[9] What we call geometry comprised all of mathematics for the Greeks. It is probable that the Greeks had no numerals in Pythagoras' time[10]: the Pythagoreans used instead arrangements of pebbles to represent numbers. Basically, there were three such arrangements, and they form the fundamental kinds or classes of numbers: "square," "oblong," and "triangular" numbers:

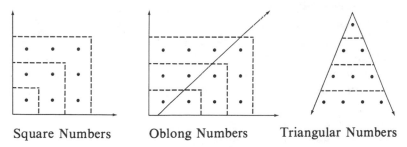

Square Numbers   Oblong Numbers   Triangular Numbers

The square numbers are made by adding "gnomons" successively to the unit. Although the *gnomon* was originally a measuring device,†, gradually it came to mean any vertical line, and then in connection with

---

†See p. 36 n. for definition and pp. 34,36 for suggestion as to its use.

Greek mathematical notation, a figure like a carpenter's square—with arms of equal length, in the case of construction of the square numbers.† (Only later did members of the series of square numbers, 1,4,9,16, etc., come themselves to be called gnomons.) It is of interest to point out that if we add the square numbers, 9 and 16, we have an illustration of the Pythagorean theorem: $9 + 16 = 25$ or $3^2 + 4^2 = 5^2$.

The oblong numbers are made by adding successively to the number 2. In this case, however, one arm is longer by one unit than the other.‡

> **T33** Aristotle *Physics* 203a10–15
> Further, the Pythagoreans identify the infinite with the even. For this, they say, when it is taken in and limited by the odd, provides things with the element of infinity. An indication of this is what happens with numbers. If the gnomons are placed around the one, and without the one, in the one construction the figure that results is always different, in the other it is always the same.

The fact that the geometrical representation of oblong numbers can be divided evenly with a line extended indefinitely and that all oblong numbers are thus divisible by two led them to identify infinity with even numbers. Simplicius explains why:

> **T34** Simplicius *Phys.* 455. 20. [K&R244]
> They meant by infinity even numbers 'since everything even' as the commentators say, 'is divisible into equal parts, and what is divisible into equal parts is infinite in respect of division into two; for division into halves goes on *ad infinitum*, while the addition of the odd limits it by putting an end to halving'. So the commentators refer the unlimited to the even in respect of divisibility into halves, and it is plain that they conceive of infinite divisibility in terms not of numbers but of magnitudes....

But of the three kinds, it is the third, the triangular numbers, which were foremost in importance for the Pythagoreans. They are formed by adding the integers successively to the unit to get, in order, 1,3,6,10, etc. The triangle formed by adding the successive numbers up to four, $1+2+3+4 = 10$, was considered to be that from which all others came and to be generated from the unit by division. It was regarded as holy and was called the *tetraktys*. There is a connec-

tetraktys

---

† •• and •••   exemplify gnomons with arms of equal length.
‡ •••• and •••• exemplify gnomons with one arm longer by one unit than the other.

tion here between these four numbers and the manner in which the point, the line, the plane, and the solid are successively generated. In other words, a unit defines a point, 2 points define a line, 3 points a plane and 4, a solid. And it will be recalled that Aristotle recounts (T31) that in order to fulfill the sacred number ten, a "counter-earth" was assumed in addition to the nine other celestial bodies.

Several things are to be noticed here regarding this conception of numbers—both for their intrinsic interest and because of their implications for Pythagoreanism in general.

(1) The three kinds of number, square, oblong and triangular, function not only to mark out specific numbers but also indicate rules for the indefinitely extendable series of numbers for each kind.

(2) We must not think of the individual pebbles as alone constitutive of any numbers. As it is the pebbles which fix the space, the *gnomon* is a spatial figure made definite by the numbers of pebbles that fix it. This is important for our understanding of the Pythagorean theory of the generation of the universe as like the generation of numbers in which a limit is imposed upon an unlimited space by the succession of appropriately fixed *gnomons*.

(3) Conceiving of numbers in this way is another instance of the inability to distinguish ideas from things, the incorporeal from the corporeal, common to the early Greek thinkers. Aristotle, to whom it was abundantly clear that numbers are abstractions, takes the Pythagoreans severely to task for identifying numbers with things.

T35 Aristotle *Met.* 1080b16–21
And the Pythagoreans also believe in one kind of number— the mathematical; only they say it is not separate but sensible substances are formed out of it. For they construct the whole universe out of numbers—only not numbers consisting of abstract units. They suppose the units to have spatial magnitude. . . .All. . .suppose numbers to consist of abstract units, except the Pythagoreans; but *they* suppose the numbers to have magnitude, as has been said before.

T36 Aristotle *Met.* 1083b11–18
. . . .that bodies should be composed of numbers, and that this should be mathematical number, is impossible. For it is not true to speak of indivisible spatial magnitudes; and however much there might be magnitude of this sort, units at least have not magnitude; and how can a magnitude be composed of indivisibles? But arithmetical number, at least,

consists of units, while these thinkers identify numbers with real things; at any rate they apply their propositions to bodies as if they consisted of those numbers.

(4) Pythagoras may have initially basked in the glory of his discovery of the theorem bearing his name, but the unfortunate fact is that this very discovery had consequences in conflict with the basic Pythagorean premise that all is number. For the Pythagoreans, "number" meant the integers; but then what integer can be assigned to the length of the hypotenuse of a right triangle with equal legs of unit length (or equal legs of any length for that matter)? In the case of the unit triangle, since $c^2 = a^2 + b^2$:

$$c = a^2 + b^2 = \sqrt{2}$$

But there is no integer corresponding to $\sqrt{2}$: we call $\sqrt{2}$ an irrational number. More generally, regardless of length, if $a = b$:

$$c = \sqrt{2a^2} = a\sqrt{2},$$

again with no integer corresponding. Subsequent discovery of such "irrationality" in the structure of the Pythagorean cosmos led members of the Brotherhood into the profoundest difficulties—difficulties constituting more than an insignificant test of their oath of secrecy.

(5) It is the Pythagoreans who developed geometry into a discipline distinct from its early practical association with the surveying of land in Egypt. Just because it was assumed to have no connection with the sense world, the study of mathematics became the way to purify and perfect the human soul by leading it away from the worldly and sensible towards the eternal and intelligible. And for much the same reasons it is still considered by many to be a central part of the liberal arts.

THE HARMONY OF OPPOSITES

Undoubtedly the most far-reaching application of mathematical inquiry by Pythagoras was his discovery of the simple proportions in the theory of harmonics. Diogenes Laertius tells us he discovered them on the monochord:[11] If a string fastened at both ends be stopped so that the lengths of the two parts are in the ratios of 2:1 or 3:2 or 4:3, we will have the octave and the major fourth and fifth respectively. The first thing to note here is that the proportions 2:1, 3:2, and 4:3 also state relationships between the elements of the holy *tetraktys*. Second, Pythagoras could not have discovered these proportions merely by observation. He must have had some kind of idea and conducted something like an experiment. Which preceded which—the idea or the fact? Perhaps he was musically "doodling" when the idea hit him. At any rate, experiment would confirm his suspicions whatever their origins. Third, stopping the string is a beautiful example of introducing a particular limit upon the otherwise unlimited vibrations. Of course, it is just that proportion which when introduced produces just that tone (middle C on the piano equals 440 vibrations). Certainly this striking instance of the reality of the particular being found in the mathematical proportion either suggested or confirmed that things are numbers. But more generally it suggested that things are a balance of opposites expressible as the imposition of the limit upon the unlimited. We have already spoken of the Pythagorean notion of the soul as an "attunement of opposite elements,"† and the phrase "the music of the spheres" still echoes today the poetic application of these same Pythagorean ideas to the movement of the heavenly bodies.

> **T37**   Aristotle *De Caelo* 290b12
> From all this it is clear that the theory that the movement of the stars produces a harmony, i.e., that the sounds they make are concordant, in spite of the grace and originality with which it has been stated, is nevertheless untrue. Some thinkers suppose that the motion of bodies that size must produce a noise, since on our earth the motion of bodies far inferior in size and in speed of movement has that effect. Also, when the sun and the moon, they say, and all the stars, so great in number and in size, are moving with so rapid a motion, how should they not produce a sound immensely great? Starting from this argument and from the observation that their speeds, as measured by their distances, are in the same ratios as musical concordances, they assert that the sound given forth by the circular movement of the stars is a harmony. Since, however, it appears unaccountable that we should not hear this music, they explain this by saying that the sound is in our ears from the very moment of birth and is thus indistinguishable from its contrary silence, since sound and silence are discriminated by mutual contrast. What happens to men, then, is just what happens to coppersmiths, who are so accustomed to the noise of the smithy that it makes no difference to them.

Truly, this idea that number is at the root of the real is one of the two or three most powerful, successful, elegant, and inspiring ideas that man

---

†See T29 p. 85.

has ever come up with. Pythagoras held the clarification and application of this idea to be the peculiar vocation of man.

THE PYTHAGOREAN COSMOS

It is of the utmost importance for the understanding of Pythagoreanism to realize that the pursuit of mathematical inquiry is designed to purify the soul of man, to allow it to regain, through rational discipline, its rightful place among the finer elements of the cosmos. But in this process of purification a vision of reality is slowly acquired, and it is to the outlines of this Pythagorean vision that we now turn.

We have already seen that for the Pythagoreans all things were numbers; that is, the things of the universe were held to be constituted by various harmonious proportions. Throughout the development of the school there were attempts to directly connect certain things, qualities and conditions with specific numbers. Justice was associated with the number four, and the connection is still with us in the phrase "four-square", meaning evenly and solidly balanced. The number five, which is the union of the first even number, two, with the first odd number, three, was the number for marriage. Not only were things numbers, but, as Aristotle points out, so were the virtues.[12]

Besides the two principles of Limit and Unlimited, we have seen how there are nine other pairs of contrasting opposites which, along with this pair, are basic for the Pythagoreans: odd and even, one and many, right and left, male and female, resting and moving, straight and curved, light and darkness, good and bad, and square and oblong. Aristotle also tells us that earth, air, fire and water are held by the Pythagoreans to be derived from these more basic opposites.† The close connection between early Pythagorean thought and that of Ionian thinkers like Anaximander is evident here in that both tend to think of all diversity as separating out from the all-inclusive reality which they identify with the One.[13]

It is the mechanism of the generative process that is the Pythagorean innovation. By imposition of the Limit on the Unlimited, the other nine pairs of opposites, the elements, and all other this-worldly diversity are generated. Defining the distinction between odd and even in terms of divisibility by two, early Pythagoreans concluded that the One or Unit is odd, i.e., that it is an instance of one of the pair of opposites "odd-even." At the same time, identifying it with the Limit, they thought of it as the generative source of the opposite pair "odd-even" as well as of everything else. Later Pythagoreans more consistently

---

†See T31pp. 85-6.

regarded the One as the first product of imposition of the Limit on the Unlimited[14] and of course thereby diverged from the Ionian view, the Limit and the Unlimited being primarily formal in character.

How the generation of the opposites from the One is to be explained successfully was a problem for the whole school. Aristotle in the following passages suggests the conception of "drawing in" or "inhaling", in which the Unlimited surrounding the One is drawn in and "limited by the limit":

T38   Aristotle *Met.* 1091a13-19

It is strange also to attribute generation to things that are eternal, or rather this is one of the things that are impossible. There need be no doubt whether the Pythagoreans attribute generation to them or not; for they say plainly that when the one had been constructed, whether out of planes or of surface or of seed or of elements which they cannot express, immediately the nearest part of the unlimited began to be constrained and limited by the limit.

T39   Aristotle *Physics* 213b23-28

The Pythagoreans, too,...held that void exists and that it enters the heaven itself, which as it were inhales it, from the infinite air. Further it is the void which distinguishes the natures of things, as if it were like what separates and distinguishes the terms of a series. This holds primarily in the numbers, for the void distinguishes their nature.

It is interesting to note that Aristotle in the first passage also speaks of the possibility of the One being constructed of seed. This suggests a biological conception of the generative process. Again, just as with the Ionians, the Pythagoreans may have thought of the cosmos as alive in some general sense. Or perhaps it is better to say that they simply did not think of a dead world in the way modern man has tended to. Reference to the void as "like what separates and distinguishes the terms of a series" is suggestive of the reality of empty space as well as of the pebbles in the *gnomon*.

As to the shape and order of their cosmos, the Pythagoreans are the first on record to hold that the earth is not the center, but moves in circular orbit about the central fire. Again, reference to Aristotle, who does not take this position, will further flesh out their view:

T40   Aristotle *De Caelo* 293a18-25

Most people say that the earth lies at the centre of the universe...but the Italian philosophers known as Pythagoreans take the contrary view. At the centre, they say, is fire, and the earth is one of the stars, creating night and day by its circular motion about the centre. They further construct another earth in opposition to ours to which they give the name counter-earth. In all this they are not seeking for theories and causes to account for observed facts, but rather forcing their observations and trying to accommodate them to certain theories and opinions of their own. But there are many others who would agree that it is wrong to give the earth the central position, looking for conformation rather to theory than to the facts of observation. Their view is that the most precious place befits the most precious thing: but fire, they say, is more precious than earth, and the limit than the intermediate, and the circumference and the centre are limits. Reasoning on this basis they take the view that it is not earth that lies at the centre of the sphere, but rather fire.

POLITICAL AND RELIGIOUS AFFINITIES OF Th.℞ ITALIAN SCHOOL

Although it is surely a gross error to evaluate ideas in terms of their origins, it is at the same time historically illuminating to recognize that Pythagoras and the Pythagoreans, a well as Parmenides, were involved in politics a strongly conservative flavor.[15] Winspear suggests some interesting connections between the Pythagoreans' cosmological and mathematical ideas and their political affinities: among them, their political concern with order and their view that the creation and maintenance of the universe are to be understood as an imposition of Limit on the Unlimited;[16] their abhorrence of conflict and their affirmation of the cosmological importance of the harmony of opposites;[17] and their opposition to democratic equality and their mathematical interest in proportionality.[18] In the last instance, proportional equality is taken as the model of *Diké*. Farrington says of the Pythagoreans:

> This mathematical philosophy appeared as a rival to the natural philosophy of the Ionians. And here it becomes immediately apparent that, as a theory of the universe, it contained less of sensuous intuition and more of abstract thought than the Ionian view. Mathematical relations now take the place of physical processes or states, like rarefaction and condensation, and tension. The universe, so it appeared to the Pythagoreans, could be better, and more quickly, understood by drawing diagrams on sand than by thinking about phenomena like raised beaches, silting up of river mouths, evaporation, felting, and so forth. Herein lay a danger. This mathematical approach was adjusted both to the religious and social preconceptions of the school.

Mathematics not only seemed to provide a better explanation of things than the Ionian view. It kept the souls of the brethren pure from contact with the earthly, the material, and suited the changing temper of a world in which contempt for manual labour kept pace with the growth of slavery. In a society in which contact with the technical processes of production became ever more shameful, as being fit only for slaves, it was found extraordinarily fortunate that the secret constitution of things should be revealed, not to those who manipulated them, not to those who worked with fire, but to those who drew patterns on the sand. For Heraclitus, who came at the end of a school of thought in which industrial technique had played a prominent role in providing the stock of ideas by which nature was explained, nothing seemed more natural than to regard fire, the chief agent in the technical manipulation of things, as the fundamental element. The substitution of number for fire as the First Principle marks a stage in the separation of philosophy from the technique of production. This separation is of fundamental importance in the interpretation of the history of Greek thought. Henceforth the banausic† association of the oven, the soldering-iron, the bellows, and the potter's wheel reduce their influence on Greek thought in comparison with the more gentlemanly pursuit of theory of numbers and geometry.[19]

The Eleatics will lead philosophy even further from its Ionian association with technique than had the Pythagoreans. Though the Pythagoreans moved from Ionian monism in the direction of a dualism rooted in the separation of soul and form on the one hand from matter and sense experience on the other, they, along with the Ionians, were still motivated by the theoretical concern of explaining the material world of sense experience in terms of their formal principles. And the connection of their theory of the harmony of opposites with empirically observed musical harmonies is obvious. Though Parmenides is reputed to have been at one time a Pythagorean,‡ he later attacked Pythagorean dualism as well as any attempt to explain the changing world of sense. The Eleatics will, in fact, deny the reality of change entirely.

It is also illuminating to recognize that Pythagoreanism, along with the thought of Xenophanes and Heraclitus, is expressive of Dionysian influence. It, as well as the thought of Xenophanes, differs from Heraclitus in being more influenced by Orphism than by unadulterated

---

†Common, menial or practical.
‡Diogenes Laertius 9. 21-3 and Strabo 6; see T42 and T43 p. 99.

Dionysiac ideas; however, "Orpheus, the ideal of the Orphic, is a Diony-sus tamed, and clothed, and in his right mind—in a word Apollo-nised."[20] But an Appollonised Dionysus is really a contradiction in terms because of the disparity between the Apollonian (or Olympia-nised) *Eidolon* soul and Dionysian *Thymos* soul.† Evidence of its attempt to reconcile these two opposed elements is to be found in the Orphic revival of worship of the heavenly bodies, particularly the sun. The sun is involved in daily and seasonal cycles; yet at the same time it lends itself to interpretation as an Olympian or Apollonian immortal God.[21] With the heavens now become the wheel of birth, individual souls are thought of as fallen from the light upper reaches to the dark earth. They have a divine origin but are imprisoned here, a belief accounting for the Orphic's preoccupation with reunion with God through purification rights. Light and darkness become symbols of good and evil, and we have a cosmic as well as a moral dualism, both reflected in the assumed conflict between soul and body.[22] Cornford sums up the philosophical consequences:

> Further, throughout the mystical systems inspired by Orphism, we shall find the fundamental contrast between the two principles of Light and Darkness, identified with Good and Evil. This cosmic dualism is the counterpart of the dualism in the nature of the soul; for, as always, *physis* and soul correspond, and are, indeed, identical in substance. The soul in its pure state consists of fire, like the divine stars from which it falls; in its impure state, throughout the period of reincarnation, its substance is infected with baser elements, and weighed down by the gross admixture of the flesh.* In the cosmologies inspired by this conception, we may expect to find, first, that the element of fire will be set in contrast with the other three,** and second, that the manifold world of sense will be viewed as a degradation from the purity of real being. Such systems will tend to be other-worldly, put-ting all value in the unseen unity of God, and condemning the visible world as false and illusive, a turbid medium in which the rays of heavenly light are broken and obscured in mist and darkness. These characteristics are common to all the systems which came out of the Pythagorean move-ment—Pythagoreanism proper, and the philosophies of Parmenides, Empedocles, and Plato.[23]

---

†See pp. 13ff.
*All this is very clearly brought out by Socrates in Plato's *Phaedo*.
**It must be remembered, too, that fire is the element of which the Measurers of Time (the heavenly bodies) consist. Diog. Laert. 8. 1. 27 (Pythagoras).

The Olympian aspect of Orphism is manifested in the development of later Pythagoreanism toward a number atomism—even to the point of convergence with that ultimate product of the Scientific tradition, the Atomism of Leucippus and Democritus. Parmenides' denial of the possibility of change because of its inexplicability in terms of the One Being will represent his reaction to the contradiction implicit in Orphism between its Dionysiac and Olympian elements. Zeno and Melissus, as his disciples will, of course, follow his example in this respect.

NOTES

1. F. M. Cornford, "Mysticism and Science in the Pythagorean Tradition," *Classical Quarterly* 16 (1922), p. 138.
2. *Ibid.*
3. Herodotus 4. 95.
4. Apollonius *Hist. Mir.* 6; Kirk & Raven, p. 218.
5. Porphyrius *Vita Pythagorae* 9; ibid. p. 217.
6. Diogenes Laertius 8. 3.
7. Plutarch *Alex. fort.* 1. 4. 328; Kirk & Raven, p. 221.
8. Iamblichus *V.P.* 199; *ibid.*
9. Porphyrius *V.P.* 37; *ibid.* p. 227.
10. George Sarton, *A History of Science: Ancient Science Through the Golden Age of Greece* (Harvard University Press, 1952; reprint ed., New York: John Wiley & Sons, Inc., Science Editions, 1964), p. 205.
11. Diogenes Laertius 8. 11.
12. Aristotle *Meta.* 1078b21, *Magna Moralia* 1182a11.
13. Cornford, *From Religion to Philosophy*, p. 210.
14. Kirk & Raven, p. 318.
15. Winspear, pp. 78ff; p. 99.
16. *Ibid.*, pp. 86-7.
17. *Ibid.*, p. 87.
18. *Ibid.* pp. 94–5.
19. Farrington, pp. 48-9.
20. Cornford, *From Religion to Philosophy*, p. 195.
21. *Ibid.*, p. 196.
22. *Ibid.*, pp. 178–180.
23. *Ibid.*, p. 197.

CHAPTER 5
The Eleatics: Parmenides

Basically, the term "Eleatic" refers to the members of the school of philosophy located at the Sicilian colony of Elea and associated with Parmenides. The term also extends to thinkers whose views closely resemble those of Parmenides. In Plato's dialogue, *The Sophist*, the principle speaker is called simply An Eleatic Stranger, conveying both of the above conditions. While Zeno falls under the first and is noted for his attacks on the opponents of Parmenides, the views of Melissus of Samos constitute an amplification of Parmenides in some important respects.†

Considered historically, Eleatic thought is a watershed in early Greek philosophy. It sounds the death-knell of the Ionian hope of explaining the manyness of nature in terms of a unitary stuff, and all subsequent Greek thinkers were bound to acknowledge this Eleatic criticism in one way or another.

PARMENIDES

Based on a passage from Plato's dialogue *Parmenides*, it is estimated that Parmenides flourished *circa* 475 B.C. Other information from the same source concerning a visit of Parmenides and Zeno to Athens is also generally accepted:

---

†Melissus and Zeno are presented in the next chapter.

T41   Plato *Parmenides* 127b[1]

According to Antiphon, then, this was Pythodorus' account. Zeno and Parmenides once came to Athens for the Great Panathenaea.† Parmenides was a man of distinguished appearance. By that time he was well advanced in years, with hair almost white; he may have been sixty-five. Zeno was nearing forty, a tall and attractive figure. It was said that he was Parmenides' favorite. They were staying with Pythodorus outside the walls in the Ceramicus. Socrates and a few others came there, anxious to hear a reading of Zeno's treatise, which the two visitors had brought for the first time to Athens. Socrates was then quite young. Zeno himself read it to them; Parmenides at the moment had gone out.

Limited additional background information concerning Parmenides' Pythagorean associations, his slight contact with Xenophanes, and his political activity is found in the following testimonia:

T42   Diogenes Laertius 9. 21-3. [Loeb]

Parmenides, a native of Elea, son of Pyres, was a pupil of Xenophanes (Theophrastus in his *Epitome* makes him a pupil of Anaximander). Parmenides, however, though he was instructed by Xenophanes, was no follower of his. According to Sotion he also associated with Ameinias the Pythagorean, who was the son of Diochoetas and a worthy gentleman though poor. This Ameinias he was more inclined to follow, and on his death he built a shrine to him, being himself of illustrious birth and possessed of great wealth; moreover it was Ameinias and not Xenophanes who led him to adopt the peaceful life of a student....Parmenides is said to have served his native city as a legislator: so we learn from Speusippus in his book *On Philosophers*.

T43   Strabo *Geography* 6.1 [Loeb]

....Elia....This is the native city of Parmenides and Zeno, the Pythagorean philosophers. It is my opinion that not only through the influence of these men but also in still earlier times the city was well governed....

T44   Plutarch *adv. Colot.* 32, 1126A [K&R 265]

Parmenides set his own state in order with such admirable laws that the government yearly swears its citizens to abide by the laws of Parmenides.

---

†An Athenian festival celebrated once every four years.

Whether or not Parmenides is the greatest of the Pre-Socratics, he certainly would be one of those considered if such a choice had to be made, and without doubt he is the most original among them. This originality makes him a pivotal figure in any interpretation of Pre-Socratic thought. He raises questions extremely damaging to the general tenor of thinking of both the Milesians and Pythagoreans, and the relation of his point of view to that of Heraclitus is as interesting as it is problematic.† All subsequent thinkers, if not his disciples, have had to come to terms with the difficulties he raised. Parmenides is said to have been a pupil of Xenophanes, and he shares with his teacher a rather "bull-headed" monistic orientation. Like Heraclitus, he shows a relatively limited interest in physical explanation.

The Milesians were, to use Cleve's term, "transformists." That is, they tried to explain how the one vital stuff constituting the *physis* of the universe could become, through transformation, the many diverse things of our everyday experience. The Parmenidean line of thought raised the embarrassing question of how a vital stuff, of the sort the Milesians assumed, could possibly become something other than itself without contradiction. The cosmological implications of his thought are that reality is a plenum—that is, a three-dimensional, continuous whole with no interstices and with nothing outside of it. This view presents difficulties for a thinker like Anaximenes, whose principle of condensation and rarefaction as the explanation of how transformations of the vital stuff take place, presupposes either such interstices or such an outside empty space. It is also a direct challenge to the position of the early Pythagoreans for, to hold as they seem to have, that the generation of the multiplicity of the world proceeds from the Unit through a kind of number atomism, requires the same assumption. It was Parmenides who forced Greek thought to forsake the monistic attempt to derive the plurality of appearances from an assumed single basic stuff and to embrace instead an original plurality of elements or atoms.

PARMENIDES' POEM

All the fragments of Parmenides we have are from a poem which was divided into three parts: a "Prologue", the "Way of Truth", and the "Way of Seeming". The goddess of the Prologue directs the young Parmenides to gain familiarity with the Way of Seeming[2] as well as the Way of Truth. The whole character of the Prologue as well as the poetic form of the whole piece suggests that Parmenides thought of himself as communicating something of a mystical or religious revelation. Besides

---

†See pp. 106ff.

the Prologue, it is estimated we possess about nine-tenths of the Way of Truth and one tenth of the Way of Seeming. The Prologue and the Way of Truth will be presented entire at this point, followed by comment and criticism. Then bits and pieces, all we have of the Way of Seeming, will be considered.

Prologue

(Frg. 1) The mares which carry me conveyed me as far as my desire reached, when the goddesses who were driving had set me on the famous highway which bears a man who has knowledge through all the cities. Along this way I was carried; for by this way the exceedingly intelligent mares bore me, drawing the chariot, and the maidens directed the way. The axle in the naves gave forth a pipe-like sound as it glowed (for it was driven round by the two whirling circles (*wheels*) at each end) whenever the maidens, daughters of the Sun, having left the Palace of Night, hastened their driving towards the light, having pushed back their veils from their heads with their hands.

There (*in the Palace of Night*) are the gates of the paths of Night and Day, and they are enclosed with a lintel above and a stone threshold below. The gates themselves are filled with great folding doors; and of these Justice, mighty to punish, has the interchangeable keys. The maidens, skillfully cajoling her with soft words, persuaded her to push back the bolted bar without delay from the gates; and these, flung open, revealed a wide gaping space, having swung their jambs, richly-wrought in bronze, reciprocally in their sockets. This way, then, straight through them went the maidens, driving chariot and mares along the carriage-road.

And the goddess received me kindly, and took my right hand in hers, and thus she spoke and addressed me:

"Young man, companion of immortal charioteers, who comest by the help of the steeds which bring thee to our dwelling: welcome!—since no evil fate has dispatched thee on thy journey by this road (for truly it is far from the path trodden by mankind); no, it is divine command and Right. Thou shalt inquire into everything: both the motionless heart of well-rounded Truth, and also the opinions of mortals, in which there is no true reliability. But nevertheless thou shalt learn these things (*opinions*) also—how one should go through all the things-that-seem, without exception, and test them.

The Way of Truth

(Frg.2) Come, I will tell you—and you must accept my word when you have heard it—the ways of inquiry which alone are to be thought: the one that *it is*, and it is not possible for *it not to be*, is the way of credibility, for it follows Truth; the other, that *it is not*, and that *it* is bound *not to be*: this I tell you is a path that cannot be explored; for you could neither recognize that which *is not*, nor express it.

(Frg.3) For it is the same thing to think and to be.*

(Frg.4) Observe nevertheless how things absent are securely present to the mind; for it will not sever Being from its connection with Being, whether it is scattered everywhere utterly throughout the universe, or whether it is collected together.

(Frg.5) It is all the same to me from what point I begin, for I shall return again to this same point.

(Frg.6) One should both say and think that Being Is; for To Be is possible, and Nothingness is not possible. This I command you to consider; for from the latter way of search first of all I debar you. But next I debar you from that way along which wander mortals knowing nothing, two-headed**, for perplexity in their bosoms steers their intelligence astray, and they are carried along as deaf as they are blind, amazed, uncritical hordes, by whom To Be and Not To Be are regarded as the same and not the same, and (*for whom*) in everything there is a way of opposing stress.***

(Frg.7, 8, §1) For this (*view*) can never predominate, that That Which Is Not exist. You must debar your thought from this way of search, nor let ordinary experience in its variety force you along this way, (*namely, that of allowing*) the eye, sightless as it is, and the ear, full of sound, and the tongue, to rule; but (*you must*) judge by means of the Reason (*Logos*) the much contested proof which is expounded by me.

(§2) there is only one other description of the way remaining, (*namely*), that (*What Is*) Is. To this way there are very many sign-posts: that Being has no coming-into-being and no destruction, for it is whole of limb, without motion, and without end. And it never Was, nor Will Be, because it Is

---

*Or, reading 'ἐστιν: 'that which is possible to think is identical with that which can Be.' (Zeller and Burnet, probably rightly).

***i.e.*, 'in two minds'.

***Cf. Heraclitus, Frg. 8.

now, a Whole all together, One, continuous; for what creation of it will you look for? How, whence (*could it have*)
sprung? Nor shall I allow you to speak or think of it as
springing from Not-Being; for it is neither expressible nor
thinkable that What-Is-Not Is. Also, what necessity impelled it, if it did spring from Nothing, to be produced later
or earlier? Thus it must Be absolutely, or not at all. Nor will
the force of credibility ever admit that anything should come
into being, beside Being itself, out of Not-Being. So far as
that is concerned, Justice has never released (*Being*) in its
fetters and set it free either to come into being or to perish,
but holds it fast. The decision on these matters depends on
the following: *It is*, or *It Is Not*. It is therefore decided—as is
inevitable—(*that one must*) ignore the one way as unthinkable and inexpressible (for it is no true way) and take the
other as the way of Being and Reality. How could Being
perish? How could it come into being? If it came into being,
it Is Not; and so too if it is about-to-be at some future time.
Thus Coming-into-Being is quenched, and Destruction also
into the unseen.*

(§3) Nor is being divisible, since it is all alike. Nor is there
anything (*here or*) there which could prevent it from holding
together, nor any lesser thing, but all is full of Being. Therefore it is altogether continuous; for Being is close to Being.

(§4) But it is motionless in the limits of mighty bonds,
without beginning, without cease, since Becoming and Destruction have been driven very far away, and true conviction
has rejected them. And remaining the same in the same
place, it rests by itself and thus remains there fixed; for
powerful Necessity holds it in the bonds of a Limit, which
constrains it round about, because it is decreed by divine law
that Being shall not be without boundary. For it is not
lacking; but if it were (spatially infinite), it would be lacking
everything.**

(§5) To think is the same as the thought that It Is; for you will
not find thinking without Being, in (*regard to*) which there is
an expression. For nothing else either is or shall be except
Being, since Fate has tied it down to be a whole and motionless; therefore all things that mortals have established,
believing in their truth, are just a name; Becoming and

---

*ἄπυστος, 'beyond perception'; ἄπαυστος, 'never-ending'.
**Reading and meaning doubtful. Diels-Kranz: 'if it lacked Limit, it would fall short of
being a Whole,' but without any certainty.

Perishing, Being and Not-Being, and Change of position, and alteration of bright colour.

(§6) But since there is a (*spatial*) Limit, it is complete on every side, like the mass of well-rounded sphere, equally balanced from its centre in every direction; for it is not bound to be at all either greater or less in this direction or that; nor is there Not-Being which could check it from reaching to the same point, nor is it possible for Being to be more in this direction, less in that, than Being, because it is an inviolate whole. For, in all directions equal to itself, it reaches its limits uniformly.

PARMENIDES' STARTING POINT

It is plain from the outset of the Way of Truth, that Parmenides' commitment to the power of thought in discerning the truth at least matches Heraclitus' faith in the *Logos* as a guide to the truth. Either something exists or nothing exists, begins Parmenides. If something exists, it is what it is and can be naught else; if nothing exists, its non-existence is likewise necessitated. But for the Greeks the faculty of thought (*Nous*) involves immediate apprehension of an object, the existence of which was presupposed by its very operation. Just as seeing implies something seen, so thinking implies something thought. Hence a non-existent object of thought becomes a contradiction in terms. The only consistent alternative is that *something* exists and that this something cannot not be. The theme recurs in Frg. 6, 7 and 8—a fact that may illustrate the claim of Frg. 5 (the original position of which in the poem is uncertain), that the point of beginning the argument makes no difference because one always returns to the same point. A summary statement by Guthrie sharply delineates Parmenides' starting point:

> All previous thinkers had taken the physical world as a datum and interested themselves in questions of its origin, the kind of basic stuff that might underlie its variegated appearance, and the mechanical processes by which it was produced. Parmenides refused to accept this datum, or any datum. Like an ancient Descartes, he asked himself what, if anything, it was impossible not to believe; and to him the answer was *est*: something exists. . .[3]

PARMENIDES AND IDEALISM

Frg. 3, "For it is the same thing to think and to be," suggests that Parmenides may have been an idealist in the sense that would make

existence mind-dependent. But the Greek conception of thought as
Nous implies otherwise: objects apprehended by *Nous* are no more
dependent on *Nous* for their existence than objects of sight are ordinar-
ily held to be dependent for their existence on being seen. It is the fact
that there is no thought without an object that is offered as the reason
for asserting the sameness of thought and its object in Frg. 7, 8. What
can be meant by "sameness" here? One consistent interpretation would
be that thought and Being are the same insofar as Being can only be
manifest to thought.

Further, eyes, ears and tongue are denigrated in favor of reason, and
perceived changes in substance, position and color are denied reality in
Frg. 7, 8: Parmenides is clearly an idealist in the Platonic sense that
would make objects of thought rather than objects of perception the
prime realities. This is, of course, no accident because of the profound
effect that Parmenides had on Plato. Another way in which Parmenides
anticipates Plato is in his claim that Being is atemporal rather than
merely everlasting—a basic characteristic of Plato's Forms. Frg. 4
declares Being to be independent of limitations of spatial location as
well, because it is an object of thought rather than of perception.

In connection with the evident religious mysticism in the Parmenidean attitude towards Being, the following comments by Werner Jaeger
are very much to the point:

> We have here a new stage in the approach to the same
> problem which the older thinkers had answered by equating
> their first principle with the Divine. Like them Parmenides
> connects the knowledge of existence with the sphere of
> religion; indeed, he does so with peculiar effectiveness. On
> the other hand, he definitely fails to identify Being with God,
> even though in later times his theory of absolute Being and
> its predicates has been construed again and again as a philo-
> sophical theology. Therefore it may well be more in keeping
> with the character of his thought if we speak of his Mystery
> of Being. This will at least do justice to the form he has given
> his doctrine....no one with a live religious sense will refuse
> to count his pure ontology as a genuine mystery and revela-
> tion; nor will he fail to be deeply stirred when he sees how
> much it meant to Parmenides to experience the nature of
> Being. To put it otherwise, the religious element lies more in
> the way the man has been affected by his discovery, and in
> his firm and decided handling of the alternatives of truth and
> appearance, than in any classification of the object of his
> research as divine.

> In the long run, however, a Greek would feel that the real
> basis of this religious attitude of 'the man who knows' must

lie in the value and significance of that which is known. . . . At
this time the strongest religious motive for viewing the world
philosophically still lies in the concept of unity. But Parmenides gives it new strength by endowing this unity with the
properties of completeness, immobility, and limitation.[4]

PARMENIDES AND HERACLITUS

Though it is only possible and not certain that Parmenides was
familiar with the writings of Heraclitus,[5] the evidence that Parmenides
had Heraclitus specifically in mind in some of his criticisms of earlier
thought is cumulative.[6] While the prime concern of both philosophers is
with a monistic reality "behind" appearances rather than with appearances themselves, comparison of the Heraclitean *Logos* with the Parmenidean Being in terms of the Dionysiac and Olympian conceptions of
the soul (source of motion) suggested by Cornford points up the basic
difference between the two. The dynamic and pervasive qualities of the
Logos are akin to the Dionysiac soul (*Thymos*), while Parmenidean
Being as an immobile object of intellect set apart and incapable of any
commerce with the changing world of appearance is expressive of the
Olympian notion of soul (*Eidolon*).
    Turning our attention to those portions of Frg. 6, 7 and 8 that
probably concern Heraclitus, it cannot always be inferred even from
what appear to be Parmenides' most direct criticisms that the two
philosophers are in every respect opposed. As a matter of fact, from an
epistemological point of view, there is a large area of agreement between
them. Both placed ultimate reliance on reason or *Logos* for determination of the truth. And for Parmenides as well as for Heraclitus, reason is
intimately associated with verbal utterance (Frg. 2, 6, 7, 75). Parmenides' criticism of vision and hearing as a means of access to Being
appears to place him in sharp opposition to Heraclitus, who speaks of
things of which there is sight, hearing and knowledge as those he honors
most (Frg. 55)†. Yet Heraclitus, too, maintained that the eyes and ears
are bad witnesses if men have barbarian souls (Frg. 107).‡ Basically,
Parmenides and Heraclitus are one in their rejection of what they
regard as the judgment of "blind, amazed, uncritical hordes" (Frg. 6).
Neither favors acceptance of what he regards as mere appearance or
seeming. All of this is, of course, not intended to minimize the importance of disagreements between them—disagreements centering on
their differing notions of the compatability of the object of thought with
change. For Heraclitus, the *Logos* was the all-embracing order of

†See p. 62.
‡See p. 64.

change which gives rise, through strife and conflict between opposites, to the variegated panoply of sense experience. Heraclitus may not have intended violation of the law of contradiction, but the Dionysiac character of his *Logos* brought it into intimate association with changes proceeding from A to not A and back again. For him there was one order of change tolerant of and responsible for the very existence of A and not A—as such, opposed—and taken as evidence of stress in the very motor of existence. It is most probably this view to which Parmenides objects in Frg. 6. For Parmenides, Being as an object of thought is necessarily unchanging, held fast in its fetters by Justice (Frg. 7, 8 §2), "held in the bonds of a Limit by powerful Necessity" (Frg. 7, 8 §4), tied down by Fate "to Be whole and motionless" (Frg. 7, 8 §5). Imagining his Being after the model of the Olympian *Eidolon* soul, Parmenides sunders its connection with the realm of becoming.

POLITICAL IMPLICATIONS OF PARMENIDES' POINT OF VIEW

The aloof character of Parmenides' Being also had consequences for political thought considerably different from those of Heraclitus. If Heraclitus is representative of the Classical stage in the development of Greek culture insofar as his *Logos* pervades the *Cosmos*, including man and his *Polis*, Parmenides is a pioneer in asserting the independence of philosophy from the practical concerns of the *Polis* and hence a forerunner of the Intellectualistic or Individualistic period of Greek cultural development. Parmenides shares with Heraclitus the view that the truth is accessible to any man that uses his endowment of reason to search it out, and in this sense he operates out of the Classical tradition. Yet the immobility of Parmenides' Being, with the consequent gap between the realms of Truth and the flux of everyday life, implies that there can be no *Cosmos* understood as an order immanent in the changing universe. This has the further consequence that the *Polis* cannot, of course, be the embodiment of such a nonexistent order.

THE GRANDFATHER OF LOGIC

Parmenides differs from all his predecessors in a most remarkable way. Whereas all previous thinkers *expressed* themselves exclusively in the language of unsupported prophetic pronouncements, Parmenides, though still assuming the prophetic mantle, ultimately rests his case on the correctness of his logic: ". . .but (*you must*) judge by means of the Reason (*Logos*) the much contested proof which is expounded by me" (Frg. 7, 8 §1). Though his arguments are somewhat halting, sometimes inconclusive, and frequently repetitious, it is clear what he is attempting: the first rational argument for a philosophical position ever made. If Aristotle is the father of logic, in that he first set forth explicitly the forms of valid inference, Parmenides is the grandfather, in that he was the first to attempt the implicit use of such forms.

Let us try to outline Parmenides' arguments for the Way of Truth, with its conclusion of the individuality, homogeneity, continuity, immobility, finitude, and sphericity of Being as expressed in Frg. 7, 8. For Parmenides, "What is, is" seems to be a tautology. If it is a tautology, "What is not, is" would be a contradiction, but the unthinkability of what is not would also follow if it is argued that thought presupposes an existing object, as suggested earlier. What is must be atemporal or eternal since it could not have come from non-Being, which is not; but even if, hypothetically, it were to come from non-Being, how could its coming to be at one time rather than another be explained? (It is assumed that perishing or destruction can be similarly dismissed.) What is, is unchanging since it is atemporal and since, as expressed by Parmenides in a manner reminiscent of Anaximander, it is held fast by Justice. (Frg. 7, 8 §2) What is, is indivisible since it is homogeneous: consequently it is continuous (Frg. 7, 8 §3). It must therefore be a whole. But it is a *unique* whole as well, because not only is it impossible for anything else to come from Being, but it is also impossible for anything else to come from non-Being. (At least the uniqueness of Being would follow if it were shown that nothing other than Being can have eternality.) Parmenides' claim that Being is finite and bounded rather than infinite appears to rest on the Greek preference for self-contained form. In his words: ". . . .because it is decreed by divine law that Being shall not be without boundary. For it is not lacking; but if it were (*spatially infinite*) it would be lacking everything." (Frg. 7, 8 §4) There was a similar Greek preference for circularity and sphericity, and Parmenides describes Being as "a well rounded sphere, equally balanced from its centre in every direction." It is to be pointed out, however, that the same conclusion would then seem to be a consequence of Parmenides' view of the homogeneity and boundedness of Being, and this may be taken to be the gist of his argument in Frg. 7, 8 §6.

SOME CRITICISMS OF HIS LOGIC

The reality of change as well as our ability to talk about it presupposes both the reality of the two characteristics serving as opposite terms of the process of change and the meaningfulness of language used to refer to them. Parmenides' argument against the possibility of change rests on the assumption that one or both of the opposites does not exist and hence cannot be intelligibly spoken of either. But as is suggested by Plato's argument against Parmenides in *The Sophist*,[7] there are at least two senses of "is": (1) "is" meaning "exists", as in "Xerxes exists" and (2) the "is" of predication, as in "Xerxes is a man." While Parmenides' logic applies to the existential "is", the "is" of predication can be used to speak meaningfully of opposites if one should wish to do so. Once this is admitted, it is clear that non-men as well as men exist, if we are willing to grant the testimony of our senses. Plato makes a similar point, and by using the same distinction between the "is" of identity and the "is" of predication, also solves a problem not explicitly dealt with by Parmenides but nonetheless implied by his thought, viz., how is it possible to deny the existence of anything if the thought of anything presupposes its existence? Plato's answer is that a statement that green men do not exist is to be interpreted as: "There do not *exist* (existential "is") any individuals such that they *are* ("is" of predication) green men.[8] Or put in another way: "X is not green" means that "X is other than green" and not that "X does not exist."

If Parmenides had been aware of the distinction between the existential "is" and the "is" of predication he might have granted it, but might have replied with the following alternative argument against the existence of the required opposites:

> *What is*, is *not what is not.*
> *Purple things* are *not chartreuse* (things which are not).
> Therefore *what is*, is not anything purple.

The relation between "what is" and "not what is not" in the first premise of the argument is one of identity. That is, "what is" and "what is not" are contradictories. On the other hand, the purple things and non-chartreuse things referred to in the second premise are not identical, since the relation between purple and chartreuse is not that of contradictories. This is to say only that there are other non-chartreuse things besides purple ones: lavender, turquoise and sepia things, for example. (Logicians refer to the relation between purple and chartreuse as that of contraries. And it is noteworthy that Aristotle declares that change occurs between contraries.) It is clear that the stated argument will not hold up if this distinction between the "is" of predication and the "is" of identity (a third sense of "is" in addition to the existential "is") is recognized.

SCIENTIFIC ASPECTS

Despite the fact that the flaws in his logic show Parmenides' arguments against the existence of change to be non sequiturs, he made important contributions to scientific thought. The conservation laws of modern physics testify to the soundness of his reasoning concerning at least the existential "is." Parmenides of course did not discover the law of conservation of mass-energy, for example, but his thinking dictates that there be some conservation laws or other, and empirical investigation has revealed mass-energy to be a conserved quantity.

Mass-energy like Parmenides' Being can be neither created nor destroyed. But mass-energy is like Parmenides' Being in a second important respect as well: it is not part of the changing world of sense experience, belonging rather to a realm of theoretical constructs separated from the perceptual world by a deep chasm. This is the chasm that divides logically defined from perceptually defined entities. It was taken as fundamental as early as Plato, but only successfully bridged in fairly recent times by recognition of the need for such concepts as "coordinating definitions," "rules of correspondence," and "epistemic correlations," all of which serve to relate theoretical notions to things perceived.[9] There is at least this much justification of the gap proclaimed by Parmenides' Way of Truth and Way of Seeming. In the following passages, Giorgio de Santillana identifies Parmenides' realm of Truth with that of mathematics and suggests that it is the theoretical construct of pure geometrical space that Parmenides "had in mind but could not yet define" when he used the term "Being." He also interprets Parmenides' argument for this concept as the first conscious step-by-step application of the principle of indifference or sufficient reason.[10]†

> Geometry as the Greeks meant it put three requirements on its space: first, it must have continuity (in a sense somewhat stronger than the mere absence of gaps between points); second, it must be the same, homogeneous throughout, so that we can move figures freely from place to place without altering their geometrical properties; and, finally, it must be isotropic, or the same in all directions. . . .

> Now it is also true that anything that satisfies these three conditions must be isomorphic with and intrinsically indistinguishable from Euclidean space. That is the fundamental reason why, when we find Parmenides stating repeatedly and emphatically that his Being satisfies his three conditions—as the reader can check by going over the text—we must conclude that whatever else his Being may have meant to him in addition, it was certainly the space of the mathematician (and Physicist) that he had in mind. . . .

---

†See p. 43 of the present volume for a definition of the principle of sufficient reason.

It is curious to note that the Pythagorean movement, which had aimed from the beginning at discovering the principle of form in nature, should have wrecked itself on a rock so much like the one the Ionians had struck. To have order, harmony, and form in the world presupposed a formal substratum which should have no form itself, but be the bearer of all form, exactly as the hydrodynamic universe of the Ionians had been a quest for a material substratum which should be sufficiently neutral in its own intrinsic properties to be modifiable into all the kinds of matter in the world.

It was Parmenides, standing at the confluence of the two traditions, who realized that the two problems were in fact one. The true conception of geometrical space, once formed, is equally well adapted to serve as a substratum for physical form, in view of its rigidity and impassibility, and for matter, if one adopts a view of matter which transforms it into an accidental and contingent property of the space it "occupies." As we shall see, that was the course taken by Parmenides, and later by Newton, and it is not surprising that he should have ascribed such a master stroke to the inspiration of the deity.[11]

THE WAY OF SEEMING

What to make of Parmenides' Way of Seeming and its relation to the Way of Truth has been a source of much perplexity among scholars. Without doubt Parmenides valued the Way of Truth over the Way of Seeming: the question is why he felt it necessary that someone acquainted with the Way of Truth should also have familiarity with the Way of Seeming (Prologue). The only reason that Parmenides himself gives us is "in order that no intellect of mortal men may outstrip you." (Frg. 7, 8 §8) Does this mean that someone acquainted with the Way of Seeming as well as the Way of Truth has a firmer grasp of reality? Or does it only mean that he demonstrates greater intellectual acumen? The latter would seem to follow if one takes at face value the conclusion of the Way of Truth that the realm of changing perception is to be relegated to non-Being. But it is difficult to accept the view that a man of Parmenides' stature would have gone to the trouble of proposing a theory of appearance of his own if demonstration of greater intellectual acumen were his only motivation. This leaves only the first alternative. Martin Heidegger sets forth an interesting though somewhat speculative version of it. He claims that it is Parmenides' view that a knowledge of seeing or appearance as such is essential to complete knowledge because Being must be distinguished from mere appearance through which it must always reveal itself and with which it is (on Heidegger's view) always intimately associated.[12] On this view, Parmenides and Heraclitus would have more in common than is usually acknowledged. A more prosaic version is that, though the Way of Truth may lead to the absolute truth, we must of necessity still deal with the appearances of the sense world as best we can, and that the Way of Seeing constitutes an attempt to do so. Such appears to have been the view of Aristotle.

> **T45**   Aristotle *Meta.* 986b28–987a2
>
> ....Parmenides seems in places to speak with more insight. For, claiming that, besides the existence, nothing non-existent exists, he thinks that of necessity one thing exists, viz. the existent and nothing else (on this we have spoken more clearly in our work on nature), (*Phys.* 1.3–ed) but being forced to follow the observed facts, and supposing the existence of that which is one in definition, but more than one according to our sensations, he now posits two causes and two principles, calling them hot and cold, i.e. fire and earth; and of these he ranges the hot with the existent, and the other with the non-existent.

And it is one with which a number of contemporary scholars concur, Guthrie[13], Cornford[14], and de Santillana[15] among them. Mathematical knowledge is certain; physical knowledge is not; the former, according to de Santillana, is the Parmenidean sphere of Being, the latter the realm of seeing. De Santillana then goes on to quote Einstein: "If it is certain, it is not physics; if it is physics, it is not certain."[16] It should be noted that this view, more than anything else, is based upon Plato's solution to the same problem.

The Way of Seeing commences with the introduction of the two opposite explanatory principles of Light and Night as well as several subsidiary pairs of opposites. The association of Light with fire is reminiscent of Heraclitus, but in general the approach is early Pythagorean.

> (Frg.7,8§7) At this point I cease my reliable theory (*Logos*) and thought, concerning Truth; from here onwards you must learn the opinions of mortals, listening to the deceptive order of my words.

> (§8) They have established (*the custom of*) naming two forms, one of which ought not to be (*mentioned*): that is where they have gone astray. They have distinguished them

as opposite in form, and have marked them off from another by giving them different signs: on one side the flaming fire in the heavens, mild, very light (*in weight*), the same as itself in every direction, and not the same as the other. This (*other*) also is by itself and opposite: dark Night, a dense and heavy body. This world-order I describe to you throughout as it appears with all its phenomena, in order that no intellect of mortal men may outstrip you.*

(Frg.9) But since all things are named Light and Night, and names have been given to each class of things according to the power of one or the other (*Light or Night*), everything is full equally of Light and invisible Night, as both are equal, because to neither of them belongs any share (of the other).**

The intent of the phrase referring to the two named forms, "one of which ought not to be (*mentioned*)" in Frg. 7, 8§8 has been a subject of debate. As Guthrie points out, it has been interpreted to mean that two forms should be mentioned (i.e., not only one); that one form should be mentioned, the other not; and that none should be mentioned (i.e., not *even* one).[17] Though the question cannot be settled here, a version of the second interpretation originally due to Aristotle and sanctioned by Cornford[18] has considerable plausibility. This is to assign Light and its associated characters to the sphere of Being, and Night with its kindred opposites to the sphere of non-Being.

T46   Aristotle *De Gen. et Cor.* 318b7-9, 13-15
....he [i.e., Parmenides] says that the things into which change takes place are two, and he asserts that these two, viz., *what is* and *what is not*, are Fire and Earth....Hence whatever the contrasted 'poles' of the changes may be— whether Fire and Earth, or some other couple—the one of them will be a 'being' and the other 'a not-being'. [See T45]

Following this interpretation, only those members of each pair associated with Light could be named and thought of. The conflict of the plurality of these forms with the unity of Parmenidean Being might be dealt with by claiming that the opposites are admittedly denizens of the realm of seeming and not to be found in the Way of Truth. Yet there is a conflict, which is what probably led H. Frankel to choose the third

---

*Or, reading γνώμη (Stein): "in order that no mortal may outstrip you in intelligence."
**Kranz takes 'ἐπεὶ with the previous line, and translates: "For nothing is possible which does not come under either of the two" (i.e., everything belongs to one or other of the two categories Light and Night).

alternative, viz., that no forms should be mentioned—only the one Being.[19]

The following two fragments setting forth part of Parmenides' plan for the Way of Seeming suggested the degree of detail that this part of the poem must have involved. The role of Necessity in holding "the limits of the stars" in Frg. 10 parallels its role in setting a limit to Being in Frg. 7, 8§4.

> (Frg.10) You shall know the nature of the heavens, and all the signs in the heavens, and the destructive works of the pure bright torch of the sun, and whence they came into being. And you shall learn of the wandering works of the round-faced moon, and its nature; and you shall know also the surrounding heaven, whence it sprang and how Necessity brought and constrained it to hold the limits of the stars.
>
> (Frg.11) (*I will describe*) how earth and sun and moon, and the aether common to all, and the Milky Way in the heavens, and outermost Olympus, and the hot power of the stars, hastened to come into being.

Presumably included as part of the plan we find such fragments as:

> (Frg.14) (*The moon*): shining by night with a light not her own, wandering round the earth.
>
> (Frg.15) (*The moon*): Always gazing towards the rays of the sun.
>
> (Frg.15a) (*Earth*): Rooted in water.
>
> (Frg. 17) On the right, boys, on the left, girls...(*in the womb*).
>
> (Frg.18) When a woman and a man mix the seeds of Love together, the power (*of the seeds*) which shapes (*the embryo*) in the veins out of different blood can mould well-constituted bodies only if it preserves proportion. For if the powers war (*with each other*) when the seed is mixed, and do not make a unity in the body formed by the mixture, they will terribly harass the growing (*embryo*) through the twofold seed of the (*two*) sexes.

Frg. 15a is reminiscent of Thales, though Guthrie feels it may have referred to the rivers of the underworld mentioned in the Odyssey (10.513f)[20]. Frg. 17 and 18 extend Parmenides' concern with the sense world to physiology and perhaps show the influence of Alcmaeon.

There is even an account of sensation and knowledge given from the viewpoint of the Way of Seeming. In introducing Frg. 16 for which he is the source, Theophrastus says:

T47   Theophrastus *De Sensu* 1ff. [K&R282–3]

The majority of general views about sensation are two: some make it of like by like, others of opposite by opposite. Parmenides, Empedocles and Plato say it is of like by like, the followers of Anaxagoras and of Heraclitus of opposite by opposite....Parmenides gave no clear definition at all, but said only that there were two elements and that knowledge depends on the excess of one or the other. Thought varies according to whether the hot or the cold prevails, but that which is due to the hot is better and purer; not but what even that needs a certain balance;

Then comes:

(Frg.16) For according to the mixture of much-wandering limbs which each man has, so is the mind which is associated with mankind: for it is the same thing which thinks, namely the constitution of the limbs in men, all and individually; for it is excess which makes Thought.

The best information we have concerning Parmenides', overall cosmological views rests on an interpretation of Aetius' and Parmenides' own Frgs. 12 and 13:

T48   Aetius 2. 7. 1. [K&R284]

Parmenides said that there were rings wound one around the other, one formed of the rare, the other of the dense; and that there were others between these compounded of light and darkness. That which surrounds them all like a wall is, he says, by nature solid; beneath it is a fiery ring and likewise what lies in the middle of them all is solid; and around it is again a fiery ring. The middlemost of the mixed rings is the primary cause of movement and of coming into being for them all, and he calls it the goddess that steers all, the holder of the keys, Justice and Necessity. The air, he says, is separated off from the earth, vaporized owing to earth's stronger compression; the sun is an exhalation of fire, and so is the circle of the Milky Way. The moon is compounded of both air and fire. Aether is outermost, surrounding all; next comes the fiery thing that we call the sky; and last comes the region of the earth.

(Frg. 12) For the narrower rings were filled with unmixed Fire, and those next to them with Night, but between (*these*) rushes the portion of Flame. And in the centre of these is the goddess who guides everything; for throughout she rules over cruel Birth and Mating, sending the female to mate with the male, and conversely again the male with the female.

(Frg. 13) First of all the gods she devised Love.

The rings referred to bring Anaximander's similar ideas to mind, but even more interesting is reference to the goddess, associated with Justice or Necessity by Aetius, and the goddess's connection with the god Love. Regarding Parmenides' cosmology as modeled on the Orphic idea of a fall of the soul from light to darkness, Cornford places the goddess at the center of the earth and is unperturbed by the apparent conflict between the association of earth with dark non-Being on the one hand, and the goddess's guiding and creative function on the other (the latter derived from her responsibility for the god Love). His resolution of the apparent difficulty is to argue that even earth, though at the low end of the scale of being, has some fire, heat and light, that is, some dynamic power remaining within it. He even suggests that Parmenides, by placing the source of love in the earth, is hinting at the movement of life interpreted as the desire for perfection.[21] Doubtful Frg. 20 appears to bear out Cornford's positioning of the goddess:

> *Doubtful*
> *(Frg.20)* but below it (*Earth?*) is a path, dreadful, hollow, muddy; this is the best path to lead one to the lovely grove of much-revered Aphrodite.

We conclude our account of the Way of Seeming with:

> (Frg.19) Thus, therefore, according to opinion, were these things created, and are now, and shall hereafter from henceforth grow and then come to an end. And for these things men have established a name as a distinguishing mark for each.

NOTES

1. Plato, *Plato: The Collected Dialogues.*
2. Guthrie, vol. 2, pp. 3-4.
3. *Ibid.*, p. 20.
4. Jaeger, *Theology of the Early Greek Philosophers*, pp. 107-8.
5. *Ibid.*, p. 23.
6. *Ibid.*, p. 32.
7. *Plato: The Collected Dialogues; Sophist* 258C-295D.
8. *Ibid.*, 255E-258C.
9. deSantillana, p. 98.
10. *Ibid.*, p. 95.
11. *Ibid.*, p. 95-97.
12. Martin Heidegger, *An Introduction to Metaphysics*, trans. Ralph Manheim (New York: Doubleday Anchor Books, 1961), p. 95.

13. Guthrie, vol. 2, pp. 56-7.
14. F. M. Cornford, *Plato and Parmenides* (Indianapolis: Bobbs-Merrill Co., Inc., Library of Liberal Arts, n.d.) pp. 50-1.
15. deSantillana, p. 102.
16. *Ibid.*
17. Guthrie, vol. 2, p. 54.
18. Cornford, *From Religion to Philosophy*, pp. 221-2.
19. Guthrie, vol. 2, p. 54.
20. *Ibid.*, pp. 65-6.
21. Cornford, *From Religion to Philosophy*, pp. 222-3.

CHAPTER 6

The Eleatics:
Melissus and Zeno

MELISSUS

Melissus is known to have led the Samians to victory over the Athenians in a naval battle in 440 B.C. The implication is that he was in his prime at that time. The following two testimonia, noting among other things that he was politically active, constitute our major sources of information concerning his life:

T49 Diogenes Laertius 9. 4. 24. [Loeb]
Melissus, the son of Ithagenes, was a native of Samos. He was a pupil of Parmenides....He took part also in politics and won the approval of his countrymen, and for this reason he was elected admiral and won more admiration than ever through his own merit....According to Apollodorus, he flourished in the 84th Olympiad (444–440 B.C.).

T50 Plutarch *Pericles* 26 [K&R298]
For when Pericles had set sail, Melissus, son of Ithagenes, a philosopher who was then in command of Samos, was so contemptuous of the small number of the Athenian ships or of their commanders' inexperience that he persuaded the Samians to attack. A battle took place which the Samians won. They took so many prisoners and destroyed so many ships that they had command of the sea, and they devoted to the prosecution of the war certain supplies which they did

not till then possess. Pericles himself, according to Aristotle,
had also been defeated by Melissus in an earlier naval battle.

The title of Melissus' book is said by Simplicius to have been "About
Nature or Reality,"[1] Simplicius being the source for all of the fragments
of Melissus we possess. Though Melissus may be presumed to have been
a younger man than Zeno and to have written his book later than Zeno
wrote his treatise, the content of Melissus' thought is so continuous with
that of Parmenides that it is more appropriate to consider it immediately after that of Parmenides. Then in the next section we can go on
to consider Zeno's criticisms of Parmenides' opponents.

MELISSUS AND PARMENIDES

If one is familiar with the writing of Parmenides, reading Melissus
may come as something of an anticlimax. In any event, acquaintance
with Parmenides makes the encounter with Melissus' writings easier to
handle because of the not inconsiderable indebtedness of Melissus to
Parmenides. As a matter of fact, this is an important reason for reading
Melissus—so that Parmenides' ideas may be better understood.
Because of the great degree of similarity between the two, it will not be
necessary to supply any detailed exposition of Melissus' ideas. Rather,
all of his fragments will be presented immediately, and a discussion of
relevant points of difference from Parmenides as well as suggestive
points of originality will follow.

(Frg.1) That which was, was always and always will be. For
if it had come into being, it necessarily follows that before it
came into being, Nothing existed. If however Nothing
existed, in no way could anything come into being out of
nothing.

(Frg.2) Since therefore it did not come into being, it Is and
always was and always will be, and has no beginning or end,
but it is eternal. For if it had come into being, it would have a
beginning (for it would have come into being at some time,
and so begun), and an end (for since it had come into being,
it would have ended). But since it has neither begun nor
ended, it always was and always will be and has no beginning
nor end. For it is impossible for anything to Be, unless it Is
completely.

(Frg.3) But as it Is always, so also its size must always be
infinite.

(Frg.4) Nothing that has a beginning and an end is either
everlasting or infinite.

(Frg.5) If it were not One, it will form a boundary in relation
to something else.

(Frg.6) If it were infinite, it would be One; for if it were two, (*these*) could not be (*spatially*) infinite, but each would have boundaries in relation to each other.

(Frg. 7, §1) Thus therefore it is everlasting and unlimited and one and like throughout (*homogeneous*).

(§2) And neither could it perish or become larger or change its (*inner*) arrangement, nor does it feel pain or grief. For if it suffered any of these things, it would no longer be One. For if Being alters, it follows that it is not the same, but that that which previously Was is destroyed, and that Non-Being has come into being. Hence if it were to become different by a single hair in ten thousand years, so it must be utterly destroyed in the whole of time.

(§3) But it is not possible for it to be rearranged either, for the previous arrangement is not destroyed, nor does a non-existent arrangement come into being. And since it is neither increased by any addition, nor destroyed, nor changed, how could it have undergone a rearrangement of what exists? For if it were different in any respect, then there would at once be a rearrangement.

(§4) Nor does it feel pain; for it could not Be completely if it were in pain; for a thing which is in pain could not always Be. Nor has it equal power with what is healthy. Nor would it be the same if it were in pain; for it would feel pain through the subtraction or addition of something, and could no longer be the same.

(§5) Nor could that which is healthy feel pain, for the Healthy—That which Is—would perish, and That which Is Not would come into being.

(§6) And with regard to grief, the same reasoning applies as to pain.

(§7) Nor is there any Emptiness; for the Empty is Nothing; and so that which is Nothing cannot Be. Nor does it move; for it cannot withdraw in any direction, but (*all*) is full. For if there were any Empty, it would have withdrawn into the Empty; but as the Empty does not exist, there is nowhere for it (*Being*) to withdraw.

(§8) And there can be no Dense and Rare. For the Rare cannot possibly be as full as the Dense, but the Rare must at once become more empty than the Dense.

(§9) The following distinction must be made between the Full and the Not-Full: if a thing has room for or admits something, it is not full; if it neither has room for nor admits anything, it is full.

(§10) It (*Being*) must necessarily be full, therefore, if [*sic*] there is no Empty. If therefore it is full, it does not move.

(Frg.8§1) This argument is the greatest proof that it (*Being*) is One only; but there are also the following proofs:

(§2) If Things were Many, they would have to be of the same kind as I say the One is. For if there is earth and water and air and fire and iron and gold, and that which is living and that which is dead, and black and white and all the rest of the things which men say are real: if these things exist, and we see and hear correctly, each thing must be of such a kind as it seemed to us to be in the first place, and it cannot change or become different, but each thing must always be what it is. But now, we say we see and hear and understand correctly,

(§3) and it seems to us that the hot becomes cold and the cold hot, and the hard soft and the soft hard, and that the living thing dies and comes into being from what is not living, and that all things change, and that what was and what now is are not at all the same, but iron which is hard is worn away by contact with the finger, and gold and stone and whatever seems to be entirely strong (*is worn away*); and that from water, earth and stone come into being. So that it comes about that we neither see nor know existing things.

(§4) So these statements are not consistent with one another. For although we say that there are many things, everlasting (?), having forms and strength, it seems to us that they all alter and change from what is seen on each occasion.

(§5) It is clear therefore that we have not been seeing correctly, and that those things do not correctly seem to us to be Many; for they would not change if they were real, but each would Be as it seemed to be. For nothing is stronger than that which is real.

(§6) And if it changed, Being would have been destroyed, and Not-Being would have come into being. Thus, therefore, if Things are Many, they must be such as the One is.

(Frg.9) If therefore Being Is, it must be One; and if it is One, it is bound not to have body. But if it had Bulk, it would have parts, and would no longer Be.

(Frg.10) If Being is divided, it moves; and if it moved, it could not Be.

POINTS OF DIFFERENCE WITH PARMENIDES

A first difference of Melissus' views from those of Parmenides lies in the contention, as in Frg. 2 above, for example, that "it Is and always was and always will be." Contrast this with Parmenides' Frg. 7,8 §2†where he claims that "it never Was, nor Will Be." For Melissus, "what is" is everlasting; for Parmenides it is atemporal.

A second way in which the two differ has to do with Parmenides' assumption that "what is" is limited and hence finite. Melissus argues instead that "what is" is infinite or unlimited on questionable grounds in Frg. 3 and continues on this assumption in Frg. 7(1). However, Aristotle attributes a better argument to someone who, according to Guthrie[2], could only have been Melissus when he says:

> **T51**   Aristotle *De Gen. et Corr.* 325a4–16
> For some of the older philosophers thought that "what is" must of necessity be "one" and immovable.... Some of them add that it is "infinite" since the limit (if it had one) would be a limit against the void.

FURTHER DEVELOPMENT OF MELISSUS' IDEAS IN RELATION TO THOSE OF OTHER THINKERS

Guthrie also points out that Parmenides nowhere explicitly uses the Greek word for emptiness or void, i.e., *kenon*.[3] In contrast, Melissus uses it several times, expressly denying its existence in Frg. 7(7). Whether Melissus was first to make use of the idea or whether he was led to deny the existence of a void in conscious criticism of the atomists, Democritus and Leucippus, the denial clearly places Melissus in opposition to them. In the same Frg. 7(7), as well as in Frg. 7 (10), Melissus supplies a proof for the immobility of Being (another point of opposition to the Atomists) resting on his denial of the existence of a void. Parmenides had never proven the immobility of Being; he had only assumed it. Still another connection between Melissus and the Atomists is to be found in Frg. 8(2) where Melissus maintains that, "If Things were Many, they would have to be of the same kind as I say the One is." The atoms of Democritus and Leucippus were many with a substantial number of the attributes of the One of the Eleatics.

There is also evidence that Melissus did battle with Empedocles' pluralistic alternative to Parmenides. His specific mention of earth,

---

†See p. 102.

water, air, and fire in the attack on pluralism in Frg. 8(2) suggests that he may have had Empedocles in mind, since Empedocles is generally believed to be the first to have enumerated them. Similarly with the denial of the possibility of rearrangement or mixture in Frg. 7(3): Empedocles speaks of mixture as the source of the many things of sense experience. Melissus' opposition to Anaximenes' notion of the many coming from the One through condensation and rarefaction is apparent from his denial of the possibility of the Dense and Rare in Frg. 7(8).

SOME POINTS OF SPECIAL INTEREST

One of the more interesting questions for debate about Melissus' ontology concerns whether he held "what is" to be material or immaterial. On the one hand, Melissus claims that Being is infinite in size and that there is no void, but in Frg. 9 he denies that it can have Body because its consequent divisability would be inconsistent with its unity. The commentators differ on this point. Aristotle interprets Melissus, in contrast with Parmenides, as holding that Being is material:

> **T52** Aristotle *Meta.* 986b 18–20
> Parmenides seems to fasten on that which is one in definition, Melissus on that which is one in matter, ...

Simplicius, on the other hand, basing his claim on Frg. 9, maintains that Melissus' One is incorporeal.

> **T53** Simplicius *Phys.* 109. 34 [K&R302]
> For he made it clear that he means that what exists is incorporeal when he wrote: "If Being is, it must be one; and being one, it must have no body. If it were to have bulk, it would have parts and be no longer one!"

The supposition that Melissus as well as Parmenides was confusedly wrestling with the emerging notion of mathematical space may perhaps resolve the difficulty.† This is so simply because the distinction between the immateriality of mathematical space and the materiality of bodies whose positions and movements it is designed to explain was not yet clear to Melissus any more than to Parmenides.

Perhaps the strangest sounding claim of Melissus, in Frgs. 7(4), 7(5), and 7(6) is that "what is" cannot feel pain or grief. A little reflection on the nature of Ionian monism should make the strangeness disappear, however. Melissus had not yet moved away from the Ionian notion that nature is alive. But then, neither had any other Greek thinker up to his time (with the possible though not certain exception of the Atomists).

---

†de Santillana makes this claim for Parmenides; See pp. 110-1 of present volume.

ZENO

Our sources of information about Zeno's life are largely the same as those for Parmenides. From Testimonia T41–T43 in the chapter on Parmenides† we can conclude that Zeno flourished *circa* 450 B.C., and that, like Parmenides, he came from Elea, was originally a Pythagorean, and was involved in politics.

RELATION TO PARMENIDES' OPPONENTS

While Melissus supported Parmenides' position with positive arguments of his own, Zeno took upon himself the critical task of dealing with Parmenides' opponents. de Santillana's hypothesis that Parmenidean Being had the character of Euclidean space is supported by the fact that Zeno, his foremost disciple, was concerned largely with problems in this area[4].

The relation between the thought of Zeno and that of Parmenides is perhaps best set forth in Plato's dialogue *Parmenides* where, referring to what was probably Zeno's only work, Plato makes Zeno say:

> **T54** Plato *Parmenides* 128c[5]
>
> ....the book is in fact a sort of defense of Parmenides' argument against those who try to make fun of it by showing that his supposition, that there is a one, leads to many absurdities and contradictions. This book, then, is a retort against those who assert a plurality. It pays them back in the same coin with something to spare, and aims at showing that, on a thorough examination, their own supposition that there is a plurality leads to even more absurd consequences than the hypothesis of the one. It was written in that controversial spirit in my young days, ...

Those who believe in plurality could include any of the Greek pluralists, and indeed any man of common sense. Nevertheless, a substantial number of scholars[6] maintain that Zeno had particularly in mind the Pythagoreans of his time, i.e., the Fifth Century number-atomists referred to by Cornford‡. They theorized that the world was made up of numbers, which they identified with collections of geometrical points as discussed in Chapter 4§. Not all of Zeno's arguments deal directly with plurality, though just about all of them presuppose it.

All of the existing fragments of Zeno, except Frg. 4 , contain arguments dealing directly with plurality. Our knowledge of his other argu-

---

†See pp. 99.
‡See pp. 82.
§See pp. 81ff.

ments, including the paradoxes of motion for which he is most famous, an argument concerning place, and one having to do with the millet seed, comes primarily through the interpretations of Aristotle and Simplicius. It will be evident from examining them that Zeno's method of argument is what we call a *reductio ad absurdum* (or what the Greeks shortly after Zeno came to call the *epicheirêma*). Essentially, this method consists in showing that a given assumption leads to conclusions that contradict one another. As a consequence, the assumption must be rejected. As used by Zeno, the *reductio ad absurdum* arguments are also *ad hominem*: that is, they take as assumptions what those believing in plurality—those for whom the arguments are intended— would be willing to grant. Aristotle distinguished what he called dialectical reasoning from demonstrative reasoning and regarded Zeno as the "inventor" or "pioneer" of dialectical reasoning.[7] While demonstrative reasoning begins with premises known to be true, dialectical reasoning starts from premises that are only commonly accepted.[8] Aside from mere intellectual exercise, the objective of reasoning on the basis of premises not known to be true is either to deal with an opponent or to throw further light on the truth.[9] Presumably Zeno had both of these objectives in mind. Frg. 3 contains a complete *reductio ad absurdum* and is presented first. Frgs. 1 and 2 each constitute only one half of each of the complete arguments from which they must have been excerpted; Frg. 4 only states the intent of such an argument.

PARADOXES OF PLURALITY

(Frg.3) (Epicheirêma showing that if Things are Many, they must be (a) finite, (b) infinite in number.

If Things are Many, they must be as many as they are and neither more nor less than this. But if they are as many as they are, they must be finite (in number).

If Things are Many, they are infinite in number. For there are always other things between those that are, and again others between those. And thus things are infinite (in number).

(Frg.2) (First half of the Epicheirêma showing that if Things are Many they must be (a) infinitely small, (b) infinitely great).

If it (a unit without magnitude) be added to another existing thing, it would not make the latter at all larger. For if a thing without magnitude is added (to another) the latter cannot gain anything in magnitude. And thus (it follows) at once that the thing added is nothing. And if when a unit is subtracted the other will not become at all less, and will not, on the other hand, increase when (this unit) is added, it is clear that the unit added or subtracted was nothing.

(Frg.1) (Second half of the Epicheirêma showing that if Things are Many, they must be (a) infinitely small, (b) infinitely great).

If Being had no size, it could not Be either.

If anything Is, it follows that each (part) must have a certain size and bulk, and distance one from the other. And the same reasoning applies also to the part preceding it; for that too will have size and there will be another part preceding it. The same reasoning, in fact, applies always: no part of the Whole will be such as to be outermost, nor will any part be unrelated to another part. Therefore, if Things are Many, they must be both small and great: so small as to have no size, so large as to be infinite.

SUGGESTION OF A PARADOX OF MOTION

(Frg.4) (From an Epicheirêma showing the impossibility of motion).

That which moves, moves neither in the place in which it is, nor in that in which it is not.

PARADOXES OF MOTION

The last mentioned fragment sounds very much as if it may have been part of what Aristotle refers to as the paradox of the flying arrow. Aristotle refers to the arrow paradox and then gives an account of all of Zeno's paradoxes of motion in the following passage:

T55   Aristotle *Phy.* 239b5-20, 30-240a4

Zeno's reasoning, however, is fallacious, when he says that if everything when it occupies an equal space is at rest, and if that which is in locomotion is always occupying such a space at any moment, the flying arrow is therefore motionless. This is false, for time is not composed of indivisible moments any more than any other magnitude is composed of indivisibles.

Zeno's arguments about motion, which cause so much disquietude to those who try to solve the problems that they present, are four in number. The first asserts the non-existence of motion on the ground that that which is in locomotion must arrive at the half-way stage before it arrives at the goal. . . .

The second is the so-called "Achilles", and it amounts to this, that in a race the quickest runner can never overtake the slowest, since the pursuer must first reach the point whence the pursued started, so that the slower must always hold a lead. This argument is the same in principle as that which depends on bisection, though it differs from it in that the spaces with which we successively have to deal are not divided into halves....

The third is to the effect that the flying arrow is at rest, which result follows from the assumption that time is composed of moments: if this assumption is not granted, the conclusion will not follow.

The fourth argument is that concerning the two rows of bodies, each row being composed of an equal number of bodies of equal size, passing each other on a race course as they proceed with equal velocity in opposite directions, the one row originally occupying the space between the goal and the middle point of the course and the other that between the middle point and the starting-post. This, he thinks, involves the conclusion that half a given time is equal to double that time. The fallacy of the reasoning lies in the assumption that a body occupies an equal time in passing with equal velocity a body that is in motion and a body of equal size that is at rest; which is false.

Leaving Aristotle's criticism aside for a moment, let us first explicate the paradoxes themselves a bit further. The first paradox, which has come to be known as the "Dichotomy," raises the question of how motion through an interval will be possible if, in order to traverse that interval, one must first traverse half of it, then one-half of the remaining half, and half of that—and so on. How, in other words, will motion be possible on the basis of the hypothesis that spatial intervals are infinitely divisible? Such an hypothesis would instead seem to require an impossibility—that is, traversal of an infinite number of subintervals. The second paradox or "Achilles" as explained by Aristotle is closely related to the first, although it does not presuppose repeated bisection and concerns the relative motion of two bodies rather than the motion of just one.

The first of the second pair of arguments rests on the assumption that time is made up of a collection of indivisible moments. The question raised is how, if a flying arrow is admitted to be at a particular location at any one of these moments (and consequently it would seem also at rest at any of these moments), it can properly be said to move. Since the fourth argument or what has come to be known as the "Stadium" involves relative motion, it has the same relation to "Arrow" as

"Achilles" has to "Dichotomy" in this respect. While Aristotle speaks of two rows of bodies in our quotation from him, in a subsequent discussion of the argument, which has not been quoted, he makes it clear that there is really a third stationary set in the center of the race course relative to which the other two sets of bodies are moving. Relative then to each other, the two sets of moving bodies will pass one another in half the time that it takes them to pass the stationary set of bodies. Aristotle's criticism—that Zeno assumes falsely that a body moving at a given velocity relative to a stationary body will pass the stationary body in the same time as it will pass another moving body—is a legitimate criticism of the argument as stated. Yet the obvious nature of this criticism as well as the attempt to relate the "Stadium" meaningfully to Zeno's other three paradoxes of motion have led some to question Aristotle's understanding of the argument. For example, Kirk & Raven:

> Indeed the only way in which any sense can be made of the argument is to suppose—and by so supposing it becomes perhaps the most telling of the whole set—that each of Zeno's ὄγκοι (a deliberately vague word meaning 'solid bodies' or 'masses') represents one such indivisible minimum of space, and that those in the rows of B and Γ are alike moving at such a speed as to pass one A in one indivisible minimum of time. Zeno is of course fully justified in asking his opponents—or those of them at least who believed in indivisible minima—to visualize such a situation....But once so much is granted, then the rest of the argument is valid. For while each B has passed two A's—which, by the data, means in two indivisible minima of time—each Γ has passed four B's—which again, by the data must have taken four indivisible minima. It is true, of course, that unless the argument is concerned with indivisble minima it is, as Aristotle says, totally invalid. But as soon as it is seen to be concerned with indivisible minima, both of space and time, then it does most ingeniously demonstrate that these so-called indivisible minima, are divisible after all. And upon the unfortunate Pythagoreans, who had hitherto confused the indivisible units of arithmetic with the points in infinitely divisible geometrical magnitudes, this last argument must finally have impressed the urgent need for revision of their suppositions.[10]

Kirk & Raven further relate the last two paradoxes of motion to the first two by claiming that, whereas not only the "Stadium" but also the "Arrow" assume both space and time to be made of indivisible minima, the first two paradoxes assume rather the infinite divisibility of both space and time. They also point out that if the former assumption is applicable to spatially extended bodies and the latter to what we differentiate as the points of geometrical space, the Pythagoreans who identified the two would be vulnerable to both sets of arguments.[11] Their interpretation is interesting and persuasive, yet the available evidence does not permit a definite decision as to whether they or Aristotle are correct.

On the basis of what Aristotle says, while "Dichotomy" and "Achilles" appear to have assumed only the infinite divisibility of space (and not of time) the "Arrow" and "Stadium" seem to have rested on the hypothesis that only time (and not space) is composed of indivisible minima. As a matter of fact, Aristotle's refutation of both "Dichotomy" and "Achilles" rests on his claim that time as well as space is infinitely divisible—presumably something which Zeno neglected to consider:

T56 Aristotle *Phys.* 233a22-33

Hence Zeno's argument makes a false assumption in asserting that it is impossible for a thing to pass over or severally to come in contact with infinite things in a finite time. For there are two senses in which length and time and generally anything continuous are called 'infinite': they are called so either in respect of divisibility or in respect of their extremities. So while a thing in a finite time cannot come in contact with things quantitatively infinite, it can come in contact with things infinite in respect of divisibility: for in this sense the time itself is also infinite—and so we find that the time occupied by the passage over the infinite is not a finite but an infinite time, and the contact with the infinites is made by means of moments not finite but infinite in number.

If one is led to think once more that perhaps Aristotle misunderstood Zeno and did not appreciate the full force of his argument, it is important to note that while Aristotle considered the above refutation an adequate answer to Zeno, he did not regard it as an adequate way of dealing with the problem as he himself (Aristotle) understood it. As will be clear from what follows, Aristotle saw the essential problem to be how it is possible for an infinite number of moments to pass, or for an infinite number of points to be traversed. He accordingly introduced the distinction between a potential infinite number of moments or points and an actual infinite number of moments or points. The only assumption consistent both with the continuity of space and time and with the possibility of traversing the infinite, Aristotle maintained, is that both space and time consist of a potentially and not an actually infinite number of unities:

T57 Aristotle *Phy.* 263a15-23, 26-30, b3-7

....although this solution is adequate as a reply to the

questioner (the question asked being whether it is possible in a finite time to traverse or reckon an infinite number of units), nevertheless as an account of the fact and explanation of its true nature it is inadequate. For suppose the distance to be left out of account and the question asked to be no longer whether it is possible in a finite time to traverse an infinite number of distances, and suppose that the inquiry is made to refer to the time taken by itself (for the time contains an infinite number of divisions); then this solution will no longer be adequate,...for motion if it is to be continuous must relate to what is continuous: and though what is continuous contains an infinite number of halves, they are not actual but potential halves. If the halves are made actual, we shall get not a continuous but an intermittent motion....to the question whether it is possible to pass through an infinite number of units either of time or of distance we must reply that in a sense it is and in a sense it is not. If the units are actual, it is not possible: if they are potential, it is possible.

Aristotle's refutation of the "Arrow" follows from the point of view he takes here. If the assumption that time consists of moments (i.e., actual moments) is denied, he says in his original statement of this paradox, the conclusion will not follow. Rather it is Aristotle's view that since time is continuous, it is potentially infinitely divisible: it consists of neither a finite nor infinite number of actual moments.

Bertrand Russell presents an overall evaluation of the significance of Zeno's paradoxes of motion, interpreting them somewhat differently from either Aristotle or Kirk & Raven, and suggesting a way of dealing with them based on the admissability of infinite numbers. Whether or not this line of approach would be in conflict with that of Aristotle is not entirely clear.

Zeno's arguments, in some form, have afforded grounds for almost all the theories of space and time and infinity which have been constructed from his day to our own...all his arguments are valid (with certain reasonable hypotheses) on the assumption that finite spaces and times consist of a finite number of points and instants, and...the third and fourth almost certainly in fact proceeded on this assumption, while the first and second, which were perhaps intended to refute the opposite assumption, were in that case fallacious. We may therefore escape from his paradoxes either by maintaining that, though space and time do consist of points and instants, the number of them in any finite interval is infinite; or by denying that space and time consist of points and instants at all; or lastly, by denying the reality of space and time altogether. It would seem that Zeno himself, as a supporter of Parmenides, drew the last of these three possible deductions, at any rate in regard to time. In this a very large number of philosophers have followed him. Many others, like M. Bergson, have preferred to deny space and time consist of points and instants. Either of these solutions will meet the difficulties in the form which Zeno raised them. But...the difficulties can also be met if infinite numbers are admissible. And on grounds which are independent of space and time, infinite number, and series in which no two terms are consecutive, must in any case be admitted. Consider, for example, all the fractions less than 1, arranged in order of magnitude. Between any two of them, there are others, for example, the arithmetical mean of the two. Thus no two fractions are consecutive, and the total number of them is infinite. It will be found that much of what Zeno says as regards the series of points on a line can be equally well applied to the series of fractions. And we cannot deny that there are fractions, so that two of the above ways of escape are closed to us.[12]

Having considered Zeno's paradoxes of plurality and motion, his major contributions to philosophy have been touched upon; but Zeno is also known to have proposed two paradoxes of somewhat less importance, to which we now briefly turn.

A PARADOX OF PLACE

Neither the Eleatics nor their opponents had a clear conception of the distinction between physical body, space, and place: in particular, place was taken to be something bodily. Aristotle refers to a paradox of Zeno apparently based on this confusion:

T58 Aristotle *Phy.* 209a24–26
....if it [i.e., place] is itself an existent, *where* will it be? Zeno's difficulty demands an explanation: for if everything that exists has a place, place too will have a place, and so on *ad infinitum.*

Based on another account of the same argument in Simplicius and an imitation of Zeno by Gorgias, Cornford suggests that it may have been part of a dilemma attempting to disprove plurality, of which he makes the following hypothetical reconstruction:

If things are many, each of them must be somewhere: either (a) in itself or (b) in another.

But (a) if it is in itself, it will be both container and contained, and one thing will be two: place and body. But what is one cannot be two.

And (b) it cannot be in another, namely its place; for if place exists, place will be in a place, and so on for ever. But this is absurd. Place, therefore, does not exist.

Therefore, if things are many, they are nowhere, and what is nowhere is nothing.[13]

Aristotle, sensibly distinguishing between a body and its place, understood as the innermost boundary of what contains body,[14] denies the necessity for the infinite regress on the grounds that the sense in which place is "in" something else differs from the sense in which a body is in place.

T59   Aristotle *Phy.* 210b23-27
Zeno's problem—that if Place is something it must be in something—is not difficult to solve. There is nothing to prevent the first place from being 'in' something else—not indeed in that as 'in' place, but as health is 'in' the hot as a positive determination of it or as the hot is 'in' body as an affection. So we escape the infinite regress.

The relation of place to that which it is "in", namely the container or body, is that of characterization to what is thereby characterized—or in this case as Aristotle puts it, of the limit to the limited.[15]

PARADOX OF THE MILLET SEED

A final argument, related by Simplicius and also attributed to Zeno by Aristotle, applies the same sort of analysis of infinite smalls to sensation that Zeno applied to plurality and motion. Recalling Parmenides' denial of the validity of sensation, it is clear that this argument, too, is directed against Parmenides' opponents.

T60   Simplicius *Phys.* 255r[16]
....the problem of Zeno the Eleatic, which he propounded to Protagoras the Sophist, "Tell me, Protagoras," said he, "does one grain of millet make a noise when it falls, or does the ten-thousandth part of a grain?" On receiving the answer that it does not, he went on: "Does a measure of millet grains make a noise when it falls, or not?" He answered, "It does make a noise." "Well," said Zeno, "does not the statement about the measure of millet apply to the one grain and the ten-thousandth part of a grain?" He assented, and Zeno

continued, "Are not the statements as to the noise the same in regard to each? For as are the things that make a noise, so are the noises. Since this is the case, if the measure of millet makes a noise, the one grain and the ten-thousandth part of a grain make a noise."

T61   Aristotle *Phys.* 250a20–24

Hence Zeno's reasoning is false when he argues that there is no part of the millet that does not make a sound; for there is no reason why any such part should not in any length of time fail to move the air that the whole bushel moves in falling. In fact it does not of itself move even such a quantity of the air as it would move if this part were by itself; for no part even exists otherwise than potentially.

NOTES

1. Simplicius *Phys.* 70. 16; Kirk & Raven, p. 299.

2. Guthrie, vol. 2, p. 106-7.

3. *Ibid.*, p. 104.

4. deSantillana, p. 96.

5. Plato, *Plato: The Collected Dialogues*, pp. 922-923.

6. Tannery, Burnet, Lee, Cornford. See Guthrie, vol. 2, pp. 83ff. and John Burnet, *Early Greek Philosophy* (1930: reprint, 4th ed. Macmillan Co.; New York: Meridian Books, 1957) p. 314.

7. Diogenes Laertius 9. 25 (cf. 8. 57); also Sextus Empiricus *Math.* 7.7; Guthrie, vol. 2, p. 82 and 82n3.

8. Aristotle *Topics* 100a25-30.

9. *Ibid.*, 101a25-101b4.

10. Kirk & Raven, pp. 296-7.

11. *Ibid.*, p. 292.

12. Bertrand Russell, *Our Knowledge of the External World* (New York: Mentor Books, New American Library, 1960), pp. 140-141.

13. Cornford, *Plato and Parmenides*, p. 149.

14. Aristotle *Phys.* 212a20-21.

15. *Ibid*, 212b26-8.

16. Arthur Fairbanks, *The First Philosophers of Greece* (London: Routledge & Kegan Paul, Ltd., 1917), p. 116-7.

PART III

MEDIATING SYSTEMS

The Pluralists
Empedocles
Anaxagoras
The Atomists
—Leucippus
—Democritus
A Revitalized Monism
Diogenes of Apollonia

CHAPTER 7

Empedocles

The philosophers treated in Chapters 7–10 either were closely associated with Athens or lived during the period of Athenian ascendency. All of these thinkers attempt to formulate systematic points of view mediating between the Ionian faith that rational explanation of the changing world of experience is possible, and the Italian school's refinement of the nature of such explanation (as with the Pythagoreans), even to the point of concluding that it is impossible (as with the Eleatics). Their mediating systems are in the mainstream of early Greek philosophy and in fact constitute its culmination.

Winspear's characterization of these thinkers as progressive materialists may be somewhat forced, but his observations offer genuine insight into the direction of their thought:

> Beginning as it did with a profound interest in change and process, the philosophy of the progressives endeavored to build up a philosophical opposition to the conservative emphasis on the changeless, the static, and the eternal. But unable (because of the acceptance of slavery) to build up any organic and all-embracing ethical universalism which it might oppose to the Pythagorean defense of an earlier and more primitive concept of organism and organic harmony, the movement of progressive thought was more and more forced to fall back on an unbridled individualism. In ethics

this culminated in the hedonism of the Cyrenaics†, and [in] physics, with the atomism of Democritus. The two systems, each in its respective sphere, have this in common, that they begin with the atomic, isolated individual and endeavor to build up a picture of cosmic or ethical truth by a sheer process of combination.[1]

One might generalize on the above observation concerning the combinatory atomism of Democritus and the individualistic hedonism of the Cyrenaics, and say that it is characteristic of every one of these mediating systems except that of Diogenes of Apollonia: all of them attempt to explain the world in terms of combinations of simpler elements and are consequently called "Pluralists." Evolution in the direction of Democritean atomism is evident in the decreasing reliance placed on extraelemental forces as one moves, say, from Heraclitus to Democritus. Heraclitus, of course, saw the *Logos* of change, embedded in change itself, as conflict: in Empedocles, Strife has been supplemented by Love, and both are factors of a different order than the elements, Earth, Air, Fire and Water. Next comes Anaxagoras, for whom conflict is entirely eliminated through the governance of an extramaterial Nous. Then finally, with Democritus, all is Atoms, the Void, and Necessity: individual atoms combining to constitute the world as it is—simply because that is the way they behave. Accompanying this, we also have the movement from Heraclitus, for whom all is qualitative, to Democritus, for whom all quality is reduced to quantitative difference, a movement foreshadowed in Anaximenes.

Although we have more fragments of the works of Empedocles than of any other early Greek thinker excepting Democritus, about one hundred and fifty, we know next to nothing about his life and activities that is reliable. There is a mass of conflicting tradition about him, including reports that he lived to be sixty, seventy-seven and ninety-seven years old. It is generally agreed that he came from Acragas in Sicily, and the most reasonable guess is that he flourished around 450 B.C.

> **T62** Diogenes Laertius 8. 2. 51 [Loeb]
> Empedocles was, according to Hippobotus, the son of Meton and grandson of Empedocles, and was a native of Acragas.... The grammarian Apollodorus in his *Chronology* tells us that "He was the son of Meton," and Glaucus says he went to Thurii, just then founded [445-444 B.C.].

---

†The Cyrenaics were a school of philosophy founded by Aristippus of Cyrene (ca.435–356 B.C.), noted chiefly for the view that the pleasure of the individual should be the aim of life.

T63 Aristotle *Meta.* 984a11-12

Anaxagoras of Clazomenae, who, though older than Empedocles, was later in his philosophical activity.

T64 Simplicius *Phys.* 25. 19 quoting Theophrastus [K&R320]

Empedocles of Acragas was born not long after Anaxagoras, and was an admirer and associate of Parmenides, and even more of the Pythagoreans.

Diogenes Laertius reports a great number of traditional stories about Empedocles, and it may be correct to conclude that the latter played an important role in the political life of his city. The tradition makes him an active democrat who saved his city from a conspiracy and refused the kingship which was offered to him. The story that in later life he was exiled from his home city would seem to conflict with the fragment (112) of his work in which the people of the city, to whom the work is addressed, are called his friends. It seems clear that he left the city, perhaps for Peloponnesus, as one source has it, and all trace of him vanished. There are also several tales about his death, the most dramatic being that he jumped into the fiery crater of Mount Etna to create the impression of divinity.

Diogenes Laertius also reports that Aristotle in a lost dialogue, *Sophist*, attributes the invention of rhetoric to Empedocles.[2] And Gorgias, the famous rhetorician and sophist, is said to have been his pupil.

THE PROBLEM OF HIS TWO WORKS

The existing fragments are from his two books, *On Nature (Periphysis)* and *Purifications (Katharmoi)*, which together are said to total about five hundred lines.[3] They give us the picture of a man who enjoyed wide and good reputation as a doctor, man of science, and religious seer.

(Frg.112) Friends, who dwell in the great town on the city's heights, looking down on yellow Acragas, you who are occupied with good deeds, who are harbours (*of refuge*) treating foreigners with respect, and who are unacquainted with wickedness: greeting! I go about among you as an immortal god, no longer a mortal, held in honour by all, as I seem (*to them to deserve*), crowned with fillets and flowing garlands. When I come to them in their flourishing towns, to men and women, I am honoured; and they follow me in thousands, to inquire where is the path of advantage, some

desiring oracles, while others ask to hear a word of healing
for their manifold diseases, since they have long been
pierced with cruel pains.

Both works are in the poetic form made popular by Parmenides and
reflect strong Eleatic and Pythagorean influences. The tradition, perhaps as an expression of this, makes him a pupil of Parmenides as well
as of Telauges, the son of Pythagoras.

There has been a problem with the fragments from the two works, at
least for modern interpreters. It centers around the question of whether
the immortality which Empedocles attributes to the soul in *Purifications* can have any possibility or even meaning in the light of his
description of the nature of things in *On Nature*. Without doubt the
perspectives differ in the two, but it does appear possible to understand
them as complementing each other and, as Kirk & Raven point out,
"unless one poem is used to throw light upon the obscurities of the
other, even more difficult problems remain to be solved."[4] There are
some things to be suggested concerning the assumption of complement-
arity, but they had best come up after the several aspects of his thought
have been presented. We shall begin with the work titled *On Nature* and
consider the *Purifications* later.

ON NATURE

A.   *Reaction to Parmenides*

Parmenides and his followers upheld the following two theses: (1) the
necessity for a monistic conception of reality and the logical inconsistency of pluralism, and (2) the incompatibility of the one Being with
both the plurality and the flux of the sense world. A corollary of this
second thesis is that the sense world is but mere appearance.† As
Guthrie points out, anyone not wishing to deny the reality of the sense
world has one of three alternatives open to him. The first is the route
taken by Diogenes of Apollonia, to be considered subsequently, and
constitutes a return to the earlier Ionian ideas, simply ignoring the
Eleatic critique. The second, taken by Plato, is to argue that the sense
world is not totally unreal but constitutes a secondary realm which,
though not a proper object of knowledge, is yet a suitable object for
opinion. The third alternative is the way of Empedocles who, though
distrustful of experience, felt that the function of knowledge is to
explain the sense world. Each of the last two alternatives attempts to
explain the plurality of changing things in everyday experience on the
basis of a plurality of unchanging constituents, thus implicitly denying

†Parmenides, Frg. 1, p. 101.

the first of the Eleatic theses, that reality is monistic and pluralism inconsistent.

Empedocles not only points out the relativity of the senses and of the whole human situation to Pausanias, to whom his treatise *On Nature* is addressed (Frg.1), but also enjoins him to accept all of the senses on an equal footing and to "use whatever way of perception makes each thing clear" (Frg.3). And he calls upon the Muse to grant the knowledge proper for "us creatures of a day to hear", telling Pausanias to "grasp (these things)", and guard them well.

(Frg.1) Pausanias, but you must listen, son of wise Anchites!

(Frg.2) For limited are the means of grasping (*i.e., the organs of sense-perception*) which are scattered throughout their limbs, and many are the miseries that press in and blunt the thoughts. And having looked at (*only*) a small part of existence during their lives, doomed to perish swiftly like smoke they are carried aloft and wafted away, believing only that upon which as individuals they chance to hit as they wander in all directions; but every man preens himself on having found the Whole: so little are these things to be seen by men or to be heard, or to be comprehended by the mind! But you, since you have come here into retirement, shall learn—not more than mortal intellect can attain.

(Frg.3) But, ye gods, avert from my tongue the madness of those men, and guide forth from my reverent lips a pure stream! I beseech thee also, much-wooed white-armed maiden Muse, convey (*to me*) such knowledge as divine law allows us creatures of a day to hear, driving the well-harnessed car from (*the realm of*) Piety! Nor shall the flowers of honour paid to fame by mortals force you at least to accept them on condition that you rashly say more than is holy—and are thereupon enthroned by the heights of wisdom!

But come, observe with every means, to see by which way each thing is clear, and do not hold any (*percept of*) sight higher in credibility than (*those*) according to hearing, nor (*set*) the loud-sounding hearing above the evidence of the tongue (*taste*); nor refuse credence at all to any of the other limbs where there exists a path for perception, but use whatever way of perception makes each thing clear.

(Frg.4) But it is of great concern to the lower orders to mistrust the powerful; however, as the trustworthy evidence of my Muse commands, grasp (*these things*), when my reasoned argument has been sifted in your innermost heart!

(Frg.5) To protect it within your silent bosom.

While these passages suggest the experience of change, the ebb and flow of life and perception, this is not to be taken as asserting the full reality of flux and the Many. Empedocles does not believe in change in the sense that something comes into existence which did not exist before.

(Frg.11) Fools!—for they have no long-sighted thoughts, since they imagine that what previously did not exist comes into being, or that a thing dies and is utterly destroyed.

(Frg.12) From what in no wise exists, it is impossible for anything to come into being; and for Being to perish completely is incapable of fulfillment and unthinkable: for it will always be there, wherever anyone may place it on any occasion.

These fragments are purely Parmenidean in thought and follow from the basic idea that "Being is." The implication is that even though things seem to change in the sense of "coming into being," they really do not. And the impossibility of such "coming into being" is asserted on the strictly Eleatic ground that, since Being is full and continuous, there is no room for anything to come into existence.

(Frg.13) Nor is there any part of the Whole that is empty or overfull.

(Frg.14) No part of the Whole is empty; so whence could anything additional come?

B. *The Elements*

Of course the denial of creation also implies the impossibility of the destruction of anything. As the next two fragments make clear, there is no real change, but only the rearranging (mixing) of what already is. Like Anaxagoras' "seeds" and in contradistinction to the atoms of Democritus, which it will be possible to describe in purely quantitative terms, Empedocles' elements (fire, air, earth and water), which are for him "what already is", retain their qualitative characteristics. Still, Empedocles idea of explaining qualitative changes in terms of a quantitative rearrangement of plurality of elements represents an important advance on Anaximenes' quantitative principle of the condensation and rarefaction of what for him was the one thing that already is (Air). It may be regarded as a consequence of Empedocles' attempt to avail himself of the Pythagorean interest in generation of things from numbers, understood as geometrical arrangements in the face of Parmenidean strictures on the One becoming Many. It is also a notion made more explicit by Anaxagoras and expanded upon by the Atomists.

(Frg.15) A wise man would not conjecture such things in his heart, namely, that so long as they are alive (which they call Life), they exist, and experience bad and good fortune; but that before mortals were combined (*out of the Elements*) and after they were dissolved, they are nothing at all.

(Frg.8) And I shall tell you another thing: there is no creation of substance in any one of mortal existences, nor any end in execrable death, but only mixing and exchange of what has been mixed; and the name 'substance' (*Physis, 'nature'*) is applied to them by mankind.

Not only does Frg.15 affirm the combining of the elements to form mortals, but it also distinguishes the apparent truth of experience that men are nothing before and after their lives from the correct belief that a wise man would hold. In the next fragment (Frg. 9), we see that although "Right" would require speech of a different kind, Empedocles himself speaks in the idiom of custom.

(Frg.9) But men, when these (*the Elements*) have been mixed in the form of a man and come into the light, or in the form of a species of wild animals, or plants, or birds, then say they that this has 'come into being'; and when they separate, this men call sad fate (*death*). The terms that Right demands they do not use; but through custom I myself also apply these names.

More specifically, Empedocles speaks of the elements, or "roots":

(Frg.6) Hear, first, the four roots of things: bright Zeus [Fire], the life-bearing Hera [Air], and Aidoneus [Earth], and Nêstis [Water] who causes a mortal spring of moisture to flow with her tears. (Aetius 1, 3, 20).

(Frg.7) (*The Elements*): uncreated.

(Frg.26) In turn they get the upper hand in the revolving cycle, and perish into one another and increase in the turn appointed by Fate. For they alone exist, but running through one another they become men and the tribes of other animals, sometimes uniting under the influence of Love into one ordered Whole, at other times again each moving apart through the hostile force of hate, until growing together into the Whole which is One, they are quelled. Thus in so far as they have the power to grow into One out of Many, and again, when the One grows apart and Many are formed, in this sense they come into being and have no stable life; but in so far as they never cease their continuous exchange, in this sense they remain always unmoved (*unaltered*) as they follow the cyclic process.

T65 Simplicius *Phys.* 25. 21. [K&R329]
He makes the material elements four in number, fire, air, water and earth, all eternal, but changing in bulk and scarcity through mixture and separation; but his real first principles, which impart motion to these are Love and Strife. The elements are continually subject to an alternate change, at one time mixed together by Love, at another separated by Strife; so that the first principles are, by his account, six in number.

In expected poetic fashion, a habit for which Aristotle continually takes him to task, Empedocles has referred to the four elements or "roots" in terms of the gods (Frg.6): Zeus is Fire, Hera, Air, Aidoneus, Earth, and Nêstis, Water. But that the references can vary is indicated in Frgs. 96 and 98, where Fire is Hephaestus, the smithy.† However referred to, they are the original elements first put forth by the Ionian thinkers. They are uncreated and it is out of the mixing of these "roots" in varying proportions that the changing things of experience come about.

C. *Love and Strife*

Both the change and direction of experience are brought about by the two opposing forces of Aphrodite or Love, and Wrath, Hate or Strife (all terms in translations of the fragments to follow). There is a cyclical process in operation in which Love and Strife alternately dominate the whole, Love bringing harmony and union, Strife disharmony and disunion. Aristotle points out that insofar as Empedocles regards Love as good, and Strife as bad, "he is the first to mention the good and bad as principles."[5] They are eternal moving principles of things.

(Frg.16) (*Love and Hate*): As they were formerly, so also will they be, and never, I think, shall infinite Time be emptied of these two.

(Frg.21) But come, observe the following witness to my previous discourse, lest in my former statements there was any substance of which the form was missing. Observe the sun, bright to see and hot everywhere, and all the immortal things (*heavenly bodies*) drenched with its heat and brilliant light; and (*observe*) the rain, dark and chill over everything; and from the Earth issue forth things based on the soil and solid. But in (*the reign of*) Wrath they are all different in form and separate, while in (*the reign of*) Love they come together and long for one another. For from these (*Elements*) come all things that were and are and will be; and trees spring up, and

---

†See p. 153.

men and women, and beasts and birds and water-nurtured
fish, and even the long-lived gods who are highest in honour.
For these (*Elements*) alone exist, but by running through
one another they become different; to such a degree does
mixing change them.

(Frg.22) For all these things—beaming Sun and Earth and
Heaven and Sea—are connected in harmony with their own
parts: all those (*parts*) which have been sundered from them
and exist in mortal limbs. Similarly all those things which
are more suitable for mixture are made like one another and
united in affection by Aphrodite. But those things which
differ most from one another in origin and mixture and the
forms in which they are moulded are completely unaccus-
tomed to combine, and are very baneful because of the
commands of Hate, in that Hate has wrought their origin.

(Frg.20) This process is clearly to be seen throughout the
mass of mortal limbs: sometimes through Love all the limbs
which the body has as its lot come together in One, in the
prime of flourishing life; at another time again, sundered by
evil feuds, they wander severally by the breakers of the shore
of life. Likewise too with shrub-plants and fish in their
watery dwelling, and beasts with mountain lairs and diver-
birds that travel on wings.

(Frg.23) As when painters decorate temple-offerings with
colours—men who, following their intelligence, are well-
skilled in their craft—these, when they take many-coloured
pigments in their hands, and have mixed them in a harmony,
taking more of some, less of another, create from them
forms like to all things, making trees and men and women
and animals and birds and fish nurtured in water, and even
long-lived gods, who are highest in honour; so let not Deception compel your mind (*to believe*) that there is any other
source for mortals, as many as are to be seen existing in
countless numbers. But know this for certain, since you have
the account from a divinity.

(Frg.35) But I will go back to the path of song which I
formerly laid down, drawing one argument from another:
that (*path which shows how*) when Hate has reached the
bottommost abyss of the eddy, and when Love reaches the
middle of the whirl, then in it (*the whirl*) all these things
come together so as to be One—not all at once but voluntar-
ily uniting, some from one quarter, others from another.
And as they mixed, they poured forth countless races of

mortals. But many things stand unmixed side by side with the things mixing—all those which Hate (*still*) aloft checked, since it had not yet faultlessly withdrawn from the Whole to the outermost limits of the circle, but was remaining in some places, and in other places departing from the limbs (*of the Sphere*). But insofar as it went on quietly streaming out, to the same extent there was entering a benevolent immortal inrush of faultless Love. And swiftly those things became mortal which previously had experienced immortality, and things formerly unmixed, changing their paths. And as they mixed, there poured forth countless races of mortals, equipped with forms of every sort, a marvel to behold.

(Frg.38) Come now, I will first tell you of (*the sun*) the beginning, (*the Elements*) from which all the things we now look upon came forth into view: Earth, and the sea with many waves, and damp Air [i.e., terrestrial air], and the Titan Aether [i.e., fiery celestial air] which clasps the circle all round.

(Frg.39) If the depths of the earth were unlimited, and also the vast Aether [i.e., Air], a doctrine which has foolishly issued forth off the tongues of many, and has been spread abroad out of their mouths, since they have seen only a little of the Whole.

With regard to the above fragments a number of considerations present themselves. In the first place, there would logically appear to be four stages in the cycle: (1) the domination of Aphrodite or Love; (2) the domination of Wrath, Hate or Strife; (3) the transition from the domination of Aphrodite or Love to that of Wrath, Hate or Strife; and (4) the transition back again. Secondly, it is not quite true to simply say that Love attracts and Strife repels, or Love creates and Strife destroys. To the extent that everything tends toward unity and to the degree that Strife dominates, there is a tendency toward complete separation of the four elements. Aristotle makes this point with respect to the first and second stages of the cycle:

T66   Aristotle *Meta*. 985a22-29
And Empedocles, though he uses the causes to a greater extent than this, neither does so sufficiently nor attains consistency in their use. At least, in many cases he makes love segregate things, and strife aggregate them. For whenever the universe is dissolved into its elements by strife, fire is aggregated into one, and so is each of the other elements; but whenever again under the influence of love they come together into one, the parts must again be segregated out of each element.

And then he goes on to add that "it would seem that Strife is the begetter of everything that exists except the One."[6] Nonetheless, Empedocles speaks as if the completely mixed state of Love is primitive, and as the following passage from *De Caelo* bears out, Aristotle thought Empedocles had sufficient reason for asserting the primacy of Love:

T67 Aristotle *De Caelo* 301a14-20

But there is no sense in starting generation from an original state in which bodies are separated in movement. Hence Empedocles omits the period when Love was gaining ascendency; for he could not have constructed the heavens by building them up out of bodies in separation, making them combine by the power of Love; since our world has its constituent elements in separation and therefore presupposes a previous state of unity and combination.

But there are other reasons for making the state of Love primary. One of them, suggested in Frg. 35, as well as other fragments to be discussed presently, is the reference to the whole cyclical process as going on in a sphere, and Frg. 38 speaks of the Aether "which clasps the circle all around," while Frg. 39 specifically takes issue with the view of Earth being unlimited in depth and Aether in height. This immediately suggests that the state of Love, which is one of homogeneity and union, is analogous to the Parmenidean One. In fact Empedocles says things about the state of Love and the One which makes them both much like the Parmenidean One.

(Frg.27) (*The Sphere under the dominion of Love*): Therein are articulated neither the swift limbs of the sun, nor the shaggy might of Earth, nor the sea: so firmly is it (*the Whole*) fixed in a close-set secrecy, a rounded Sphere enjoying a circular solitude.

(Frg.27a) There is no strife nor unseemly war in his limbs.

(Frg.28) But he (*God*) is equal in all directions to himself and altogether eternal, a rounded Sphere enjoying a circular solitude.

(Frg.29) For there do not start two branches from his back; (*he has*) no feet, no swift knees, no organs of reproduction; but he was a Sphere, and in all directions equal to himself.

Another reason for considering the oneness of the state of Love as primary lies in the position of the One in Pythagorean thought. The One is that from which everything else proceeds and, as we shall see later, is basic to the religious views of Empedocles. Hippolytus speaks directly to this point:

T68 Hippolytus *Ref.* 7. 29. [K&R356]

This is just what Empedocles says about his own birth—'Of

These I too am now one, a fugitive from the gods and a
wanderer.' He calls by the name of god, that is to say, the
One and its unity, in which he Himself dwelt before he was
snatched thence by Strife and born into this world of plurality which Strife has organized.

One of the reasons for supposing the compatability of *On Nature*
with the *Purifications* lies in the similar descriptions of the One contained in both (Frg. 29, above, from the former and Frg. 134,† from the
latter). There are bound to be difficulties here, but there appears to be a
sense in which the explanation of the qualitative changes of experience
in terms of the continuous quantitative mixing of unchanging elements
is a mediating mechanism between the Parmenidean One and the
Pythagorean One. There is no way of telling whether Empedocles
intended to do any such thing, but the introduction of the Love-Strife
(One-Many) cycle allows, on the one hand, an explanation of the
process of generation and decay, the changes and developments in
experience, and the fall of the soul in terms of the Pythagorean One. On
the other hand, it allows retention of the Parmenidean distinction
between the real One and the appearance of Many. True, the One of
Empedocles includes the notion of mixing and movement from One to
Many, but in the last paragraph of the fragment below, Frg. 17, the tone
is completely Eleatic. The general impression given is that the Love-
Strife cycle might go on within the unchanging One.

> (Frg.17) I shall tell of a double (*process*): at one time it
> increased so as to be a single One out of Many; at another
> time again it grew apart so as to be Many out of One. There
> is a double creation of mortals and a double decline: the
> union of all things causes the birth and destruction of the
> one (*race of mortals*), the other is reared as the elements
> grow apart, and then flies asunder. And these (*elements*)
> never cease their continuous exchange, sometimes uniting
> under the influence of Love, so that all become One, at other
> times again each moving apart through the hostile force of
> Hate. Thus insofar as they have the power to grow into One
> out of Many, and again, when the One grows apart and
> Many are formed, in this sense they come into being and
> have no stable life; but insofar as they never cease their
> continuous exchange, in this sense they remain always
> unmoved (*unaltered*) as they follow the cyclic process.
>
> But come, listen to my discourse! For be assured, learning
> will increase your understanding. As I said before, revealing

---

†See p. 164.

the aims of my discourse, I shall tell you of a double process. At one time it increased so as to be a single One out of Many; at another time it grew apart so as to be Many out of One—Fire and Water and Earth and the boundless height of Air, and also execrable Hate apart from these, of equal weight in all directions, and Love in their midst, their equal in length and breadth. Observe her with your mind, and do not sit with wondering eyes! She it is who is believed to be implanted in mortal limbs also; through her they think friendly thoughts and perform harmonious actions, calling her Joy and Aphrodite. No mortal man has perceived her as she moves in and out among them. But *you* must listen to the undeceitful progress of my argument.

All these (*Elements*) are equal and of the same age in their creation; but each presides over its own office, and each has its own character, and they prevail in turn in the course of Time. And besides these, nothing else comes into being, nor does anything cease. For if they had been perishing continuously, they would Be no more: and what could increase the Whole? And whence could it have come? In what direction could it perish, since nothing is empty of these things? No, but these things alone exist, and running through one another they become different things at different times, and are ever continuously the same.

(Frg.30) But when great Hate had been nourished in its limbs, and had rushed up into honour, when the time was fulfilled which, alternating, is fixed for them (*Love and Hate*) by a broad oath.

(Frg.31) For all the limbs of the god trembled in succession.

(Frg.36) As they came together, Hate returned to the outermost (*bound*).

(Frg.37) (*Fire increases Fire*), Earth increases its own substance, Aether (*increases*) Aether.

In Frg. 17 there are two slightly differing descriptions of the two transitional stages between Love and Strife, and both stages are regarded as creative of "mortals." Empedocles calls the two stages a "double process," and the question "Is the world in its present stage moving towards the dominance of Love or Strife?" almost asks itself. An answer will be attempted when the process of generation is considered.† But more important for our understanding of the whole cycle is

---

†See p. 153ff.

the fact that even though Empedocles has spoken of the four "roots", along with Love and Strife, as ultimate, there is a phrase in Frg. 17 in which Love and Strife are said to "each preside over his own office." (The term "office" suggests a function with rules for fulfillment.) Further, in Frg. 30 "a broad oath" binding both alternately hints there are laws or structures even more basic. But it is generally agreed that there is no distinction between the material thing and the abstract principle of its function in Empedocles. The abstract is as yet beyond conception.

D.   *Cosmogony and Cosmology*

Earlier we considered the nature of the mixed state of Love. When, in turn, under the domination of Strife, the motion of separation began to prevail, and the four elements began to separate out and aggregate (Frg. 37)—"all the limbs of the god trembled in succession" (Frg. 31), as Empedocles puts it. From Frg. 36, as well as from Frg. 35, the impression arises that Strife is introduced from "the outermost limits of the circle" and returns there after its period of dominance. The following fragments and references concern various aspects of this separating out.

T69   Aetius 2. 6. 3. [K&R332]
Empedocles holds that aither was the first to be separated off, next fire, and after that earth. From the earth, as it was excessively constricted by the force of rotation, sprang water. From water air came by evaporation. The heavens arose from the aither, the sun from fire, while terrestrial things were compressed from the other elements.

T70   [Plutarch] *Strom. ap.* Eusebium *P.E.* 1. 8. 10. [K&R332]
Empedocles of Acragas. . . holds that the air that was separated off from the original mixture of the elements flowed around in a circle; and after the air fire ran outwards and, having nowhere else to go, ran upwards under the solidified periphery around the air. There are, he says, two hemispheres revolving round the earth, one consisting entirely of fire, the other of a mixture of air with a little fire; this latter he supposes to be night. Their motion arises from the fact that the accumulation of fire in one region gives it preponderance there.
(Frg. 51) Mightily upwards (*rushes Fire*).
(Frg. 52) Many fires burn below the surface (*of the Earth*).
(Frg.53) For so (*the Aether*) chanced to be running at that time, though often differently.

(Frg.54) (*Fire by nature rose upwards*), but Aether sank down with long roots upon the Earth.

(Frg.55) Sea, the sweat of Earth.

(Frg.56) Salt was solidified, pressed by the forceful rays (*of the sun*).

T71   Aristotle *De Gen. et Corr.* 334a1-4

For though Strife 'dissociated', it was not by Strife that the 'Ether' was borne upwards. On the contrary, sometimes he attributes its movement to something like chance ('For *thus*, as it ran, it *happened* to meet them there, though often otherwise'), while at other times he says it is the *nature* of fire to be borne upwards.

T72   Aristotle *Phys.* 196a21-23

Empedocles. . .says that the air is not always separated into the highest region, but 'as it may chance.'

It is not possible to determine the exact order in which the separating out comes about. T69 and T70 give slightly differing versions. Frgs. 51-56 shed some light upon the positioning of the elements, but Aristotle (T71 and T72) questions whether there is not a factor of chance in the whole process and refers specifically to Frg. 53. That chance is operative in the generation of individual things is made clear in the above and following fragment, and one might conjecture that it is not impossible for the same kind of factor to operate in reverse during the separating out period so that the elements could aggregate in a different order each time.

(Frg.59) But as the one divinity became more and more mingled with the other (*i.e., Love and Hate*), these things fell together as each chanced, and many other things in addition to these were continuously produced.

Frgs. 40-48 and T73, 74, 75, which are next presented, tell of the composition of and relationship between the sun and moon and indicate that Empedocles knew that the moon's light is reflected sunlight and how eclipses came about. The two references to Aetius tell about the nature of the fixed stars and their positioning on the outer rim. How they can consist of fire and be attached to the frozen rim is not easy to see. Perhaps only the free planets are stars of fire and the fixed stars like our moon shine with borrowed light, but this too is pure speculation.

(Frg.40) Sharp-shooting sun and gracious moon.

(Frg.41) But (*the sun*) collected in a ball travels round the great sky.

(Frg.42) (*The moon*) cuts off his (*the sun's*) rays, whenever she goes below him, and she throws a shadow on as much of the Earth as is the breadth of the bright-eyed moon.

(Frg.43) Thus the ray (*of sunshine*) having struck the broad surface of the moon (*returns at once in order that, running, it may reach the heavens*).

(Frg.44) (*The Sun, having been round the Earth, by reflection from the heavenly light*) flashes back to Olympus with serene countenance.

(Frg.45) There whirls round the Earth a circular borrowed light.

(Frg.46) As the nave of the chariot (*-wheel*) whirls round the goal, (*so does the moon circle closely round the Earth*).

(Frg.47) She gazes at the sacred circle of her lord (*the sun*) opposite.

(Frg.48) It is the Earth that makes night by coming in the way of the (*sun's*) rays.

T73 [Plutarch] *Strom. ap.* Eusebium *P.E.* 1.8.10. [K&R333]†
The sun is not in its nature fire, but rather a reflection of fire like that which comes from water. The moon, he says, was composed of air that had been shut in by fire; this air was solidified, like hail. The moon gets its light from the sun.

T74   Aetius 2.13.2. [K&R333]
Empedocles says that the stars are made of fire, composed of the fiery element which the air originally contained but squeezed out at the first separation.

T75   Aetius 2.13.11. [K&R333]
Empedocles says that the fixed stars were attached to the ice (i.e., the frozen periphery), while the planets were unattached.

As we have previously seen, every cosmologist has had the problem of explaining why or how the earth continues to maintain its position at the center of the cosmos, and in T76 we have the reason given by Empedocles. Some interpreters take this passage from Aristotle as evidence that Empedocles was familiar with centripetal and centrifugal forces, but it seems more reasonable to say, with Kirk & Raven, that here we have one of the few arguments from observation that occur among the early Greek philosophers of Nature (Physis).

T76   Aristotle *De Caelo* 295a14-23
... all those who try to generate the heavens to explain why the earth came together at the center. They then seek a reason for its staying there; and some say, in the manner explained, that the reason is to size and flatness, others, like Empedocles, that the motion of the heavens, moving about it at a higher speed, prevents movement of the earth, as the water in a cup, when the cup is given circular motion, though it is often underneath the

---

†Continuation of **T70**.

bronze, is for the same reason prevented from moving with the downward motion which is natural to it.

E. *The Evolution of Life*

There is a very basic and very Pythagorean characteristic about the mixing process that produces all the many things in our changing experience. Empedocles conceived of the nature of each existing particular as the result of a specific proportion in the combination of "roots." How he could know just what proportions produce what things is no clearer than for the Pythagoreans generally, but that he thought of the matter in this way is clear from the next two fragments.

(Frg.96) But the Earth obligingly in its broad vessels received two parts out of the eight of shining Nêstis, four of Hephaestus. And these became the white bones fitted together by the cementing of Harmony, divinely originated.

(Frg.98) The Earth, having been finally moored in the harbours of Love, joined with these in about equal proportions: with Hephaestus, with moisture, and with all-shining Aether, either a little more (*of Earth*) or a little less to their more. And from these came blood and the forms of other flesh.

In the fragments dealing with the generation and birth of things to which we now turn, we find in Empedocles something very like a theory of evolution. No doubt the essential features of a survival of the fittest theory are present, as the following passage from Aristotle makes clear. And mention of the role of "accidental compounding" in this passage parallels our modern notion of mutation.

T77 Aristotle *Phys.* 198b29–33
Wherever then all the parts came about just what they would have been if they had come to be for an end, such things survived, being organized spontaneously in a fitting way; whereas those which grew otherwise perished and continue to perish, as Empedocles says his 'man-faced ox-progeny' did.

But there is nothing organic about the evolution in Empedocles. Despite appearances to the contrary, it is a matter of chance combinations in which the product represents only a proportionality among the elements. Empedocles' evolution lacks any conception of growth, but then, in our own day such interpretations of evolution are still with us. The reduction of qualitative change to quantitative mixture is a salient feature of the Empedoclean contribution to thought, and, as we mentioned before, has had a long history since.

The following passage from Aetius is descriptive of four developmental phases of the cosmic cycle.

T78   Aetius 5. 19. 5. [K&R336]
Empedocles held that the first generation of animals and
plants were not complete but consisted of separate limbs not
joined together; the second, arising from the joining of these
limbs, were like creatures in dreams; the third was the generation of the whole-natured forms; and the fourth arose no
longer from the homoeomerous substances such as earth or
water, but by generation in some cases as the result of the
condensation by their nourishment, in others because femi-
nine beauty excited the sexual urge; and the various species of
animals were distinguished by the quality of the mixture in
them.

Following Kirk & Raven, it seems reasonable to consider the stages in
Aetius in pairs, with the first and second coming before the complete union
of Love and the last two as the result of the introduction of Strife. Part of the
evidence for such understanding lies in the following passages from
Aristotle and Simplicius.

T79   Aristotle *De Caelo* 300b26-31
There is a further question, too, which might be asked. Is it
possible or impossible that bodies in unordered movement
should combine in some cases into combinations like those of
which bodies of nature's composing are composed, such, I
mean, as bones and flesh? Yet this is what Empedocles asserts
to have occurred under Love. 'Many a head' says he, 'came to
birth without a neck'.

T80   Aristotle *De Anima* 430a28-30
And Empedocles said that 'where heads of many a creature
sprouted without necks' they afterwards by Love's power were
combined.

T81   Aristotle *De Gen. et Corr.* 334a6-8
He combines the assertion that the Order of the World is the
same *now*, in the reign of Strife, as was it *formerly* in the reign of
Love.

T82   Simplicius *De Caelo* 587. 24 [K&R339]
By 'in the period of Love' he means, not when Love was already
in control, but when it was going to be.

In what follows, the fragments and references concerned with the
generation of living things will be grouped as they belong in one of the
phases described by Aetius (T78). In this grouping, we continue to follow
the interpretation of Kirk & Raven[7] except where indicated.
First: "separated limbs"

(Frg.57) On it (*Earth*) many foreheads without necks sprang
forth, and arms wandered unattached, bereft of shoulders, and
eyes strayed about alone, needing brows.

(Frg.58) Limbs wandered alone.

Second: "creatures in dreams"

(Frg.60) Creatures with rolling gait and innumerable hands.

(Frg.61) Many creatures were created with a face and breasts on both sides; offspring of cattle with the fronts of men, and again there arose offspring of men with heads of cattle; and (*creatures made of elements*) mixed in part from men, in part of female sex, furnished with hairy limbs.

Third: "Whole-natured forms"

(Frg.62) Come now, hear how the Fire as it was separated sent up the night-produced shoots of men and much-lamenting women; for my tale is not wide of the mark nor ill-informed. At first, undifferentiated shapes of earth arose, having a share of both elements Water and Heat. These the Fire sent up, wishing to reach its like, but they did not exhibit a lovely body with limbs, nor the voice and organ such as is proper to men.

The third stage is clearly brought about by the introduction of Strife and the beginnings of the aggregation of the elements. Just what a "whole-natured form" would be is far from clear. Though Kirk & Raven cite Simplicius as believing that such would have no parts at all and Aristotle as holding them to be "merely a form of seed," they give no interpretation themselves. Cleve takes the view that the reference of Simplicius is a commentary upon Aristotle's interpretation in terms of seed or "sperma," the whole forming an opinion not unrelated to our current understanding of the basic forms of life. The passage is worth quoting.

T83 Simplicius *Phys.* 382. 17 [Cleve II 365–6]

"Whole-natured", namely, is in the first place that which in all its parts completely is whatever it is, since not yet any differentiation has taken place in it. For every part of the sperma is all the parts of the (future) body, whereas no part of the body is all the other parts, because then already differentiation has occurred within them, and the "whole-natured" has already been split asunder.

Fourth: "by generation"

A rereading of the last half of T78† will make clear that in this fourth phase we are obviously in our own world, to which the next fragments refer.

(Frg. 71) But if your belief concerning these matters was at all lacking—how from the mixture of Water, Earth, Aether and Sun (*Fire*) there came into being the forms and colours of mortal things in such numbers as now exist fitted together by Aphrodite.

---

†See p. 154.

(Frg.72) How also tall trees and fish of the sea.

(Frg.73) And as at that time Cypris, when she had drenched earth with rain-water, busying herself in preparation of the forms, gave them to swift Fire to strengthen them.

(Frg.74) (*Aphrodite*): bringing the tuneless tribe of prolific fish.

(Frg.75) Of (*the animals*), those that are of dense composition on the outside and rare within, having received this flabbiness under the hands of Cypris.

(Frg.76) This is (*found*) in the hard-backed shells of the sea-dwellers, especially the sea-snails and the stone-skinned turtles. There you will see earth dwelling on the surface of the flesh.

(Frg.77,78) (*Trees*) retentive of their leaves and retentive of their fruit, flourish with abundance of fruit all the year round, in accordance with Air (*i.e., Vapour, Moisture, in their composition*).

(Frg.79) Thus eggs are borne, first by the tall olive trees.

(Frg.80) Which is the reason why pomegranates are late-ripening and apples remain juicy for so long (?).

(Frg.81) Wine is the water from the bark, after it has fermented in the wood.

(Frg.82) Hair, and leaves, and the close feathers of birds, and the scales that grow on stout limbs, are the same thing.

(Frg.83) But hedgehogs have sharp-shooting hairs that bristle on their backs.

(Frg.148) Earth that envelops mortals (*the body*).

The last thirteen fragments are clearly from the sections *On Nature* concerned with the explanations and descriptions of the various forms of life, the influences of the elements on their natures, and the interdependence of those forms of life on one another. A second and smaller group of eight fragments (63-70) is concerned with embryology and is self-explanatory even if it poses interesting and unanswered questions.

(Frg.63) But the substance of (*the child's*) limbs is divided (*between them*), part in the man's (*body and part in the woman's*).

(Frg.64) Upon him comes Desire also, reminding him through sight.

(Frg.65) And they (*male and female seed*) were poured into pure parts. Some of it forms women, (*namely*) that which has encountered Cold, (*and conversely that which encounters Hot produces males*).

(Frg.66) The divided meadows of Aphrodite.

(Frg.67) For in the warmer part the stomach (*i.e., the womb*) is productive of the male, and for this reason men are swarthy and more powerfully built and more shaggy.

(Frg.68) On the tenth day of the eighth month (*the blood*) becomes a white putrefaction (*milk*).

(Frg.69) Double-bearing: (*women, as bearing in both the seventh and ninth months*).

(Frg.70) Sheepskin: (*the membrane, or caul, round the unborn child*).

(Frg.153a) In seven times seven days (the unborn child is *found*).

F. *Epistemology*

Before we can take up Empedocles' general theory of perception and of sight, smell and hearing in particular, his theory of effluences, emanations, or images must be considered. In commentary upon,

(Frg.89) Realising that from all created things there are effluences, . . .

Plutarch writes:

T84   Plutarch *Quaest. Nat.* 19. 916d [K&R343]
Consider the matter in Empedocles words, 'knowing that there are effluences of all things that came into being.' Not only animals and plants and earth and sea, but also stones and brass and iron continuously give off many a stream; for everything is worn away and perishes from continual motion of a ceaseless flux.

Some commentators explain the existence of effluences in terms of the power of Strife to break down continually what was thoroughly mixed. It has also been suggested that the Empedoclean view that like knows or perceives like is possible only because of the separation out and aggregation of the four elements under Strife. It is possible to become one with the divine under Love, but knowing the divine requires the force of Strife. As we shall presently see, both are needed for the salvation of the soul.

The phenomena referred to in the following fragments are either explained by the theory of effluences and the like-to-like doctrine or are exemplifications of it.

(Frg.90) Thus sweet seized on sweet, bitter rushed towards bitter, sour moved towards sour, and hot settled upon hot.

(Frg.91) (*Water is*) more able to agree with wine, but unwilling (*to mix*) with oil.

(Frg.92) (*The sterility of mules is due to the quality of their seed: both the male and female seed are soft substances which when mixed produce a hard substance, as when*) brass is mixed with tin.

(Frg.93) The berry of the grey elder mingles with the linen.

(Frg.101) Tracking down with its nostrils the portions of animal limbs, all those (*portions*) that, when living, they left behind from their feet on the tender grass.*

(Frg.109) We see Earth by means of Earth, Water by means of Water, divine air by means of Air, and destructive Fire by means of Fire; Affection by means of Affection, Hate by means of baneful Hate.

(Frg.109a) (*Reflections are emanations onto the mirror from the objects mirrored.*)

It is by virtue of the Fire in the eye that we are able to see. According to Empedocles' theory, both eye and object are active, fiery rays from the eye mingling with effluences from the object. In fragment 84, below, sight is explained not too clearly by the fact that the tissues of the fire-containing pupils allow fire out but keep the water surrounding the pupil from coming in. The commentary by Theophrastus explains this, again not too clearly, in terms of pores or passageways throughout the body, suitably sized to the sense involved.

(Frg.84) As when a man, thinking to make an excursion through a stormy night, prepares a lantern, a flame of burning fire, fitting lantern-plates to keep out every sort of winds, and these plates disperse the breath of the blowing winds; but the light leaps out through them, in so far as it is finer, and shines across the threshold with unwearying beams: so at that time did the aboriginal Fire, confined in membranes and in fine tissues, hide itself in the round pupils; and these (*tissues*) were pierced throughout with marvellous passages. They kept out the deep reservoir of water surrounding the pupil, but let the Fire through (*from within*) outwards, since it was so much finer.

T85   Theophrastus *De Sensu* 7 [K&R343]

Empedocles has the same theory about all the senses maintaining that perception arises when something fits into the passages of any of the senses. So one sense cannot judge the objects of another, since the passages of some are too wide, of others too narrow, for the object perceived, so that some

---

*The hunting dog is referred to.

things pass straight through without making contact while others cannot enter at all.

Even though vision occurs because like attracts like, nevertheless, as Frgs. 85-88 make clear, it is Aphrodite (Love) who makes the different elements blend to form eyes or any of the other parts of things. Frg.94 is perhaps part of his attempt to explain the nature of our perception of color on the same theory. Frg. 99 characterizes the ear as a bell for receiving the appropriate effluences, and we have already seen in Frg. 101† how the understanding of smells is based upon the same doctrine.

(Frg.85) But the benevolent flame (*of the eye*) happened to obtain only a slight admixture of earth.

(Frg.86) Out of which (*Elements*) divine Aphrodite built tireless eyes.

(Frg.87) Aphrodite, having fastened them (*eyes*) together with clamps of affection.

(Frg.88) One vision is produced by both (*eyes*).

(Frg.94) And the black colour in the bottom of a river arises from the shadow, and the same thing is seen in deep caves.

(Frg.95) When first they (*the eyes*) grew together in the hands of Cypris. . .(*explanation of why some creatures see better by day, others by night*).

(Frg.99) (*The ear is a kind of*) bell. (*It is*) a fleshy shoot.

Equally as interesting is Empedocles' view that the seat of thinking is not in the head but in the heart, and that it is an affair of the blood. Theophrastus sets the context for the relevant fragments.

T86 Theophrastus *De Sensu* 9. [K&R344]
And he has the same theory about wisdom and ignorance. Wisdom is of like by like, ignorance of unlike by unlike, wisdom being either identical with or closely akin to perception. For having enumerated how we know each thing by its equivalent, he added at the end that 'out of these things are all things fitted together and constructed, and by these do they think and feel pleasure and pain'. So it is especially with the blood that they think; for in the blood above all other parts the elements are blended.

(Frg.104) And in so far as the rarest things came together in their fall. . .

(Frg.105) (*The heart*) nourished in the seas of blood which courses in two opposite directions: this is the place where is

---

†See p. 158.

found for the most part what men call Thought; for the
blood round the heart is Thought in mankind.

(Frg.103) Thus all (*creatures*) have intelligence, by the will of
Fortune.

(Frg.107) For from these (*Elements*) are all things fitted and
fixed together, and by means of these do men think, and feel
pleasure and sorrow.

(Frg.106) The intelligence of Man grows towards the material that is present.

(Frg.108) Insofar as their natures have changed (*during the
day*), so does it befall men to think changed thoughts (*in
their dreams*).

For those of us brought up on the distinction in kind between mind and
body, thought and feeling, Empedocles' view is a strange one, but if man
is one organism, then something not completely unlike this view of
Empedocles might well provide a more unified view than we now
possess. On this view, thought, consciousness, and awareness of sensation are very closely connected. Most of us would agree with Frg. 103 if
"sentience" were substitued for "intelligence"; but upon reflection, the
line between the two is not easily drawn. Whatever its limitations,
thought and feeling are inseparably grounded together at their base in
the whole organism via the blood. This suggests that awareness of
conciousness is an active force—"the intelligence of man grows towards
the material that is present"—throughout the creature, and that the
sense organs are avenues for the reaching out of consciousness and
intelligence rather than passive receivers of sense data. This is not far
from the contemporary view that thought is intentional.

Before concluding this section, we turn to what is undoubtedly one of
the most fascinating of the Empedoclean passages. It deals with respiration. As the blood goes from center to circumference of the body and
back again, air is pushed out and sucked in, alternately. In a closed
system with no void, such as the cosmos of Empedocles, it is a reasonable account.

(Frg.100) The way everything breathes in and out is as
follows: all (*creatures*) have tubes of flesh, empty of blood,
which extend over the surface of the body; and at the mouths
of these tubes the outer-most surface of the skin is perfo-
rated with frequent pores, so as to keep in the blood while a
free way is cut for the passage of the air. Thus, when the thin
blood flows back from here, the air, bubbling, rushes in a
mighty wave; and when the blood leaps up (*to the surface*),
there is an expiration of air. As when a girl, playing with a
water-catcher of shining brass—when, having placed the

mouth of the pipe on her well-shaped hand she dips the vessel into the yielding substance of silvery water, still the volume of air pressing from inside on the many holes keeps out the water, until she uncovers the condensed stream (*of air*). Then at once when the air flows out, the water flows in in an equal quantity. Similarly, when water occupies the depths of the brazen vessel, and the opening or passage is stopped by the human flesh (*hand*), and the air outside, striving to get in, checks the water, by controlling the surface at the entrance of the noisey strainer until she lets go with her hand: then again, in exactly the opposite way from what happened before, as the air rushes in, the water flows out in equal volume. Similarly when the thin blood, rushing through the limbs, flows back into the interior, straightway a stream of air flows in with a rush; and when the blood flows up again, again there is a breathing-out in equal volume.

(Frg.102) Thus all (*creatures*) have a share of breathing and smell.

The device used by the girl referred to by Empedocles in Frg. 100 is called a clepsydra, and his reference to it has been interpreted by some to indicate that he was here availing himself of an experiment in the modern sense. Whether this is a legitimate conclusion or whether Empedocles was merely illustrating his view by appealing to an item of common experience will be left to the reader to judge.

With all of these ideas in mind, it is evident that it was not merely poetic license that moves Empedocles to tell Pausanias to "grasp (these things), when my reasoned argument has been sifted in your innermost heart," (Frg. 4), "to protect it within your silent bosom" (Frg. 5), and in, Frg. 15, to say "a wise man would not conjecture such things in his heart". Empedocles' epistemology also makes clearer the sense in which he defends the senses as bearers of knowledge, and yet distinguishes the appearances of sense and the truth of reason.

(Frg.111) You shall learn all the drugs that exist as a defense against illness and old age; for you alone will I accomplish all this. You shall check the force of the unwearying winds which rush upon the earth with their blasts and lay waste the cultivated fields. And again, if you wish, you shall conduct the breezes back again. You shall create a seasonable dryness after the dark rain for mainkind, and again you shall create after summer drought the streams that nourish the trees and (which will flow in the sky). And you shall bring out of Hades a dead man restored to strength.

Whether Empedocles is speaking literally or figuratively in the above fragment, the point is that the divine wisdom which Pausanias was in a position to receive will be efficacious in this world even as the knowledge of Empedocles has been recognized and used in the world (Frg. 12).†More important still, the individual must retain this wisdom as the way of salvation against the normal preoccupations and "miserable trifles" of man.

> (Frg.110) If you press them (*these truths?*) deep into your firm mind, and contemplate them with good will and a studious care that is pure, these things will all assuredly remain with you throughout your life; and you will obtain many other things from them; for these things of themselves cause each (*element*) to increase in the character, according to the way of each man's nature. But if you intend to grasp after different things such as dwell among men in countless numbers and blunt their thoughts, miserable (*trifles*), certainly these things will quickly desert you in the course of time, longing to return to their own original kind. For all things, be assured, have intelligence and a portion of Thought.

THE PURIFICATIONS

The last quoted, Frgs. 110 and 111, from the *On Nature* are freighted with the religious meaning found in the *Purifications* to which we now turn. Of course, the question remains how there can be a stable soul to be saved if all is a continuous mixing. Perhaps the best introduction to the religious views of the *Purifications* is through those fragments in which Empedocles talks about his own situation. It will be recalled that in Frg. 112‡, after giving greetings to the people of Acragas, Empedocles says: "I go about among you as an immortal god, no longer a mortal, held in honour by all, as I seem (to them to deserve), crowned with fillets and flowering garlands." And he is beseeched by countless people for "the path to advantage, some desiring oracles" or a "word of healing."

> (Frg.113) But why do I lay stress on these things, as if I were achieving something great in that I surpass mortal men who are liable to many forms of destruction?

> (Frg.114) Friends, I know that Truth is present in the story that I shall tell; but it is actually very difficult for men, and the impact of conviction on their minds is unwelcome.

†See p. 142.
‡See p. 139.

(Frg.115) There is an oracle of Necessity, an ancient decree of the gods, eternal, sealed fast with broad oaths, that when one of the divine spirits whose portion is long life sinfully stains his own limbs with bloodshed, and following Hate has sworn a false oath—these must wander for thrice ten thousand seasons far from the company of the blessed, being born throughout the period into all kinds of mortal shapes, which exchange one hard way of life for another. For the mighty Air chases them into the Sea, and the Sea spews them forth onto the dry land, and the Earth (*drives them*) towards the rays of the blazing Sun; and the Sun hurls them into the eddies of the Aether. One (*Element*) receives them from the other, and all loathe them. Of this number am I too now, a fugitive from heaven and a wanderer, because I trusted in raging Hate.

(Frg.117) For by now I have been born as boy, girl, plant, bird, and dumb sea-fish.

(Frg.118) I wept and wailed when I saw the unfamiliar land (*at birth*).

The key appears in Frg. 115 where we read "that when one of the divine spirits whose portion is long life sinfully stains his own limbs with bloodshed" and ends with "Of this number am I too now." This certainly indicates his own special nature. But in the light of the phrase in Frg.113, "as if I were achieving something great in that I surpass mortal men," coupled with the invitation to wisdom which *On Nature* extends to Pausanias, Empedocles appears to regard all men as more or less in the same predicament and as having the same opportunity. He certainly did not write the *Purifications* for a select few, but to the people of Acragas. Only in this light do the next two fragments make sense.

(Frg.146) And at the last they become seers, and bards, and physicians, and princes among earth-dwelling men, from which (*state*) they blossom forth as gods highest in honour.

(Frg.147) Sharing the hearth of the other immortals, sharing the same table, freed from the lot of human griefs, indestructible.

Although it is not specifically affirmed, there are enough points of similarity between the condition outlined in Frgs. 146 and 147 and the following fragments telling the condition from which Empedocles was "exiled" to suggest that the former condition represents a return from exile and a fulfillment.

(Frg.119) How great the honour, how deep the happiness from which (*I am exiled*)!

(Frg.128) And for them there was no god Ares, nor Battle-Din, nor Zeus the King, nor Cronos nor Poseidon, but only Cypris the Queen. These men sought to please her with pious gifts—with painted animals and perfumes of cunningly-devised smell, with sacrifice of unmixed myrrh and of fragrant incense, and by casting libations of yellow honey on the ground. And the altar was not drenched with the unmixed blood of bulls, but this was the greatest pollution among men, to devour the goodly limbs (*of animals*) whose life they had reft from them.

(Frg.129) There was living among them a man of surpassing knowledge, who had acquired the extremest wealth of the intellect, one expert in every kind of skilled activity. For whenever he reached out with his whole intellect, he easily discerned each one of existing things, in ten and even twenty lifetimes of mankind.

(Frg.130) And all creatures, both animals and birds, were tame and gentle towards men, and friendliness glowed between them.

The condition of this fulfillment will be inquired into presently, but first the fragments concerned with the nature of the divine.

(Frg.131) If for the sake of any mortal, immortal Muse, it has pleased thee that my poetic endeavours should be of concern to thee, now once again, in answer to my prayer, stand beside me, Calliopeia, as I expound a good theory concerning the blessed gods!

(Frg.132) Happy is he who has acquired the riches of divine thoughts, but wretched the man in whose mind dwells an obscure opinion about the gods!

(Frg.133) It is not possible to bring God near within reach of our eyes, nor to grasp him with our hands, by which route the broadest road of Persuasion runs into the human mind.

(Frg.134) For he is not equipped with a human head on his body, nor from his back do two branches start; (*he has*) no feet, no swift knees, no hairy genital organs; but he is Mind, holy and ineffable, and only Mind, which darts through the whole universe with its swift thoughts.

(Frg.135) But that which is lawful for all extends continously through the broad ruling Air and through the boundless Light.

We have already seen that the shedding of blood caused the original fall (Frg. 115). The following fragments detail this primal sin:

(Frg.136) Will ye not cease from this harsh-sounding slaughter? Do you not see that you are devouring one another in the thoughtlessness of your minds?

(Frg.137) The father having lifted up the son slaughters him with a prayer, in his great folly. But they are troubled at sacrificing one who begs for mercy. But he, on the other hand, deaf to (*the victim's*) cries, slaughters him in his halls and prepares the evil feast. Likewise son takes father, and children their mother, and tearing out the life, eat the flesh of their own kin.

(Frg.138) Having drained off their life with bronze...

(Frg.145) Therefore you are distraught with dire sins, and shall never ease your heart of your grievous sorrows!

And Empedocles gives a graphic picture of the fate of each Hate-choosing soul. The last three fragments of the next group, 125–127, indicate some of the forms such souls assume.

(Frg.120) 'We have come into this roofed cavern.' (*Spoken by those who escort the souls to Earth*).

(Frg.121) The joyless land where are Murder and Wrath and the tribes of other Dooms, and Wasting Diseases and Corruptions and the Works of Dissolution wander over the Meadow of Disaster in the darkness.

(Frg.122) Here were the Earth-Mother (Chthoniê) and the far-seeing Sunshine-Nymph (Hêliopê), bloody Discord, and Harmony with her serious mien, Beauty and Ugliness, the Speed-Nymph and the Nymph of Delay; and lovely Infallibility and dark-eyed Uncertainty.

(Frg.123) (*The female figures*) Growth and Decay, Rest and Waking, Movement and Immobility, much-crowned Majesty, and Defilement, Silence and Voice.

(Frg.124) Alas, oh wretched race of mortals, direly unblessed! Such are the conflicts and groanings from which you have been born!

(Frg.125) For from living creatures he made them dead, changing their forms, (*and from dead, living*).

(Frg.126) (*A female divinity*) clothing (*the soul*) in the unfamiliar tunic of flesh.

(Frg.127) In the (*realm of*) animals they become lions that have their lair in the mountains, and their bed on the ground; and in (*the realm of*) fair-tressed trees, (*they become*) laurels.

In distinctly Pythagorean fashion Empedocles recommends certain matters of diet and ritual abstinence as the means of purification.

(Frg.139) (*Hymn of repentance for sins of diet*): 'Alas that a pitiless day did not destroy me before I planned evil deeds of eating with my lips!'

(Frg.140) Keep entirely away from laurel-leaves!

(Frg.141) Wretches, utter wretches, keep your hands off beans!

(Frg.144) To fast from sin.

But certainly ritual purification is only one part of the whole cycle and perhaps only a necessary condition for salvation. The inescapable conclusion from the fragments is that the principle means of purification is the attainment of knowledge and wisdom. This is the very heart of the Pythagorean teaching, that the soul is purified through knowledge. From this point of view, *On Nature* is seen to be as specifically religious a document in purpose as the *Purifications*, with the ultimate cleansing coming through the understanding of the processes of nature. The divine laws which apply to all creation are distinguished from local and passing human custom (Frg.139). The former are grasped by men in "long-sighted thoughts" (Frg.11). It is by knowing that we are reunited with the One. There is a distinct parallel between the Love-Strife cycle of the macrocosm and the contamination-purification cycle of the human microcosm. Perhaps this is the only answer to the problem of how a stable soul could possible be an entity in the cosmic cycle.

Returning to the theme of the relation of Empedocles' thought to that of Parmenides, it will be recalled that Empedocles does not deny apparent change. The Empedoclean One is more Pythagorean than Parmenidean in that it is the source of the Change and the Many of experience. But even the One is really a Many in that the four Roots are harmoniously mixed but not homogenized in the One. These Roots are each conceived in Parmenidean fashion, that is, as unchanging, and the changes that appear under the force of Love and Strife in the cycle of One to Many and back again are really only quantitative alterations in the proportions of these Roots. This explanation of appearance in terms of reality gives reality to appearance, and under no pretext is one supposed to ignore experience or what the senses tell us, although the wise man will understand (go beyond) the flux of experience. It is this activity which purifies the Soul and helps complete the cycle of return to the One.

For the sake of completeness, the following fragments are presented. They do not seem to fit anywhere.

(Frg.10) Death the Avenger.

(Frg.18) Love (*Philia*).*

(Frg.19) Adhesive Love (*Philotês*).**

(Frg.24) Touching on summit after summit, not to follow a single path of discourse to the end.

(Frg.25) For what is right can well be uttered even twice.

(Frg.32) The joint connects two things.

(Frg.33) As when fig-juice binds white milk.

(Frg.34) Having kneaded together barley-meal with water.

(Frg.49) Of night, lonely, blind-eyed.

(Frg.50) Iris brings from the sea a wind or a great rain-storm.

(Frg.97) The spine (acquired its present form by being broken when the animal turned its neck).

(Frg.116) (*The Grace*) loathes intolerable Necessity.

(Frg.142) Him will the roofed palace of aegis-bearing Zeus never receive, nor yet the roof of Hades and of the piteous voice.

(Frg.143) (*Wash the hands*) cutting off (*water*) from five springs into (*a vessel of*) enduring bronze.

(Frg.149) Cloud-gathering Air.

(Frg.150) Full-blooded liver.

(Frg.151) Life-giving Aphrodite.

(Frg.152) (*Old age, the evening of life; evening, the old age of the day: a similar metaphor in Empedocles*).

(Frg.153) Baubô.***

---

*Love in the widest sense, not merely *Eros*.
**Quoted by Plutarch to show that Empedocles does not use epithets idly for the sake of fine writing, but in order to bring out the exact nature or function of something.
***Connected with Demeter in Orphic mythology; said to have been used by Empedocles to mean "belly."

NOTES

1. Winspear, p. 116.
2. Diogenes Laertius 8. 57.
3. *Ibid.*, 77.
4. Kirk & Raven, p. 323.
5. Aristotle *Meta.* 985a4.
6. *Ibid.*, 1000a26.
7. Kirk & Raven, pp. 336-9.

CHAPTER 8

Anaxagoras

Anaxagoras, a native of Clazomenae, was in his prime about 460 B.C. Clazomenae is in Ionia and Anaxagoras is in the Ionian tradition. Living in Athens for thirty years, he was an intimate associate of Pericles, and brought the fruits of the Ionian tradition to Athens in her Golden Age. Because Diogenes Laertius attributes but one book to Anaxagoras,[1] and because in Plato's *Apology*, Socrates disparagingly mentions that Anaxagoras' work was available for but a drachma (a small sum) in the "orchestra",[2] Kirk & Raven conclude that it must have been fairly short, the fragments we possess constituting at least an eighth of the original.[3] Anaxagoras was motivated by a purely scientific curiosity uncomplicated by any of the mysticism that characterized Empedocles' approach to philosophy; he consequently found prose rather than verse the most suitable vehicle of expression. Diogenes Laertius, the source of much of our information concerning him, also provides some further important details and anecdotal material:

> **T87**   Diogenes Laertius 2. 3. 6–8, 12–14. [Loeb]
> Anaxagoras, the son of Hegesibulus or Eubulus, was a native of Clazomenae....He was eminent for wealth and noble birth, and furthermore for magnanimity, in that he gave up his patrimony to his relations. For when they accused him of neglecting it, he replied, "Why then do you not look after it?" And at last he went into retirement and engaged in physical investigations without troubling himself about public affairs. When someone inquired, "Have you no

concern in your native land?" "Gently," he replied, "I am greatly concerned with my fatherland," and pointed to the sky.

He is said to have been twenty years old at the invasion of Xerxes and to have lived seventy-two years. Apollodorus in his *Chronology* says that he was born in the 70th Olympiad [500-497 B.C.] and died in the first year of the 88th Olympiad [428 B.C.]. He began to study philosophy at Athens ...when he was twenty and at Athens they say he remained for thirty years....

Of the trial of Anaxagoras different accounts are given. Sotion in his *Succession of the Philosophers* says that he was indicted by Cleon on a charge of impiety, because he declared the sun to be a mass of red-hot metal: that his pupil Pericles defended him, and he was fined five talents and banished. Satyrus in his *Lives* says that the prosecutor was Thucydides, the opponent of Pericles, and the charge one of treasonable correspondence with Persia as well as of impiety; and that sentence of death was passed on Anaxagoras by default. When news was brought him that he was condemned...his comment on the sentence was, "Long ago nature condemned both my judges and myself to death" ....Hermippus in his *Lives* says that he was confined in the prison pending his execution; that Pericles came forward and asked the people whether they had any fault to find with him in his own public career; to which they replied that they had not. "Well," he continued, "I am a pupil of Anaxagoras; do not then be carried away by slanders and put him to death. Let me prevail upon you to release him." So he was released; but he could not brook the indignity he had suffered and committed suicide.

Aristotle relates that Anaxagoras was older than Empedocles, though "later in his philosophical activity...,"† and the closeness of association between Anaxagoras and Pericles is also attested to by Plato:

T88 Plato *Phaedrus* 270a[4]
All the great arts need supplementing by a study of nature; your artist must cultivate garrulity and high-flown speculation; from that source alone can come the mental elevation and thoroughly finished execution of which you are thinking, and that is what Pericles acquired to supplement his inborn capacity. He came across the right sort of man, I fancy, in Anaxagoras, and by enriching himself with high

---

†See T63, p. 139.

speculation and coming to recognize the nature of wisdom and folly—on which topics of course Anaxagoras was always discoursing—he drew from that source and applied to the art of rhetoric what was suitable thereto.

RELATION TO PARMENIDES AND ZENO

Anaxagoras' ontology can best be understood in the context of the thought of Parmenides and Zeno. Parmenides had denied that "what is" can come from "what is not." Anaxagoras agreed: what is commonly called coming into being and passing away is really only the mixing together and separation of a plurality of unchanging constituents.

> (Frg.17) The Greeks have an incorrect belief on Coming into Being and Passing Away. No Thing comes into being or passes away, but is mixed together or separated from existing Things. Thus they would be correct if they called coming into being 'mixing', and passing away 'separation-off.'

> (Frg.10) How can hair come from not-hair, and flesh from not-flesh?

Anaxagoras applies the logic of Parmenides even more stringently than Empedocles, for whom substances other than fire, air, earth and water could come into being and pass away through mixing and separation. For Anaxagoras, all substances assumed the status of Empedocles' four elements. How is this possible? The answer is that for Anaxagoras the unchanging constituents are infinitely great in number, each being infinitely divisible. Each thing of common sense experience is further assumed to possess some proportion of every constituent and in this sense everything is in everything (Frg. 6)—in the hot something of the cold, and in the cold something of the hot, for example (Frg. 8). Aristotle amplifies this last point:

> **T89** Aristotle *Phys.* 187b2–6
> But things, as they say, appear different from one another and receive different names according to the nature of the particles which are numerically predominant among the innumerable constituents of the mixture. For nothing, they say, is purely and entirely white or black or sweet, bone or flesh, but the nature of the thing is held to be that of which it contains the most.

These assumptions concerning the character of the unchanging constituents and the composition of the changing composites permit Anaxagoras to maintain that each thing (composite as well as constituent, it would seem) is both infinitely great and infinitely small. Each thing is infinitely great in that it contains an infinity of kinds of constituents and/or an infinity of parts; each thing is infinitely small in that the constituents are in all cases infinitely divisible. Herein we have Anaxagoras' answer to Zeno, who had regarded simultaneous infinite greatness and infinite smallness as a *reductio ad absurdum* of pluralism. Anaxagoras' justification of the infinite divisibility of things in Frg. 3 because "it is impossible that Being should not Be" is a particularly apt application of Eleatic logic.

(Frg.3) For in Small there is no Least, but only a Lesser: for it is impossible that Being should Not-Be;* and in Great there is always a Greater. And it is equal in number to the small, but each thing is to itself both great and small.

(Frg.6) And since there are equal (*quantitative*) parts of Great and Small, so too similarly in everything there must be everything. It is not possible (*for them*) to exist apart, but all things contain a portion of everything. Since it is not possible for the Least to exist, it cannot be isolated, nor come into being by itself; but as it was in the beginning, so now, all things are together. In all things there are many things, and of the things separated off, there are equal numbers in (*the categories*) Great and Small.

(Frg.8) The things in the one Cosmos are not separated off from one another with an axe, neither the Hot from the Cold, nor the Cold from the Hot.

Frg. 8 can be interpreted to mean either that the hot and cold as constituents are in everything, thus not separated from one another in this sense; or that the hot and cold as observed both contain hot and cold constituents, differing only in the differing proportions of hot and cold in each.

HOMOEOMERISM

A point of some controversy with respect to Anaxagoras' ontology concerns the idea of "homoeomerism," which appears often in Aristotle's comments on Anaxagoras and in subsequent commentators as well. According to one such reference of Aristotle,

T90 Aristotle *De Gen. et Corr.* 314a19-21

Anaxagoras posits as elements the 'homoeomeries' viz. bone, flesh, marrow, and everything else which is such that part and whole are the same in name and nature.

---

*τό μή was emended by Zeller to τομῆ, which Burnet accepts: 'it cannot be that what is should cease to be by being cut.'

The difficulty is that his notion conflicts with the contention of Frg. 6 that "in everything there must be everything." If the constituents of things are homoeomeries, all the parts of a bone for example would have to be pieces of bone; on the view of Frg. 6, a bone as a changing composite would have to contain some proportion of each of the infinite number of unchanging constituents. One solution adopted by Cornford, Tannery and Burnet, among others,[5] is to assume that when Anaxagoras maintains that everything is in everything he is speaking only of opposites such as hot-cold, wet-dry, dense-rare, bright-dark, which he indeed does mention in Frgs. 4, 8, 12, 15 and 16. Guthrie and Kirk & Raven, on the other hand, both find this solution unsatisfactory.[6] Guthrie argues that it is unlikely that Anaxagoras himself ever used the Greek word *homoiomere* and that:

> All that Aristotle is doing is to indicate what sort of sub-
> stances Anaxagoras regarded as elemental, and this he can
> do most simply by saying that they are the substances which
> *he himself* [i.e., Aristotle] calls homoeomerous; and to
> remove any shadow of doubt he adds examples—flesh,
> bone, marrow, etc.[7]

The implication intended is not only that what Aristotle calls homoeomeries, viz., flesh, bone and marrow, are, for Anaxagoras, elements, but that Anaxagoras' elements have the characteristic of what Aristotle calls homoeomeries. This view remains consistent with the notion that the expression "in everything there must be everything" really refers to everything and not just to opposites.

In Frg. 11, Anaxagoras distinguishes Mind from all other things—it alone is unmixed with anything else:

> (Frg. 11) In everything there is a portion of everything except
> Mind; and some things contain Mind also.

This distinction, as well as what Anaxagoras will say about Mind in subsequent fragments, is the basis for marking a separation between his theory of matter and his theory of Mind. Like Empedocles, though a pluralist with regard to his theory of matter, Anaxagoras is yet a dualist in distinguishing matter from the driving force of the universe—as is suggested by Theophrastus.

> **T91**   Theophrastus *Phys. Op.* Frg. 4 *ap.* Simplicium *Phys.*
> 27. 17. [K&R375]
> Anaxagoras would appear to make his material principles
> infinite, but the cause of motion and coming into being one
> only, namely Mind. But if we were to suppose that the
> mixture of all things was a single substance, indefinite both
> in form and in extent, then it follows that he is really

affirming two first principles only, namely the substance of the infinite and Mind.

A DESCRIPTIVE ACCOUNT OF ANAXAGORAS' COSMOGONY AND COSMOLOGY: IMPLICATIONS OF HIS THEORY OF MATTER

So far, consideration has been given to Anaxagoras' theory of matter. The implications of this theory of matter will be pursued in the immediately ensuing descriptive account of his cosmogony and cosmology. An examination of the dynamics of this cosmogony and cosmology will follow, for Mind, on Anaxagoras' view, is the ultimate moving force of all that occurs.

The Ionian orientation of Anaxagoras becomes evident in his cosmogony. He assumes, as did Anaximander, that the world as we know it once came from one primeval, undifferentiated mass through a process of rotation.†

(Frg.1) (*Opening sentences from his book 'On Natural Science'*): All Things* were together, infinite in number and in smallness. For the Small also was infinite. And since all were together, nothing was distinguishable because of its smallness. For Air and Aether dominated all things, both of them being infinite. For these are the most important (*Elements*) in the total mixture, both in number and in size.

(Frg.2) Air and Aether are separated off from the surrounding multiplicity, and that which surrounds is infinite in number.

(Frg.7) So that the number of the things separated off cannot be known either in thought or in fact.

(Frg.15) The dense and moist and cold and dark (*Elements*) collected here, where now is Earth, and the rare and hot and dry went outwards to the furthest part of the Aether.

(Frg.16) From these, while they are separating off, Earth solidifies; for from the clouds, water is separated off, and from the water, earth, and from the earth, stones are solidified by the cold; and these rush outward rather than the water.

(Frg.5) These things being thus separated off, one must understand that all things are in no wise less or more (for it is

---

†There is reference to "revolution" in Frgs. 12 and 13, and the term "circulate" is used in Frg. 9. See p. 178.

*Where χρήματα is used, 'Things' is spelled with a capital. See *Companion*, pp. 266-7.

not possible for them to be more than All), but all things are
forever equal (*in quantity*).

UNDIFFERENTIATED CHARACTER OF THE ORIGINAL MIXTURE, AND ANAXAGORAS' "SEEDS"

In the following portion of Frg. 4, Anaxagoras both develops a point
made in Frg. 1 to the effect that "since all were together, nothing was
distinguishable...," and makes mention of an infinite number of
"seeds" in the original mixture. The term "seeds" was one much used by
later commentators in describing Anaxagoras' position, though it
appears to be in conflict with his advocacy of the infinite divisibility of
all constituents.

> (Frg.4§2) Before these things were separated off, all things
> were together, nor was any colour distinguishable, for the
> mixing of all Things prevented this, (*namely*) the mixing of
> moist and dry and hot and cold and bright and dark, and
> there was a great quantity of earth in the mixture, and seeds
> infinite in number, not at all like one another. For none of
> the other things either is like any other. And as this was so,
> one must believe that all Things were present in the Whole.

Aristotle analyzes with some approval Anaxagoras' position with
respect to the indistinguishability or undifferentiated character of the
primeval mixture:

T92   Aristotle *Meta.* 989b6–15
For when nothing was separated out, evidently nothing
could be truly asserted of the substance that then existed. I
mean, e.g., that it was neither white nor black, nor grey nor
any other colour, but of necessity colourless; for if it had
been coloured, it would have had one of these colours. And
similarly, by this same argument, it was flavourless, nor had
it any similar attribute; for it could not be either of any
quality or of any size, nor could it be any definite kind of
thing. For if it were, one of the particular forms would have
belonged to it, and this is impossible, since all were mixed
together; for the particular form would necessarily have
been already separated out.

Guthrie, in attempting to reconcile the notion of "seeds" with infinite
divisibility, interprets the notion of "seeds" to convey the "remarkably
mature conception of different kinds of matter as retaining, in however
small a quantity, the same infinite number of ingredients in unchanging
proportions."[8] In a note to this interpretation he adds:

The infinity of ingredients in the same unequal proportions in any portion of matter, however small, is the cornerstone of his (i.e., Anaxagoras') cosmology, for it ensures that even in the original fusion, however large or small a portion to be taken, there is the lack of homogeneity which makes possible the later emergence of distinctions in perceptible bulk. The acceptability of the infinite regress (if one likes to call it that) is the great discovery which enables him to parry, and even destroy, the weapons of Zeno.[9]

It should be added that the "conception of different kinds of matter as retaining, in however small a quantity, the same infinite number of ingredients in unchanging proportions" also permits the following three assumptions already attributed to Anaxagoras to be embraced without contradiction: (1) that everything is in everything; (2) that everything as elemental is homoeomerous; and (3) that everything is infinitely divisible. Bone, for example, is in everything insofar as everything contains it in some proportion. At the same time, other things may differ from one another in the proportion of bone that they contain. But no matter how much a piece of bone is divided (even *ad infinitum*), it will still remain bone, and no matter how much anything else is divided, it will still contain bone in the invariable proportion appropriate to it (i.e., both bone and non-bone retain their homoeomerous character). It is clear too that, if Guthrie's interpretation is correct, Empedocles' idea of explaining apparent qualitative differences in terms of quantitative differences relating to a plurality of "things which are" is made more explicit by Anaxagoras.

OTHER WORLDS

In concluding our consideration of Anaxagoras' theory of matter, we direct our attention to the rather odd first half of Frg. 4:

(Frg.4 §1) Conditions being thus, one must believe that there are many things of all sorts in all composite products, and the seeds of all Things, which contain all kinds of shapes and colours and pleasant savours. And men too, were fitted together, and all other creatures which have life. And the men possessed both inhabited cities and artificial works just like ourselves, and they had sun and moon and the rest, just as we have, and the earth produced for them many and diverse things, of which they collected the most useful, and now use them for their dwellings. This I say concerning Separation, that it must have taken place not only with us, but elsewhere.

Did Anaxagoras mean to contend in this fragment that there are other universes besides the one with which we are familiar? Reference to the "one Cosmos" in Frg. 8 would suggest otherwise. Perhaps as Kirk & Raven suggest[10], we had best be guided by Simplicius' caution here:

T93 Simplicius *Phys.* 157. 9 [K&R389]

Having said, however, 'there are many things. . .and tastes' and 'men have been formed. . .have life', he adds 'the men have. . .and use it'. That he is hinting at another world in addition to our own is clear from the phrase, which he uses more than once, 'just as we have'. And that he does not regard this other world as a perceptible world which preceded this world in time is clear from the words 'of which they garner the best into their houses and use it.' For he did not say 'used' but 'use.' Nor does he mean that they are now inhabiting other regions of the same world as our own. For he did not say 'they have the sun and the moon just as we too have' but 'sun and moon, as we have'—as if he were talking of a different sun and moon. But it is debatable whether or not these considerations are valid.†

DYNAMICS OF ANAXAGORAS' COSMOGONY AND COSMOLOGY: HIS THEORY OF MIND

While Empedocles made use of the two nonmaterial principles of Love and Strife in explaining why things happen, Anaxagoras uses the single nonmaterial principle of Mind. To call these explanatory principles "nonmaterial" in the case of either philosopher is something of a half-truth because there was as yet no clear conception of the nonmaterial: Anaxagoras' Mind as well as Empedocles' Love and Strife were still thought of in semi-material terms. In contrast with Empedocles' conception of motion and change as proceeding in an ever-continuing cycle, Anaxagoras, according to Aristotle, thought of it as initiated by Mind from an original state of rest:

T94 Aristotle *Phys.* 250b 25-27

Anaxagoras. . .says that all things were together and at rest for an infinite period of time, and that then Mind introduced motion and separated them.

Not only is Mind the originator of movement for Anaxagoras, but it is also "the finest of all things and the purest and has complete understanding of everything and has the greatest power" (Frg.12). In all of these respects it is reminiscent of Heraclitus' *Logos*—though Anaxago-

---

†Differences in wording between the passages of Anaxagoras, referred to by Simplicius, and the preceding fragment are due to differences in translation.

ras nowhere refers to it as God. The fragments relevant to the functioning of mind in Anaxagoras' cosmogony and cosmology are as follows:

(Frg.12) Other things all contain a part of everything, but Mind is infinite and self-ruling, and is mixed with no Thing, but is alone by itself. If it were not by itself, but were mixed with anything else, it would have had a share of all Things, if it were mixed with anything; for in everything there is a portion of everything, as I have said before. And the things mixed (*with Mind*) would have prevented it, so that it could not rule over any Thing in the same way as it can being alone by itself. For it is the finest of all Things, and the purest, and has complete understanding of everything, and has the greatest power. All things which have life, both the greater and the less, are ruled by Mind. Mind took command of the universal revolution, so as to make (*things*) revolve at the outset. And at first things began to revolve from some small point, but now the revolution extends over a greater area, and will spread even further. And the things which were mixed together, and separated off, and divided, were all understood by Mind. And whatever they were going to be, and whatever things were then in existence that are not now, and all things that now exist and whatever shall exist—all were arranged by Mind, as also the revolution now followed by the stars, the sun and moon, and the Air and Aether which were separated off. It was this revolution which caused the separation off. And dense separates from rare, and hot from cold, and bright from dark, and dry from wet. There are many portions of many things. And nothing is absolutely separated off or divided the one from the other except Mind. Mind is all alike, both the greater and the less. But nothing else is like anything else, but each individual thing is and was most obviously that of which it contains the most.

(Frg.14) Mind, which ever Is, certainly still exists also where all other things are, (*namely*) in the multiple surrounding (*mass*) and in the things which were separated off before, and in the things already separated off.

(Frg.13) And when Mind began the motion, there was a separating-off* from all that was being moved; and all that

---

*"I [Freeman] follow Burnet in taking ἀπεκρίνετο as impersonal; Diels-Kranz make Nous the subject, and translate: 'Mind severed itself from the whole.' But the reference is to three events: the starting of the revolution by Mind; the separation of a portion from the Whole; and the internal sifting under the revolution."

Mind set in motion was separated (*internally*); and as things were moving and separating off (*internally*), the revolution greatly increased this (*internal*) separation.

(Frg.9) Thus these things circulate and are separated off by force and speed. The speed makes the force. Their speed is not like the speed of any of the Things now existing among mankind, but altogether many times as fast.

Frg. 9 suggests a complaint which Plato has Socrates express in the *Phaedo*:

T95 Plato *Phaedo* 97c, 98b[11]

However, I once heard someone reading from a book, as he said, by Anaxagoras, and asserting that it is mind that produces order and is the cause of everything. This explanation pleased me. Somehow it seemed right that mind should be the cause of everything, and I reflected that if this is so, mind in producing order sets everything in order and arranges each individual thing in the way that is best for it. . . .

It was a wonderful hope, my friend, but it was quickly dashed. . . I discovered that the fellow made no use of mind and assigned it to no causality for the order of the world, but adduced causes like air and aether and water and many other absurdities.

It would seem that Socrates' complaint was justified at least to the extent that Anaxagoras, with his Ionian proclivities, was more interested in exploring the operation of mechanical factors than of teleological factors in the cosmic process. Yet the foundations for a teleological analysis are present. Mind is not only the originator of the initial movement but, despite its separation from all else, continues to rule living things (Frg. 12) and "exists also where all other things are" (Frg.14).

SENSATION AND KNOWLEDGE

Theophrastus attributed a theory of sensation to Anaxagoras that is interesting both in its claim that we only perceive through contrast with our own state, and in its association of perception with pain:

T96 Theophrastus *De Sensu* 27ff. [K&R394]

Anaxagoras thinks that perception is by opposites, for like is not affected by like. . . .A thing that is warm or as cold as we are does not either warm us or cool us by its approach, nor can we recognize sweetness or bitterness by their like; rather we know cold by warm, fresh by salt and sweet by bitter in

porportion to our deficiency in each. For everything, he
says, is in us already. . . .Every perception is accompanied by
pain, a consequence that would seem to follow from his
hypotheses; for everything unlike produces pain by its contact; and the presence of this pain becomes clear either from
too long a duration or from an excess of sensation.

Fragments of Anaxagoras giving some clues to his theory of knowledge are as follows:

(Frg.21b) (*We are inferior to the animals in strength and
swiftness*) but we have experience, memory and wisdom and
skill for our use alone (*and so can collect their products*).

(Frg.21) Through the weakness of the sense-perceptions, we
cannot judge truth.

(Frg. 21a) Visible existences are a sight of the unseen (*i.e.,
the present gives a view of the future*).

Frg. 21b suggests Anaxagoras' awareness of the practical utility of
knowledge. The same theme appears in Aristotle's claim that

T97 Aristotle *De Part. Anima.* 687a7
Anaxagoras says, then, that it is his possession of hands that
makes man the wisest of living things.

Frg. 21 shows Anaxagoras to have shared the view of others of the
Pre-Socratics that the senses are not to be trusted, and Sextus, to whom
we owe the fragment, attributes to him the following proof of this view:

T98 Sextus Empiricus *Math.* 7, 9 [Guthrie 2.319]
If we take two colors, black and white, and pour one into the
other drop by drop, our sight will not be able to pick out the
gradual alterations although they exist in reality.

Nevertheless, despite the misleading italicized explanation attached to
Frg. 21a, it is commonly interpreted as applicable to the relation
between sense experience and Anaxagoras' infinity of constituent seeds,
and serves as evidence that he was no sceptic.

PHYSICAL SCIENCE

For Anaxagoras the heavens were not divine; they were but another
field for rational investigation. This is quite evident from an account by
Hippolytus:

T99 Hippolytus *Ref.* 1. 8. 3–10 [K&R391]
The earth (he thinks) is flat in shape, and stays suspended
where it is because of its size, because there is no void and
because the air, which is strong, keeps the earth afloat on it.
(4) Of the moisture on the earth, the sea came from the

waters in the earth, the evaporation of which gave rise to all
that has emerged, and from the rivers that flow into it. (5)
Rivers owe their origin partly to rain, partly to the waters in
the earth; for the earth is hollow, and in its hollows contains
water.... (6) The sun, the moon and all the stars are red-hot
stones which the rotation of the aither carries round with it.
Beneath the stars are certain bodies, invisible to us, that are
carried round with the sun and moon. (7) We do not feel the
heat of the stars because they are so far from the earth;
moreover, they are not as hot as the sun because they occupy
a colder region. The moon is beneath the sun and nearer to
us. (8) The sun exceeds the Peloponnese in size. The moon
has not any light of its own but derives it from the sun. The
stars in their revolution pass beneath the earth. (9) Eclipses
of the moon are due to its being screened by the earth, or,
sometimes, by the bodies beneath the moon; those of the sun
to screening by the moon when it is new.... (10).... He held
that the moon was made of earth, and had plains and ravines
on it.

Some evidence of the detail into which Anaxagoras' investigations in
this area carried him is suggested by the following two fragments:

(Frg.18) It is the sun that endows the moon with its
brilliance.

(Frg.19) We give the name Iris to the reflection of the sun on
the clouds. It is therefore the sign of a storm, for the water
which flows round the cloud produces wind or forces out
rain.

Similarly in biology for the next fragment which supposedly means that
the white of an egg is for the unhatched bird what mother's milk is to a
mammal:

(Frg.22) Bird's milk (*used to mean 'white of egg'*).

A DUBIOUS FRAGMENT

Freeman gives the following account of an apparently dubious fragment which is mentioned only for the sake of completeness.

(Frg.20) (*Translation, purporting to be from Galen's commentary on Hippocrates, into Arabic and then Hebrew. But
it is uncertain if the author quoted in the passage, called
'Ansaros' in Hebrew, is Anaxagoras; some have thought
that the material is from Hesiod. It deals principally with the*

rising and setting of the Pleiads and the seasonal work connected with this period.)

ANAXAGORAS, EMPEDOCLES AND THE ATOMISTS

In summing up Anaxagoras' contributions, the relation of his theory of matter both to Empedocles and the Atomists is of particular interest. While Empedocles attempted to answer the Eleatics by explaining qualitative differences and changes in terms of differing quantitative proportions of the unchanging elements fire, air, earth and water, the status of other than elemental substances was still subject to the Eleatic criticism of how they could have come to be if once they were not. Empedocles' unsatisfactory reply was that, strictly speaking, they do not come to be, but we only speak as if they do (Empedocles' Frg. 9).†
Anaxagoras' view that all is in all not only retains Empedocles' derivation of qualitative difference from difference in quantity, but also meets the Eleatic criticism by assuming that there never was a time when any substance was not. All substances are equally elemental, differing from one another only in the proportion of other substances that they and their homoeomerous parts contain, no matter how far divided. In affirming the infinite divisibility of all substances, Anaxagoras differed from Empedocles as well as from the Atomists. And in making differences in quality a function of differences in quantity he at the same time does not reduce them to quantitative differences as do the Atomists— and as did even Empedocles for nonelemental qualities. For Anaxagoras, every qualitative difference is as much a part of the nature of things as is its quantitative explanation. On the other hand, while for Empedocles there is a difficulty concerning the reality status of nonelemental qualities, for the Atomists there is an embarassment with respect to all qualities not attributable to quantitatively describable atoms. If Anaxagoras' theory of matter represents an ingenious alternative on this score, he is also more contemporary than the Atomists in simultaneously embracing teleological and mechanical explanation. Whereas the Atomists insist that all causation is by blind (i.e., purposeless) necessity, present day Cyberneticists find nothing at all contradictory in the study of purposive mechanisms.

---

†See p. 143.

NOTES

1. Diogenes Laertius 1. 16.
2. Plato *Apology* 26d.

3. Kirk & Raven, p. 365.

4. Plato, *Plato's Phaedrus,* trans. R. Hackforth (Cambridge: Cambridge University Press, 1952).

5. Guthrie vol. 2. p. 284; Kirk & Raven, p. 367.

6. *Ibid.*; Kirk & Raven, pp. 376 and 381.

7. Guthrie, vol. 2, p. 283.

8. Guthrie, vol. 2, p. 298.

9. *Ibid.*, vol 2, p. 298, n2.

10. Kirk & Raven, p. 390.

11. Plato, *Plato: The Last Days of Socrates*, rev. ed., trans. Hugh Tredennick (London: Penguin Classics, 1969) pp. 155–156.

CHAPTER 9

The Atomists: Leucippus
And Democritus

Leucippus and Democritus were both from Abdera in Thrace. Leucippus flourished about 430 B.C., and Democritus in approximately 420 B.C. Practically nothing is known of the life of Leucippus; Epicurus and Hermarchus seem even to have denied his existence:

T100 Diogenes Laertius 10. 13 [Loeb]
Both Epicurus and Hermarchus deny the very existence of Leucippus the philosopher, though by some and by Apollodorus the Epicurean he is said to have been the teacher of Democritus.

Though there is no doubt that Democritus existed, the situation with respect to knowledge of his life is but little better than with Leucippus. That he traveled widely is attested to in a spurious fragment,[1] and this is generally agreed to have been the case. There is other anecdotal material that has come down to us, but it is all suspect. Democritus was called the Laughing Philosopher by Cicero and Horace, presumably because this was his reaction to human folly.[2] A good deal of what we know of Democritus' life comes from Diogenes Laertius:

T101 Diogenes Laertius 9. 34, 41 [Loeb]
Democritus was the son of Hegesistratus, though some say of Athenocritus, and others again of Damasippus. He was a native of Abdera or, according to some, of Miletus.... Afterwards he met Leucippus and according to some, Anaxagoras, being forty years younger than the latter.... As

regards chronology, he was, as he says himself in the *Lesser Diacosmos*, a young man when Anaxagoras was old, being forty years his junior. He says that the *Lesser Diacosmos* was compiled 730 years after the capture of Troy. [Frg. 5, 1st part]† According to Apollodorus in his *Cronology* he would thus have been born in the 80th Olympiad [460–547 B.C.], but according to Thrasylus in his pamphlet entitled *Prolegomena to the Reading of the Works of Democritus*, in the third year of the 77th Olympiad [470–469 B.C.], which makes him, adds Thrasylus, one year older than Socrates.

It is generally agreed that Democritus is the author of the *Little World Order* (or *Little World System*) mentioned in the preceding *testimonium*. Another work, the *Great World Order*, was commonly attributed to him in Hellenistic times, but Diogenes Laertius reports that Theophrastus attributed it to Leucippus,[3] and this is the view generally now held. Though the charge of plagiarizing should probably be discounted, the following two fragments mentioning the *Great World Order* appear under Leucippus' name:

(Frg.1) (*Title of book:* The Great World-Order, *here attributed to Democritus*).

(Frg.1a,§1) (*Restoration of Herculanean Papyrus in which Democritus is accused of plagiarising from 'The Great World-Order' of Leucippus*).

Another of Leucippus' fragments‡ is associated with a second work generally credited to him, viz., a work titled "On Mind."

Democritus was a prolific writer, and Thrasyphus, a Roman scholar of the first century A.D., arranged these works in tetralogues, or groups of four, according to subject matter: *Ethics* (Tetralogies 1 and 2); *Natural Science* (3 to 6); *Mathematics* (7 to 9); and *Technical Works* (12 and 13). In addition, there was a group of works titled "Causes," another group of doubtful authenticity on various subjects, a large number of maxims, and some forged works on magic. The unfortunate thing is that none of these works has been preserved and that we are left once more with but fragments. Still more unfortunate is the fact that the fragments dealing with Democritus' natural philosophy, where he contributed most, are but a small proportion of the total and in many cases are but the titles of his works. Despite this sad situation, the number of available fragments is still embarrassingly large when considered in

---

†Freeman's version of Frg.5, 1st part: "(*In the 'Small-World-Order,' Democritus said he was*) a young man in the old age of Anaxagoras. (He said he wrote the book 730 years after the fall of Troy,...).'" The 2nd part of Frg.5 appears on p. 186.
‡Leucippus, Frg.2; see p. 187.

relation to the objective of including all fragments of each thinker in this volume. Although Leucippus' fragments are few in number (three in all) and all appear in this chapter, Freeman supplies 298 supposedly authentic fragments of Democritus. This has necessitated some selection with the following results:

Democritus' Fragments

	Number Appearing in Freeman	Approximate Proportion Appearing in This Book
Relating to:		
Natural Philosophy	68	72%
Ethics	195 ⎫	33%
Politics	35 ⎭	
TOTAL	298	42%

It will be noticed that the proportion of fragments included dealing with natural philosophy is considerably greater than the proportion of ethical and political fragments. This is both because of the greater number of the latter and the greater importance of Democritus' ideas in natural philosophy, even though Democritus' remaining fragments in natural philosophy are fragmentary indeed.

ONTOLOGY: THE ATOMIC THEORY

The atomic theory was first formulated by Leucippus and more fully developed by Democritus.[4] Presumably, most of what is known of Leucippus' views on the subject must have originally come from his book *The Great World-Order*. The second paragraph of Leucippus' Frg. 1a indicates that:

(Frg.1a, §2.) *Certain terms of the Atomic Theory can probably be traced to Leucippus, e.g.,*

> Atoms ('uncuttables').
> Close–pressed (*units*).
> Great Void.
> Absection.
> Rhythm (*meaning 'form'*).
> Contact (*meaning 'arrangement'*).
> Aspect (*meaning 'position'*).
> Entanglement.
> Eddy.

It is difficult to distinguish further the respective contributions of Leucippus and Democritus because in most cases commentators either referred to the two philosophers together or ignored Leucippus entirely.[5] Probably the more general aspects of Democritus' ontology were contained in his book titled: (Frg. 4c) 'Small World-Order', which included, among other things, the claim

> (Frg.5 [2nd part]) (... *that Anaxagoras' views on the sun were not original but ancient, and he* [i.e., Democritus] *ridiculed his views on the arrangment of the universe and on Mind*).†

Mention of Anaxagoras raises the question of the relation of the Atomists to the other pluralists, i.e., to Empedocles and Anaxagoras as well as the Eleatics (Parmenides, Melissus, and Zeno) who set the context for all three pluralist systems. As their very name indicates, the pluralists (including the Atomists) were in agreement in their affirmation of the plurality of Being; of course they all differed from the Eleatics in this respect. On the other hand, the Atomists accepted along with other pluralists the Eleatic stricture on the coming into being and passing away of what is, though at the same time taking the un-Eleatic course of attempting to explain apparent change in terms of unchanging constituents of their own choice. Whereas Empedocles identified "what is" with the four elements, and Anaxagoras spoke of "what is" as composed of an infinity of infinitely divisible "seeds", Leucippus and Democritus presupposed an infinity of indivisible atoms. One contrast of the atoms with Anaxagoras' seeds is of course their indivisibility. Another difference of the atoms not only from Anaxagoras' "seeds" but also from Empedocles' elements (which may have been regarded by him as atomic in character) is their lack of qualitative differentiation. Whereas the elements of Empedocles as well as the seeds of Anaxagoras carry qualitative differences such as taste and color down to the microscopic level, differences among the atoms of Leucippus and Democritus partake only of a spatial character. The Atomists were the first to make what later became known as the distinction between primary and secondary qualities—that is, between quantitative characteristics assumed to be in objects independent of our perception of them, and qualitative characteristics dependent for their existence on interaction between object and observer. A third contrast of the Atomists with both Empedocles and Anaxagoras concerns an issue on which the latter find themselves in agreement with Parmenides and Melissus but which sets the Atomists in opposition—namely, the question of the existence of empty space, or the Void. Whereas the differing combina-

---

†This fragment has been broken into two parts. The first part appears on p. 184, n†.

tions of unchanging constituents necessary to produce the changing panoply of perception were made possible for Empedocles and Anaxagoras through a kind of interpenetration or mixture not presupposing any empty space separating the constituents, Leucippus and Democritus held that the motion of atoms requires a Void. Their counter to Eleatic logic in this respect will be examined shortly.

Finally, we return to the specific point on which Democritus is known to have attacked Anaxagoras (Frg.5), namely, his views on Mind. Empedocles' resort to Love and Strife to explain motion would undoubtedly be subject to the same sort of attack—a line of criticism probably resting both on the nonmaterial and teleological character of such explanations. For Leucippus and Democritus, in contrast, everything must be explained in terms of movements in a void of material atoms governed by necessity—another notion to be further explored.

The surviving fragments are painfully small and inadequate:

> *On the Atoms*——
> (Frg.168) (Simplicius: *The Democriteans call the atoms 'nature'....For they said that these were*) scattered about.
> (Frg.141) Form (*for 'atom'*).
> *On the Dependence of Sensed Qualities on the Observer and the Existence of the Void*——
> (Frg.9 [1st part]) Sweet exists by convention, bitter by convention, color by convention; atoms and Void (*alone*) exist in reality...†
> (Frg.156) Naught exists just as much as Aught.
> *On the Operation of Necessity(Leucippus' Fragment)*——
> (Frg.2) (Leucippus, From a treatise "On Mind") Nothing happens at random; everything happens out of reason and by necessity.

Most of our knowledge of atomistic ontology, therefore, comes from the commentators.

A. *Atoms and the Void*

Use of the word "Form" by Democritus in Frg. 141 to refer to the atoms, and presumably in the title of the work referred to in Frg.5i *On The Different Forms*‡ as well, brings to attention an interesting comparison with Plato, who also used the term "Form" to refer to what

---

†This fragment has been broken into two parts. The second part appears on p. 201.
‡See p. 200 and note.

for him were the ultimate realities. It is all the more striking because of the contrast of Democritus' materialism with Plato's idealism. A relevant similarity in the view of the two men is that Democritus' atoms as well as Plato's Forms are objects of reason rather than experience and, as Guthrie points out, represent differing adaptations of the Pythagorean concern with form.[6] Sextus Empiricus makes some interesting observations on the former point:

> **T102**   Sextus Empiricus *Adv. Math.* 7.6.[7]
>
> The disciples both of Plato and Democritus held that only intelligible objects are real. Democritus thought so because there is no sensible substratum in nature, for the atoms which give rise to things by combining have a nature devoid of all sensible quality; Plato held this view because the sensible are always in process of becoming, but never really are.

The rationale behind Leucippus' formulation of the Atomic Theory is suggested by Aristotle:

> **T103**   Aristotle *De Gen. et Corr.* 325a 4–8, 24–37
>
> For some of the older philosophers* thought that 'what is' must of necessity be 'one' and immovable. The void, they argue, 'is not': but unless there is a void with a separate being of its own, 'what is' cannot be moved—nor again can it be 'many', since there is nothing to keep things apart. . . .
>
> Leucippus, however, thought he had a theory which harmonized with sense-perception and would not abolish either coming-to-be and passing-away or motion and the multiplicity of things. He made these concessions to the facts of perception: on the other hand, he conceded to the Monists that there could be no motion without a void. The result is a theory which he states as follows: 'The void is a "not-being", and no part of "what is" is a "not-being"; for what "is" in the strict sense of the term is an absolute plenum. This plenum, however, is not "one": on the contrary, it is a "many" infinite in number and invisible owing to the minuteness of their bulk. The "many" move in the void (for there is a void): and by coming together they produce "coming-to-be", while by separating they produce "passing-away". Moreover, they act and suffer action wherever they chance to be in contact (for *there* they are not "one"), and they generate by being put together and becoming intertwined. From the genuinely-one, on the other hand, there

---

*The reference is to Parmenides, Melissus, and (probably) Zeno.

never could have come-to-be a multiplicity, nor from the genuinely-many a "one"; that is impossible...'

The Atomist's answer to Melissus' challenge that if things were a many they would have to be the same as the Parmenidean One† is now clear: it is "Precisely so."

The status of the Void was somewhat ambiguous, but for the Atomists it was certainly not Nothing, as with the Eleatics. It must have some kind of reality in order to make possible the divisibility of compound bodies as well as the motion of atoms. The atoms themselves, as befits tiny Parmenidean Ones, contain no void and are consequently indivisible. There are an infinite number of them.

T104 Aristotle *On Democritus ap.* Simplicium *De Caelo* 295. 1. [K&R407]

Democritus...calls space by these names—'the void', 'nothing', and 'the infinite', while each individual atom he calls 'hing' (i.e. 'nothing' without 'not'), the 'compact' and 'being'. He thinks that they are so small as to elude our senses, but they have all sorts of forms and shapes and differences in size. So he is already enabled from them, as from elements, to create by aggregation bulks that are perceptible to sight and the other senses.

T105 Simplicius *De Caelo* 242. 18. [K&R407]

They (sc. Leucippus, Democritus, Epicurus‡) said that the first principles were infinite in number, and thought they were indivisible atoms and impassible owing to their compactness, and without any void in them; divisibility comes about because of the void in compound bodies.

B. *Necessary Motion of the Atoms*

Perhaps the work referred to in Frg. 8a (*Title*) *On Changes of Form* contained some of the material to be discussed in this section.

Atomism represents the terminus of what Cornford calls the scientific tradition in early Greek philosophy in that reality for the Atomists is defined exclusively in terms of spatial form, a characteristic associated with *Eidolon soul* or *Psyche.* The requirement for any lifelike driving force transcending the spatial individuality of the atoms—a requirement manifesting itself in the felt need of Empedocles and Anaxagoras to resort to nonmaterial principles of explanation—has been entirely eliminated.

---

†Melissus, Frg. 8; See p. 121.

‡Hellenistic philosopher (341-270 B.C.) originator of Epicureanism, who taught that pleasure is the Good and accepted the atomism of Leu_ippus and Democritus.

Now the life is wrung out of matter; motion, no longer a
spontaneous activity, lies not within, but between, the impe-
netrable atoms. Instead of life, nothing is left but the change
of space relations; and the governance of the world returns
to *Ananke-Moira.*[†8]

Kirk & Raven infer from the following quotation of Aetius that, for
Democritus, an original random motion of the atoms was assumed.

T106   Aetius 1. 3. 18. [K&R414]
Democritus named two (sc. properties of atoms), size and
shape; but Epicurus added a third to these, namely weight.
. . .—Democritus says that the primary bodies (i.e. the solid
atoms) do not possess weight but move in the infinite as the
result of striking one another.

The basis of their argument is that Aetius specifically states that Democritus attributed only size and shape to the atoms, and not weight.
Weight, a factor which would account for an original motion in one
direction only, was only later added as a property by Epicurus. But then
how are we to explain testimonia such as the following?

T107   Aristotle *De Gen. et Corr.*, 326a10-11
And yet Democritus says 'the more any indivisible exceeds,
the heavier it is. . .'

T108   Theophrastus *De Sensu* 61. [K&R414]
Democritus distinguishes heavy and light by size. . . .Never-
theless in compound bodies the lighter is that which contains
more void, the heavier that which contains less. Sometimes
he expressed it thus, but elsewhere he says simply that the
fine is light.

Kirk & Raven answer (and claim the support of other authorities) that,
for Democritus, though weight is not an original property of the atom,
it nonetheless operates in vortices as a result of the tendency of bulky
objects toward the center.‡ The vortex is identified with necessity
because each vortex is responsible for the formation of a plurality of
worlds through determination of the collisions and combinations of
atoms caught in that vortex:

T109   Diogenes Laertius 9. [Loeb]
All things happen by virtue of necessity, the vortex being the
cause of the creation of all things, and this he calls necessity.

---

†See pp. **10, 22 , 189**
‡Kirk & Raven, p. 416. The whirlpool and its action in bringing floating objects toward its
center is illustrative of what is intended here.

T110 Aetius 1. 26. 2. [K&R413]
(On the nature of necessity) Democritus means by it the resistance and movement and blows of matter.

Why vortices should begin from the original random motion is not clear; their existence seems to constitute an additional underived assumption. It will be recalled that for Anaxagoras, who also spoke of the cosmos as originating in a vortex, it was mind that ruled the vortex.†

COSMOGONY

Most likely, the elements of Democritus' cosmogony were to be found in his book, *Small World-Order*. There are but two surviving fragments bearing on this, however. One concerns the formation of vortices, the other an effect of their operation—namely, the association of like with like. (The same effect seems to be involved in what Anaxagoras calls the process of "separating off," which for him resulted from rotation of the vortex.‡)

(Frg.167) An eddy, of all manner of forms, is separated off from the Whole.

(Frg.164) Living creatures consort with their kind, as doves with doves, and cranes with cranes, and similiarly with the rest of the animal world. So it is with inanimate things, as one can see with the sieving of seeds and with the pebbles on beaches. In the former, through the circulation of the sieve, beans are separated and ranged with beans, barley-grains with barley, and wheat with wheat; in the latter, with the motion of the wave, oval pebbles are driven to the same place as oval, and round to round, as if the similarity in these things had a sort of power over them which had brought them together.

The formation of each of the plurality of worlds and their constituent compound bodies is contingent upon differences in the combinations of atoms produced by the necessary operation of the vortex. These in turn are dependent on the types of possible difference among the atoms themselves, both singly and in combination. On this subject Aristotle says:

T111 Aristotle *Meta.* 985b 14–19
_____ These differences, they say, are three—shape and order and

†Anaxagoras' Frg. 12; see p. 177.
‡Anaxagoras, Frgs. 12 and 13; see pp. 177.

position. For they say the real is differentiated only by
'rhythm' and 'inter-contact' and 'turning'; and of these
rhythm is shape, inter-contact is order, and turning is position; for A differs from N in shape, AN from NA in order,
from H in position.

There is no contradiction with the earlier referred to claim of Aetius that
the atoms differ only in shape and size because there the atoms were
considered only singly, and Aristotle must here be including the concept
of size under the heading "shape." Aristotle also speaks of the atoms as
differing in size as well as shape.

T112   Aristotle *Phys.* 203b1

. . .for him (*i.e.* Democritus) the common body is a source of
all things, differing from part to part in size and in shape.

Accounts of the view of Leucippus and Democritus concerning the
origin of a plurality of worlds follow. In this age of space exploration
one cannot but be struck by the imaginative power of their ideas.

T113   Diogenes Laertius 9. 31. [Loeb]

He (Leucippus) declares the All to be unlimited, . . .part is
full and part empty. . . .Out of them arise the worlds unlimited in number and into them they are dissolved. This is how
the worlds are formed. In a given section many atoms of all
manner of shapes are carried from the unlimited into the
vast empty space. These collect together and form a single
vortex, in which they jostle against each other and, circling
round in every possible way, separate off, by like atoms
joining like. And, the atoms being so numerous that they can
no longer revolve in equilibrium, the light ones pass into the
empty space outside, as if they were being winnowed; the
remainder keep together and, becoming entangled, go on
their circuit together, and form a primary spherical system.
This parts off like a shell, enclosing within it atoms of all
kinds; and, as these are whirling round by virtue of the
resistence of the centre, the enclosing shell becomes thinner,
the adjacent atoms continually combining when they touch
the vortex. In this way the earth is formed by portions
brought to the centre coalescing. And again, even the outer
shell grows larger by the influx of atoms from outside, and,
as it is carried round in the vortex, adds to itself whatever
atoms it touches. And of these some portions are locked
together and form a mass, at first damp and miry, but, when
they have dried and revolve with the universal vortex, they
afterwards take fire and form the substance of the stars.

T114   Hippolytus *Ref.* 1. 13. 2. [K&R411]
Democritus holds the same view as Leucippus about the elements, full and void...he spoke as if the things that are were in constant motion in the void; and there are innumerable worlds, which differ in size. In some worlds there is no sun and moon, in others they are larger than in our world, and in others more numerous. (3) The intervals between the worlds are unequal; in some parts there are more worlds, in others fewer; some are increasing, some at their height, some decreasing; in some parts they are arising, in others failing. They are destroyed by collision one with another. There are some worlds devoid of living creatures or plants or any moisture.

An additional point of information concerning the atoms—that they are not only infinite in number but also in the variety of their shapes—is evident from Aristotle's account of the dependency of the characters of compound bodies on atomic shape and arrangement.

T115   Aristotle *De Gen. et Corr.* 314a21
Democritus and Leucippus say that there are invisible bodies, infinite both in number and in the varieties of their shapes, of which everything else is composed—the compounds differing one from another according to the shapes, 'positions', and 'groupings' of their constituents.

Their origin is explained as follows:

T116   Aristotle *On Democritus ap.* Simplicium *De Caelo* 295. 11. [K&R418]
As they (sc. the atoms) move they collide and become entangled in such a way as to cling in close contact to one another, but not so as to form one substance of them in reality of any kind whatever; for it is very simple-minded to suppose that two or more could ever become one. The reason he gives for atoms staying together for a while is the intertwining and mutual hold of the primary bodies; for some of them are angular, some hooked, some concave, some convex, and indeed with countless other differences; so he thinks they cling to each other and stay together until such time as some stronger necessity comes from the surrounding and shakes and scatters them apart.

ASTRONOMY, THE EARTH AND NATURAL PHENOMENA

Democritus must have written at considerable length on astronomy, the earth, meteorology, and miscellaneous natural phenomena because the list of such titles included among his fragments is long:

(Frg.5a) '*On Cosmography.*'
(Frg.5b) '*On the Planets.*'
(Frg.5c) '*On Nature* or *On the Nature of the Universe.*'
(Frg.11b) '*Heavenly Causes.*'
(Frg.11c) '*Aerial Causes.*'
(Frg.11d) '*Surface Causes.*'
(Frg.11e) '*Causes of Fire and Things in Fire.*'
(Frg.11f) '*Causes of Sounds.*'
(Frg.11i) '*Mixed Causes.*'
(Frg.11k) '*On the Magnet.*'
(Frg.11r) '*The Great Year*,' or, '*Astonomy-Calendar.*'
(Frg.14a) '*Contest according to the Water-Clock*' (?)
(Frg.14b) '*Description of the Heavens.*'
(Frg.14c) '*Description of the Earth.*'
(Frg.15, in part) '*Voyage Round the World.*'†
(Frg.15a) '*Description of the Pole.*'
(Frg.15b) '*Description of the Rays.*'

All fragments dealing with the content of Democritus' views in these areas are discussed below. They are scanty indeed.

The first concerns "The Great Year":‡

(Frg.12) (*The Great Year of Philolaus and Democritus is of 82 years with 28 intercalary months.*)

Frg. 14, not quoted in its entirety here, includes several references to an astronomical calendar or calendars attributed to Democritus. A calendar of weather signs observed by Democritus is also part of this fragment:

(Frg.14, §7) (PTOLEMAEUS). *Weather signs observed by Democritus in Northern Greece. He said that the most important day was the fifteenth day after the equinox.*

Sept.	14	Swallow leaves. (Change of weather).
	26	Rain and wind-disturbances.
Oct.	5	Storm. Sowing-time.
	29	Cold or frost.
Nov.	13	Storm on land and sea.
	27	Disturbed sea and sky.
Dec.	5	Storm.
	10	Thunder, lightning, rain, wind.
	27	Very stormy.
	29	Change of weather.

---

†See p. 195-6 for complete fragment.
‡Meaning not clear.

Jan.	4	South wind as a rule.
	20	Rain.
	24	Great storm.
Feb.	6	West wind begins.
	8	West wind blows.
	24	The days called halcyon.
Mar.	7	Cold winds. Bird-days (nine).*
	18	Change of weather, Cold wind.
	27	Change of weather.
Apr.	24	Change of weather.
May	28	Rain.
June	3	Rain.
	22	Good day.
	28	West wind, morning rain, then strong north winds for 7 days.
July	16	Rain. Squalls.
	26	South wind and heat.
Aug.	19	Change of weather, with rain and wind.

8.   (JOANNES LYDUS' CALENDAR).

Jan.	15	South-west wind with rain.
	18	Dolphin sets; Change of weather usually.
	23	South-west wind blows.
Mar.	17	Setting of Pisces, *on the day of the Bacchanalia.*
Sept.	2	Change of wind, and prevalence of rain.
Oct.	6	Rise of Kids; north wind blows.
Nov.	25	The Sun in Sagittarius.

(End of Extracts from Calendar)

The next fragment suggests that Democritus must have attempted a natural explanation of the cause of eclipses:

(Frg.161) (SCHOLIAST on Apollonius Rhodius: *Eclipses were called 'down-drawings' up to the time of Democritus, with reference to the ancient belief that sorceresses could draw down the sun and moon and so cause eclipses.*)

The last fragment to be mentioned here, one from which the title *Voyage round the World* was taken, credits Democritus with the notion that the earth is rectangular. According to Guthrie[9], neither Leucippus nor Democritus regarded it as spherical: whereas for Leucippus it was drum shaped, for Democritus it was concave (as well as rectangular).

(Frg.15) *'Voyage round the World.'* (AGATHÊMERUS: *After Anaximander, descriptions of a Voyage Round the*

---

* Bird-days are those on which migrant birds appear; bird-winds are those which bring migrant birds.

World were written by Hecataeus, Hellanicus, and Damas-
tes of Sigeion copying for the most part Hellanicus.
Democritus and Eudoxus followed, and some others. The
ancients described the world as round, with Greece in the
centre, and Delphi the centre of Greece. But Democritus, a
man of wide experience, was the first to describe it as
rectangular, the length half the width. Dicearchus the
Peripatetic concurred).

There is further spotty information to be had from the commentators
concerning Democritus' views on astronomy, the earth, and natural
phenomena, but it cannot be discussed here. We shall have to rest
content with Guthrie's overall evaluation of Democritus' thought in this
area, viz., that though he had a few original ideas, his views were in
general conservative and in the Ionian tradition.[10]

BIOLOGY AND MEDICINE

Titles of works in biology and medicine were:
  (Frg.11g) *'Causes of Seeds, Plants and Fruits.'*
  (Frg.11h) *'Causes of Animals.'* (3 Books).
  (Frg.26b) *'Prognosis.'*
  (Frg.26c) *'On Diet.'*
  (Frg.26d) *'On Medical Method.'*
  (Frg.26e) *'Causes of Seasonable and Unseasonable Things.'*
  (Frg.26f) *'On Farming.'*
But only a few relevant fragments remain:
  On Biology—
  (Frg.22) The eagle has black bones.
  (Frg.126) (*All creatures*) which move along their path in a
  wavelike manner.
  On Health and Medical Matters—
  (Frg.234) Men ask in their prayers for health from the gods,
  but do not know that the power to attain this lies in
  themselves; and by doing the opposite through lack of
  control, they themselves become the betrayers of their own
  health to their desires.
  (Frg.32) Coition is a slight attack of apoplexy. For man
  gushes forth from man, and is separated by being torn apart
  with a kind of blow.
  (Frg.127) Men get pleasure from scratching themselves: they
  feel an enjoyment like that of lovemaking.

(Frg.148) The navel forms first in the womb, as an anchorage against tossing and wandering, a cable and a rope for the fruit, engendered and future.

(Frg.120) Pulse-beat (*word for*).

On Farming—

(Frg.27) (COLUMELLA: *Democritus and Mago say that vine-yards should face north for the best crops*).

(Frg.27a) (COLUMELLA: *Democritus and Mago say that bees can be generated from a dead cow*).

(Frg.28) (COLUMELLA: *Democritus in his book 'On Farming' says that it is foolish to encircle a garden with walls: if made of sun-dried bricks, they cannot stand the weather; if of stone, they cost more than they are worth; and to surround a large piece of land with a wall demands a large inheritance.*)

Again, further scanty information, though available from commentators, cannot here be considered. Guthrie's estimate is that Democritus attempted to interpret the biological and medical views of his time in terms of atomic theory, but that there is little evidence of great originality.[11]

LOGIC AND MATHEMATICS

Democritus' logical works included:

(Frg.8b) '*On Strengthening Arguments*.'

(Frg.10b) '*On Logic*' or '*The Canon*'. (3 books).

(Frg.11a) '*On Difficult Problems*.'

On the strength of the fact that he wrote a work "On Logic" as well as some references from Aristotle, it has been claimed for Democritus "that he was the first to have written a separate work on logic, and first to have not only offered a philosophical system but also consciously reflected on the logic of that system, and also [was] the first to offer a strictly logical definition of his ideas."[12]

Listed among his works on mathematics were:

(Frg.11l) '*On Difference of Comprehension*' or '*On the Contact of Circle and Sphere*.'

(Frg.11m) '*On Geometry*.'

(Frg.11n) '*On Geometrical Problems*.'

(Frg.11o) '*Numbers*.'

(Frg.11p) '*On Disproportionate Lines and Solids*.'

(Frg.11q) '*Projections*.'

From the number of works listed, Democritus must have been a serious mathematician. The two surviving fragments of consequence are concerned with the problem of divisibility. The first may be taken to mean that Democritus regarded the sphere as a polyhedron with so many small angular faces that they are not perceptible. The second fragment might be interpreted as an unresolved dilemma, but Guthrie feels that Democritus probably opted for the first alternative in line with his handling of the problem of the sphere.[13] The suggested interpretation of both fragments is consistent with the view that bodies are made up of a collection of indivisible atoms.

> (Frg.155a) (ARISTOTLE: *Democritus treats the sphere as a sort of angle when cutting it*).

> (Frg.155) If a cone were cut by a plane parallel to the base*, what ought one to think of the surfaces resulting from the section: are they equal or unequal? If they are unequal, they will make the cone have many steplike indentations and unevennesses; but if they are equal, the sections will be equal, and the cone will appear to have the same property as a cylinder, being made up of equal, not unequal, circles, which is most absurd.

MAN

A. *Man a Part of Nature*

For Democritus, man is part of nature and was the subject of the second part of his book *On Nature*:

> (Frg.5d) *'On Nature' (Second Part), or 'On the Nature of Man', or 'On Flesh.'*

But man is also the universe in microcosm and that part of it with which we are most familiar.

> (Frg.34) Man is a universe in little (*Microcosm*).

> (Frg.165) I say the following about the Whole...Man is that which we all know.

B. *The Soul and Life*

Democritus' view of soul is that it is made up of spherical atoms capable of permeating everywhere and setting other things in motion through their own natural movement. The atoms of which souls are composed are akin to atoms of fire which are of the same shape. One is reminded of Heraclitus in this respect. Breathing is essential to life because it is the only way of retaining soul atoms in the body in the face

---

*'By which is clearly meant a plane indefinitely near to the base.' Heath, *Greek Mathematics*, I, pp. 179-180.

of their material tendency to be dispersed by environmental forces. At death, not only the body, but also the soul is destroyed.[14]

T117   Aristotle *De Anima* 403b 29, 404c16

Some say that what originates movement is both preeminently and primarily soul; believing that what is not itself moved cannot originate movement in another, they arrived at the view that soul belongs to the class of things in movement. This is what led Democritus to say that soul is a sort of fire or hot substance; his forms or atoms are infinite in number; those which are spherical he calls fire and soul, and compares them to the motes in the air which we see in shafts of light coming through windows; the mixture of seeds of all sorts he calls the elements of the whole of Nature (Leucippus gives a similar account); the spherical atoms are identified with soul because atoms of that shape are most adapted to permeate everywhere, and to set all the others moving by being themselves in movement. This implies the view that soul is identical with what produces movement in animals. That is why, further, they regard respiration as the characteristic mark of life; as the environment compresses the bodies of animals, and tends to extrude those atoms which impart movement to them, because they themselves are never at rest, there must be a reinforcement of these by similar atoms coming in from without in the act of respiration; for they prevent the extrusion of those which are already within by counteracting the compressing and consolidating force of the environment; and animals continue to live only as long as they are able to maintain this resistance....Democritus roundly identifies soul and mind, for he identifies what appears with what is true—that is why he commends Homer for the phrase 'Hector lay with thought distraught'*; he does not employ mind as a special faculty dealing with truth, but identifies soul and mind.

Aristotle includes Democritus among those who believe not only that the soul is the source of motion, but also that it has a cognitive function. He further maintains that Democritus identifies soul with mind, though there is some doubt about this claim. To the contrary, the evidence seems to indicate that, though Democritus maintained that soul permeates the entire body, he also held the view that mind is concentrated in the head,[15] a view which would make equation of the two impossible.

---

*2. 23. 698.

A way of resolving the difficulty would perhaps be to regard mind as a concentration of soul atoms in the head.

T118   Aristotle *De Anima* 404b27-29, 405a8-12
Some thinkers, accepting both premises, viz. that the soul is both the originative of movement and cognitive, have compounded it of both and declared the soul to be a self-moving number. . . .

Democritus has expressed himself more ingeniously than the rest on the grounds for ascribing each of these two characters to soul; soul and mind are, he says, one and the same thing, and this thing must be one of the primary and indivisible bodies, and its power of originating movement must be due to its fineness of grain and the shape of its atoms; he says that of all the shapes the spherical is the most mobile, and that this is the shape of the particles of both fire and mind.

C.   *Perception, Thought and Knowledge*

Democritus' writings on the subjects of perception, thought and knowledge included:

(Frg.0b) '*On the Character of the Sage.*'
(Frg.5e) '*On Mind.*'
(Frg.5f) '*On Perception.*'
(Frg.5g) '*On Tastes.*'
(Frg.5h) '*On Colours.*'
(Frg.5i) '*On the Different Forms.*'†
(Frg.10a) '*On Images*' or '*On Foresight.*' (?)

Consistent with his atomistic ontology, Democritus attempts to explain all knowledge, perception as well as thought, in terms of atomic theory. All sensation and thought thus depend on physical contact of the observer or thinker with atoms of some sort streaming from the object sensed or thought of, and are in this respect analogous with the sense of touch. Aristotle comments unsympathetically on this last point, [16] and Aetius speaks of the required physical contact as dependent on impinging images. [17] The first of the following fragments shows that Democritus himself used the word for "image" in the indicated context, and the second shows the dependency of at least "opinion" (i.e., sense experience) on impinging atoms. The second fragment also introduces a sceptical theme stemming from the view expressed in Frg. 9 that what is perceived or thought is not apprehended as it is in itself, but is dependent as well on the bodily constitution of the observer or thinker.

†According to Freeman (*Companion,* p. 297) it was in this work that Democritus stated his theory of knowledge. Fragments 6, 7, and 8 below are all known to be from this work..

(Frg.123) (*Word for*) image (*as effluence from objects*).

(Frg.7) We know nothing about anything really, but Opinion is for all individuals an inflowing (*? of the Atoms*). (*From 'On the Forms'*.)

(Frg.9 [2nd part]) We know nothing accurately in reality, but (*only*) as it changes according to the bodily condition, and the constitution of those things that flow upon (*the body*) and impinge upon it.†

The next fragments repeat the theme of the consequent obscurity of knowledge:

(Frg.8) It will be obvious that it is impossible to understand how in reality each thing is (*From 'On the Forms'*).

(Frg.6) One must learn by this rule that Man is severed from reality (*From 'On the Forms'*).

(Frg.10) It has often been demonstrated that we do not grasp how each thing is or is not.

(Frg.117) We know nothing in reality; for truth lies in an abyss.

Certainly, however, Democritus is no sceptic, and he does distinguish perception and thought with respect to their degree of obscurity. Thought does permit genuine knowledge of a sort: how else could the atomic theory be justified? It can do this because of its finer capacity for distinguishing the impinging images.

(Frg.11) There are two sorts of knowledge, one genuine, one bastard (*or 'obscure'*). To the latter belong all the following: sight, hearing, smell, taste, touch. The real is separated from this. When the bastard can do no more—neither see more minutely, nor hear, nor smell, nor taste, nor perceive by touch—and a finer investigation is needed, then the genuine comes in as having a tool for distinguishing more finely. (*From 'The Canon'*).

Apparently, however, thought is still dependent on the evidence of the suspect senses.

(Frg.125) Colour exists by convention (*usage*), sweet by convention, bitter by convention.

(*Reply of the senses to Intellect*): 'Miserable Mind, you get your evidence from us, and do you try to overthrow us? The overthrow will be your downfall'.

†This fragment has been broken into two parts. The first appears on p. 187.

Unfortunately, there is no information at all concerning Democritus' treatment of the sense of touch and only one comment by Theophrastus concerning his explanation of the sense of smell:

T119   Theophrastus *De Sensu* 82[18]

As for smell, he says nothing definite except that something subtile emanating from heavy substances is the cause of odor. But what its character is, and by what this process is effected—which is perhaps the most important point of all—on this we have never a word.

The following quotations from Theophrastus, Aristotle, and Aetius must suffice to suggest how he dealt with the other senses.

T120   Theophrastus *De Sensu* 50. [K&R421]

Democritus explains sight by the visual image, which he describes in a peculiar way; the visual image does not arise directly in the pupil, but the air between the eye and the object of sight is contracted and stamped by the object seen and the seer; for from everything there is always a sort of effluence proceeding. So this air, which is solid and variously coloured, appears in the eye, which is moist (?); the eye does not admit the dense part, but the moist passes through.

T121   Aristotle *De Sensu* 442b11[19]

...white is smooth, he says, and black is rough. But flavors he reduces to shapes.

T122   Theophrastus *De Sensu* 66 [K&R423]

Bitter taste is caused by small, smooth, rounded atoms, whose circumference is actually sinuous; therefore it is both sticky and viscous. Salt taste is caused by large, not rounded atoms, but in some cases jagged ones.

T123   Aetius 4. 19. 3. [K&R423]

Democritus says that the air is broken up into bodies of like shape and is rolled along together with the fragments of the voice.

D.   *Culture*

The tenth and eleventh tetralogies of Thrasyllus indicate that Democritus was author of works titled:

15c '*On Rhythm and Harmony.*'
16a '*On Poetry.*'

18a *'On the Beauty of Words.'*
18b *'On well-sounding and ill-sounding Letters.'*
20a *'On Homer, or a Correct Diction and Vocabulary.'*
25a *'On Song.'*
25b *'On Phrases.'*
26a *'On Nomenclature.'*

In addition, the thirteenth tetralogy includes a work titled:

28a *'On Painting.'*

Since Democritus held that man is part of a changing nature, it is natural to suppose that he subscribed to an evolutionary view of culture that was prevalent in his time. According to this view, society, civilization, and the arts evolved by necessity through application of intelligence to the practical problems of human existence. Guthrie maintains that, though Democritus was not the author of such a view, "it can scarcely be doubted that he adhered to it," basing his argument in addition on the notion that the following two fragments presuppose it.[20]

(Frg.154) We are pupils of the animals in the most important things: the spider for spinning and mending, the swallow for building, and the songsters, swan and nightingale, for singing, by way of imitation.

(Frg.144) (*Music is the youngest of the arts*) For it was not necessity that separated it off (*i.e. created it*), but it arose from the existing superfluity.

For Democritus man's nature is a product of what he learns as transmitted by culture:†

(Frg.33) Nature and instruction are similar; for instruction transforms the man, and in transforming, creates his nature.

Language, one of culture's major instruments, has evolved by necessity along with culture. There is no reason, for example, why a thing should be called by one name rather than another, and in this sense names might be said to arise by chance (though nonetheless through operation of necessary causes);

(Frg.26) (PROCLUS: *Pythagoras and Epicurus agree with Cratylus, but Democritus and Aristotle agree with Hermogenes, the former that names arise by nature, the latter that they arise by chance. Pythagoras thought that the Soul gave the names, deriving them like images of reality from the mind. But Democritus thought that the proof of their chance origin was fourfold: (1) the calling of different things*

---

†Also see Protagoras' view as referred to on p. 245.

by the same name; (2) having several names for the same
thing; (3) change of name; (4) lack of name.)

But

(Frg.145) Speech is the shadow of action.

indicates nonetheless a close tie between language and reality.

Somewhat surprisingly, it would seem, the sober and rational Democritus saw value in the view of poetry as divinely inspired and of the poet as overtaken by a kind of madness. Perhaps instead this only indicates the breadth of his perspective. Democritus was attempting to explain all aspects of human experience; he was not undertaking to explain anything away.

(Frg.17) (*There is no poetry without madness*).

(Frg.18) What a poet writes with enthusiasm and divine inspiration is most beautiful.

(Frg.21) Homer, having been gifted with a divine nature, built an ordered structure of manifold verse.

Presumably the last fragment came from Democritus' book on Homer.

E. *Religion*

Among Democritus' works of religious significance surely were:

(Frg.oc) '*On those in Hades.*'

(Frg.1) '*On Hades.*'

Because of the religious importance of the number three and the fact that Amaltheia is a figure of Greek religious mythology, the following may have been on the same topic.

(Frg.1b) '*Tritogeneia' (taken to mean 'threefold in origin,'*
on the Threeness of things).

(Frg.2b) '*The Horn of Amaltheia.*'

Since soul atoms are dispersed at death along with those of the body, it is safe to assume that Democritus did not subscribe to the existence of souls in Hades. Nor does his ontology permit belief in a monotheistic God of the traditional sort: supposed evidence of such a God can be better explained in terms of natural causes:

(Frg.30) Of the reasoning men, a few, raising their hands thither to what we Greeks call the Air nowadays, said: 'Zeus considers all things and he knows all and gives and takes away all and is King of all.'

(Frg.152) There is no lightning sent from Zeus which does not contain the pure light of Aether.

Nonetheless, Aetius gives a definition of Democritus' God as "mind in spherical fire,"[21] presumably making reference to the spherical soul atoms to be found in the air† which are the material sources of both mind and soul. Thought for Democritus can assent to no more than this; yet perception is not to be denied. Sextus Empiricus, in the passage from which Frg. 166 is taken, relates that:

> **T124** Sextus Empiricus *Math.* 9. 24. 19. [Guthrie 2. 478] Democritus says that certain images come to men, some of which are beneficent and others maleficent (whence he desired to meet with 'propitious images'). They are large, indeed gigantic, and hard to destroy though not indestructible, and they show men the future in advance, by their appearance and by uttering sounds.

Such images are, according to Democritus' theory of perception, interpreted in materialistic terms as streams of impinging atoms, and again, according to his theory of perception, must have their source in objective realities of some sort. Once more we have Democritus attempting to explain, yet refusing to explain away, what was taken as reliable experience in his time. The following fragment, which might be interpreted as asserting a connection of sorts between religious language and what it expresses, need not be taken to affirm a natural connection of the sort explicitly denied by Democritus in his treatment of names:‡

> (Frg142) (*The names of the gods are*) vocal images (*i.e. express their nature*).

The next fragments suggest Democritus' views concerning the relation between the presumably beneficent gods and human life.§ The gods are good and expect man likewise to be good; yet men must take full responsibility for leading their lives well. The gods are neither scapegoats nor crutches.

> (Frg.217) They alone are dear to the gods to whom crime is hateful.

> (Frg.175) But the gods are the givers of all good things, both in the past and now. They are not, however, the givers of things which are bad, harmful or non-beneficial, either in the past or now, but men themselves fall into these through blindness of mind and lack of sense.

---

†The brilliant upper air was referred to as "aether," which sometimes meant fire and sometimes air.
‡See Frg. 26., p. 203.
§See also Frg. 234, p. 196.

ETHICS AND POLITICS

From their titles, it is clear that Democritus wrote at least the following works on ethics:

> (Frg.2) *'Tritogenia' of the three-fold character of Athene as Wisdom.'*†
> (Frg.2a) *'On Courage.'*
> (Frg.2c) *'On Cheerfulness or Well-Being.'*
> (Frg.4a) *'Ethical Notes.'*

We have no record of any work specifically on the subject of politics, though about thirty-five fragments fall into this category.

By far the largest proportion of Democritus' fragments are of ethical or political import (upwards of 230 out of a total of 298 supposedly genuine fragments)‡ and, though a good many of them are but banal aphorisms, some are of apparently conflicting content, and doubts have been expressed as to the authenticity of others. For these reasons it is difficult to judge whether or not Democritus had a unified ethical or political system.

Yet there is nothing in the fragments to conflict with Democritus' ontology, and despite reservations by some, they appear to be substantial in content. Because, too, Democritus was such a systematic thinker in other areas, an attempt has been made to present the more significant ethical and political fragments in semisystematic fashion. Their very great number precluded including them all. Considerations of space have also prohibited reference to commentators, though in this case they are not especially helpful.

A. *Ethics*

Happiness is a matter of a virtuous and wise soul rather than of externals——

> (Frg.171) Happiness does not dwell in flocks of cattle or in gold. The soul is the dwelling-place of the (*good and evil*) genius.
>
> (Frg.40) Men find happiness neither by means of the body nor through possessions, but through uprightness and wisdom.
>
> (Frg.216) Imperturbable wisdom is worth everything.

But one need not have wisdom oneself to be virtuous—

---

†taken to mean moral wisdom.
‡See chart on p. 185.

(Frg.53) Many who have learnt Reason, nevertheless live according to reason.

(Frg.39) One must either be good, or imitate a good man.

* * * * * *

External circumstances cannot be blamed for human misfortune: rather it is a lack of human intelligence——

(Frg.119) Men have fashioned an image of Chance as an excuse for their own stupidity. For Chance rarely conflicts with Intelligence, and most things in life can be set in order by an intelligent sharpsightedness.

(Frg.172) Those same things from which we get good can also be for us a source of hurt, or else we can avoid the hurt. For instance, deep water is useful for many purposes, and yet again harmful; for there is a danger of being drowned. A technique has therefore been invented: instruction in swimming.

(Frg.173) For mankind, evil comes out of what is good, if one does not know how to guide and drive correctly. It is not right to place such things in the category of evil, but in that of good. It is possible also to use what is good for an evil end* if one wishes.

(Frg.83) The cause of error is ignorance of the better.

Yet human suffering stems from within and requires the healing of wisdom——

(Frg.149) (*Inside, we are*) a complex store-house and treasury of ills, with many possibilities of suffering.

(Frg.288) Disease of the home and of the life comes about in the same way as that of the body.

(Frg.31) Medicine heals diseases of the body, wisdom frees the soul from passions.

(Frg.285) One should realise that human life is weak and brief and mixed with many cares and difficulties, in order that one may care only for moderate possessions, and that hardship may be measured by the standard of one's needs.

* * * * * *

Happiness is a tranquil cheerfulness attained through moderation of activity and enjoyment, limitation of desires, and avoidance of competition for worldly possessions——

---

*The MS. reading ἀλκήν is emended by Diels-Kranz to ἀλκῇ and translated: 'It is possible to use what is good as a help against evil.'

(Frg.189) The best way for a man to lead his life is to have been as cheerful as possible and to have suffered as little as possible. This could happen if one did not seek one's pleasures in mortal things.

(Frg.3) The man who wishes to have serenity of spirit should not engage in many activities, either private or public, nor choose activities beyond his power and natural capacity. He must guard against this, so that when good fortune strikes him and leads him on to excess by means of (*false*) seeming, he must rate it low, and not attempt things beyond his powers. A reasonable fullness is better than overfullness.

(Frg.191) Cheerfulness is created for men through moderation of enjoyment and harmoniousness of life. Things that are in excess or lacking are apt to change and cause great disturbance in the soul. Souls which are stirred by great divergences are neither stable nor cheerful. Therefore one must keep one's mind on what is attainable, and be content with what one has, paying little heed to things envied and admired, and not dwelling on them in one's mind. Rather must you consider the lives of those in distress, reflecting on their intense sufferings, in order that your own possessions and condition may seem great and enviable, and you may, by ceasing to desire more, cease to suffer in your soul. For he who admires those who have, and who are called happy by other mortals, and who dwells on them in his mind every hour, is constantly compelled to undertake something new and to run the risk, through his desire, of doing something irretrievable among things which the laws prohibit. Hence one must not seek the latter, but must be content with the former, comparing one's own life with that of those in worse cases, and must consider oneself fortunate, reflecting on their sufferings, in being so much better off than they. If you keep to this way of thinking, you will live more serenely, and will expel those not-negligble curses in life, envy, jealousy and spite.

(Frg.159) (*Democritus said*): If the body brought a suit against the soul, for all the pains it had endured throughout life, and the ill treatment, and I were to be the judge of the suit, I would gladly condemn the soul, in that it had partly ruined the body by its neglect and dissolved it with bouts of drunkenness, and partly destroyed it and torn it in pieces with its passion for pleasure—as if, when a tool or a vessel were in a bad condition, I blamed the man who was using it carelessly.

(Frg.235) All who derive their pleasures from the stomach, overstepping due season in eating or drinking or sexual pleasure, have pleasures that are but brief and short-lived, (*that is*), only while they are eating and drinking, but pains that are many. For this desire is always present for the same things, and when people get what they desire, the pleasure passes quickly and they have nothing good for themselves except a brief enjoyment; and then again the need for the same things returns.

(Frg.236) It is hard to fight desire; but to control it is the sign of a reasonable man.

(Frg.70) Immoderate desire is the mark of a child, not a man.

(Frg.147) Pigs revel in mud.

But this is not an ascetic view: the objective of the happy life is a maximum of pleasure——

(Frg.4) Pleasure and absence of pleasure are the criteria of what is profitable and what is not.

(Frg.209) For a self-sufficiency in food, there is never a 'short night'. (*i.e. those who have independence of means do not suffer from insomnia*).

(Frg.210) A rich table is provided by luck, but a sufficient one by wisdom.

(Frg.211) Moderation multiplies pleasures, and increases pleasures.

(Frg.207) One should choose not every pleasure, but only that concerned with the beautiful.

(Frg.73) Virtuous love consists in decorous desire for the beautiful.

*   *   *   *   *   *

While some care for nothing but appearances, some who speak of virtue most, practice it least; it is virtuous action that counts——

(Frg.195) Images conspicuous for their dress and ornament, empty of heart.

(Frg.53a) Many whose actions are most disgraceful practice the best utterances.

(Frg.55) One should emulate the deeds and actions of virtue, not the words.

But good intentions are essential to virtuous action——

(Frg.68) The worthy and the unworthy man (*are to be known*) not only by their actions, but also their wishes.

(Frg.62) Virtue consists, not in avoiding wrong-doing, but in having no wish thereto.

(Frg.190) One must avoid even speaking of evil deeds.

(Frg.89) An enemy is not he who injures, but he who wishes to do so.

Ultimately, virtue is a matter of individual conscience——

(Frg.264) One must not respect the opinion of other men more than one's own; nor must one be more ready to do wrong if no one will know than if all will know. One must respect one's own opinion most, and this must stand as the law of one's soul, preventing one from doing anything improper.

(Frg.244) Do not say or do what is base, even when you are alone. Learn to feel shame in your own eyes much more than before others.

(Frg.41) Refrain from crimes not through fear but through duty.

The virtuous man is a man of strong character——

(Frg.214) The brave man is not only he who overcomes the enemy, but he who is stronger than pleasures. Some men are masters of cities, but are enslaved to women.

(Frg.61) Those whose character is well-ordered have also a well-ordered life.

But a strong character is not natural to man, and is only acquired through practice——

(Frg.198) The animal needing something knows how much it needs, the man does not.

(Frg.57) Good breeding in cattle depends on physical health, but in men on a well-formed character.

(Frg.59) Neither skill nor wisdom is attainable unless one learns.

(Frg.242) More men become good through practice than by nature.

(Frg.208) The self-control of the father is the greatest example for the children.

Yet the old are not necessarily wiser than the young——

(Frg.183) There is an intelligence of the young, and an unintelligence of the aged. It is not time that teaches wisdom, but early training and natural endowment.

* * * * * *

Death is not to be feared; life is to be enjoyed——

(Frg.297) Some men, not knowing about the dissolution of mortal nature, but acting on knowledge of the suffering in life, afflict the period of life with anxieties and fears, inventing false tales about the period after the end of life.

(Frg.199) People are fools who hate life and yet wish to live through fear of Hades.

(Frg.200) People are fools who live without enjoyment of life.

(Frg.201) People are fools who yearn for long life without pleasure in long life.

(Frg.230) The life without festival is a long road without an inn.

(Frg.160) (*To live badly is*) not to live badly, but to spend a long time dying.

B. *Politics*

The wise man as an individual transcends the limitations of his communal origin in the city state——

(Frg.246) Life in a foreign country teaches self-sufficiency; for bread and bed are the sweetest cures for hunger and fatigue.

(Frg.247) To a wise man, the whole earth is open; for the native land of a good soul is the whole earth.

Yet the greatest undertakings require communal action (though one can perhaps detect a degree of sarcasm in the following comment)——

(Frg.250) The greatest undertakings are carried through by means of concord, including wars between City-States: there is no other way.

* * * * * *

In society, happiness for the individual can be found only in obedience to the law——

(Frg.47) Well-ordered behaviour consists in obedience to the law, the ruler, and the man wiser (*than oneself*).

(Frg.174) The cheerful man, who is impelled towards works that are just and lawful, rejoices by day and by night, and is strong and free from care. But the man who neglects justice,

and does not do what he ought, finds all such things dis-
agreeable when he remembers any of them, and he is afraid
and torments himself.

(Frg.215) The reward of justice is confidence of judgment
and imperturbability, but the end of injustice is the fear of
disaster.

(Frg.45) The wrongdoer is more unfortunate than the man
wronged.

For this reason the art of statecraft is of the utmost importance——

(Frg.252) One must give the highest importance to affairs of
the State, that it may be well run; one must not pursue
quarrels contrary to right, nor acquire a power contrary to
the common good. The well-run State is the greatest protection, and contains all in itself; when this is safe, all is safe;
when this is destroyed, all is destroyed.

(Frg.157) Learn thoroughly the art of statesmanship, which
is the greatest, and pursue its toils, from which men win
great and brilliant prizes.

*   *   *   *   *   *

Those who rule must be both strong and wise——

(Frg.267) Rule belongs by nature to the stronger.

(Frg.75) It is better for fools to be ruled than to rule.

And slavery as part of the Greek cultural context is presupposed——

(Frg.270) Use slaves as parts of the body: each to his own
function.

*   *   *   *   *   *

The function of law is to aid individuals in the pursuit of virtue,
reason and persuasion being far more effective in this task than compulsion or money——

(Frg.248) The law wishes to benefit men's life; and it is able
to do so, when they themselves wish to receive benefit; for it
shows to those who obey it their own particular virtue.

(Frg.245) The laws would not prevent each man from living
according to his inclinations, unless individuals harmed
each other; for envy creates the beginning of strife.

(Frg.181) The man who employs exhortation and persuasion will turn out to be a more effective guide to virtue than

he who employs law and compulsion. For the man who is prevented by law from wrongdoing will probably do wrong in secret, whereas the man who is led towards duty by persuasion will probably not do anything untoward either secretly or openly. Therefore the man who acts rightly through understanding and knowledge becomes at the same time brave and upright.

(Frg.51) In power of persuasion, reasoning is far stronger than gold.

Democritus was a democrat——

(Frg.102) In all things, equality is fair, excess and deficiency not so, in my opinion.

(Frg.251) Poverty under democracy is as much to be preferred to so-called prosperity under autocracy as freedom to slavery.

(Frg.226) Freedom of speech is the sign of freedom; but the danger lies in discerning the right occasion.

But in the interests of Justice, enemies of the State must be ruthlessly rooted out and punished——

(Frg.256) Justice is to do what should be done; injustice is to fail to do what should be done, and to put it aside.

(Frg.193) It is the business of intelligence to guard against a threatened injustice, but it is the mark of insenibility not to avenge it when it has happened.

(Frg.259) As has been laid down (*by me*) regarding beasts and reptiles which are inimical (*to man*), so I think one should do with regard to human beings: one should, according to ancestral law, kill an enemy of the State in every ordered society, unless a law forbids it. But there are prohibitions in every State: sacred law, treaties and oaths.

(Frg.260) Anyone killing any brigand or pirate shall be exempt from penalty, whether he do it by his own hand, or by instigation, or by vote.

(Frg.262) Those who do what is deserving of exile or imprisonment or other punishment must be condemned and not let off. Whoever contrary to the law acquits a man, judging according to profit or pleasure, does wrong, and this is bound to be on his conscience.

* * * * * *

It is only right that elected officials should be called to account for their mistakes; on the other hand, the just magistrate must be protected from wrong-doers——

> (Frg.265) Men remember one's mistakes rather than one's successes. This is just; for as those who return a deposit do not deserve praise, whereas those who do not do so deserve blame and punishment, so with the official: he was elected not to make mistakes but to do things well.

> (Frg.266) There is no means under the present constitution by which magistrates can be prevented from wrong-doing, however good they may be. For it is not likely for anyone else (*any more*) than for oneself, that he will show himself the same man in different circumstances.* But we must also make arrangements to see that if a magistrate does no wrong, and convicts wrong-doers, he shall not fall under the power of the latter; rather, a law or some other means must defend the magistrate who does what is just.

RELATION OF THE PLURALISTS TO OTHER EARLY GREEK THINKERS

Many treatments of the Pre-Socratics cease with Democritus, who is often regarded as the furthest point of development of early Greek thought. With respect to the Pluralists, this may be so. But there is at least one mediating figure not caught up in combinatory atomism: Diogenes of Apollonia. Diogenes attempted to preserve the old Ionian monism in the face of the Eleatic onslaught by speaking of one element, Air, interspersed with Void and changing into the various things of experience through condensation and rarefaction. His thought is a legitimate alternative to pluralism—an alternative no more or less logically sound in the light of Parmenidean logic—and one which preserves the vitality of an immanent stuff to explain reality. Where Diogenes shows the mediating tendency, however, is in his complete neglect of the Heraclitean theme of the constructive role of conflict, and in his claim that the one element, Air, is intelligent. It is an approach that brings to mind Anaxagoras' Nous, while at the same time echoing the old Ionian conception of *Physis*.

In addition to Diogenes', two other lines of inquiry will subsequently be introduced. They are included not only because they serve to throw the achievement of the natural philosophers into sharper relief, but also

---

*i.e., power may corrupt even the best.

because of their intrinsic interest. The strict empiricism of the Medical Tradition, beginning with Alcmaeon of Croton and continuing in the Hippocratic writings, will serve mainly to highlight the speculative tendency of mainstream thinkers, while the Sophists' concentration on ethical and political problems will underscore the intense interest of mainstream thinkers in nonhuman nature. As expressive of underlying social forces, the Sophists will also mark both the conclusion of early Greek philosophy and the beginning of a new movement, commencing with the Socratic return to fundamentals and the monumental synthetic achievements of Plato and Aristotle.

NOTES

1. Kathleen Freeman, *Ancilla to the Pre-Socratic Philosophers* (Oxford: Basil Blackwell & Mott, 1962), Frg. 299, p. 119.

2. Cicero *De Or.* 2. 58. 235; Horace *Ep.* 2. 1. 194; Guthrie, vol. 2 p. 387 and n4.

3. Diogenes Laertius 9. 45; Kirk & Raven, p. 403.

4. Kirk & Raven, p. 402.

5. *Ibid.*

6. Guthrie, vol. 2, p. 395, n2.

7. Milton C. Nahm, *Selections from Early Greek Philosophy*, 4th ed. (New York: Appleton-Century-Crofts, 1964), p. 162.

8. Cornford, *From Religion to Philosophy*, p. 158.

9. Guthrie, vol. 2, pp. 422-3.

10. *Ibid.*, p. 426.

11. Guthrie, vol. 2, p 470

12. *Ibid.*, p. 483. Guthrie gives as reference E. Frank, *Plato und die sogenannten Pythagoreer* (Hall, 1923), p. 81 and n205.

13. *Ibid.*, p. 488.

14. Aetius 4. 7. 4; Nahm, p. 174.

15. Guthrie, vol. 2, pp. 432-3.

16. Aristotle *DeSensu* 442a29; Kirk & Raven, p. 421.

17. Aetius 4. 8. 10; Kirk & Raven, p. 421.

18. Malcolm Stratton, *Theophrastus and the Greek Physiological Psychology Before Aristotle* (London: George Allen & Unwin, Ltd., 1917), p. 109.

19. Nahm, p. 176.

20. Guthrie, vol. 2, pp. 473-4.

21. Aetius. 1. 7. 16; Guthrie, vol. 2, p. 480.

CHAPTER 10

Diogenes of Apollonia

T125   Diogenes Laertius 9. 57. [Loeb]
Diogenes of Apollonia, son of Apollothemis, was a natural
philosopher and a most famous man. Antisthenes calls him
a pupil of Anaximenes; but he lived in Anaxagoras' time.

Diogenes lived in the latter half of the Fifth Century B.C. and probably
came from the Milesian colony of Apollonia on the Black Sea rather
than from Apollonia in Crete, as was once thought. Though in the
Milesian tradition, he lived too late to have been a pupil of Anaximenes,
and even Laertius' claim that he was a contemporary of Anaxagoras
must be interpreted in the light of an observation by Theophrastus that
he was "almost the youngest of those who occupied themselves with
these matters (i.e., physical studies)"[1]. Jaeger takes the fact that Diogenes was the butt of the comic poets Aristophanes and Philemon, as
evidence that he must have spent considerable time in Athens.[2]

  Simplicius gives the following account of Diogenes' work:

T126   Simplicius *Phys.* 151. 20 [K&R428]
...it must be realized that several books were written by this
Diogenes (as he himself mentioned in *On nature*, where he
says that he had spoken also against the physicists—whom
he calls 'sophists'—and written a *Meteorology*, in which he
also says he spoke about the material principle, as well as *On
the nature of man*); in the *On nature*, at least, which alone of
his works came into my hands, he proposes a manifold

demonstration that in the material principle posited by him
is much intelligence.

DIOGENES' IMPORTANCE

Diogenes is omitted in many popular treatments of the Pre-Socratics
because of his supposed eclecticism and because his thinking is regarded
as a throwback to earlier, more primitive ideas. That Diogenes was an
eclectic is not only attested to by Theophrastus,[3] but is evident from a
perusal of his fragments: Diogenes is indebted to Anaxagoras and
Leucippus, as Theophrastus maintains,[4] and also to Anaximenes and
Heraclitus. But the combination produces an original result—one constituting a legitimate post-Parmenidean alternative to the pluralistic
systems of Empedocles, Anaxagoras, and the Atomists. Diogenes
rejects all of them for a return (with some important differences) to
Ionian monism.

The return to Ionian monism involves the idea, going back as far as
Thales, that nature is alive, with all of its attendant teleological implications. If atomism is seen with Cornford as the logical outcome of the
scientific tendency in philosophy, Diogenes stands in strong opposition
to that outcome. With the pluralists, the dynamic living force assumed
common to all things by Greek thinkers before Parmenides first retires
to a position outside of them, i.e., Empedocles' Love and Strife and
Anaxagoras' Mind, only to be entirely eliminated from the scene by
Leucippus and Democritus, whose atoms need only necessity to guide
them. In sharp contrast, not only teleological guidance, but intelligent
guidance is for Diogenes the foundation of everything that happens in
the universe.

CONTRA THE PLURALISTS AND AIR AS PHYSIS

Diogenes' first fragment sets forth his approach to philosophy:
(Frg.1) In starting any thesis, it seems to me, one should put
forward as one's point of departure something incontrovert-
ible; the expression should be simple and dignified.
Diogenes' own point of departure is that of Anaximenes: everything is a
manifestation of the one substance, Air. In order to maintain this thesis
he must, as Guthrie suggests[5], not only counter the pluralists but also
show how it is possible to maintain in the face of Parmenidean logic that
the many can come from the one.

Frg. 2 contains not only an initial statement of the thesis but also the
required attack on the pluralists. Essentially, Diogenes' criticism is that,

unless the plurality of realities assumed by the pluralists to exist has a common substance it will be impossible for them to interact with one another. Whether the objection is legitimate and whether the felt need of all the pluralists for a unifying factor or factors (Empedocles' Love and Strife, Anaxagoras' Mind, and even the Atomists' Necessity), counts in any way toward answering it will be left to the reader.

> (Frg.2) It seems to me, to sum up the whole matter, that all existing things are created by the alteration of the same thing, and are the same thing. This is very obvious. For if the things now existing in this universe—earth and water and air and fire and all the other things which are seen to exist in this world: if any one of these were different in its own (*essential*) nature, and were not the same thing which was transformed in many ways and changed, in no way could things mix with one another, nor could there be any profit or damage which accrued from one thing to another, nor could any plant grow out of the earth, nor any animal or any other thing come into being, unless it were so compounded as to be the same. But all these things come into being in different forms at different times by changes of the same (*substance*), and they return to the same.

Subsequent fragments go on to develop the idea that Air is in itself "everlasting and immortal" despite the fact that it is manifold in form (Frg. 8), and that it must also be intelligent in order to explain how it happens that "all things have their measure" and "the best possible arrangment" (Frg.3). The dependence of both life and intelligence on breathing of air are also offered as "important indications" of the truth of the claim that Air is the same as soul or life and intelligence (Frg.4). All of these ideas are quite similar to Anaxagoras' conception of the nature of Mind. The difference is that Diogenes' air is a material rather than an immaterial principle.

> (Frg.7) And this (*Element*) itself is a body both everlasting and immortal; whereas of other things, some come into being and others pass away.

> (Frg.8) But this seems to me to be clear, that it is great and strong, everlasting and immortal and manifold in form.

> (Frg.3) Such a distribution would not have been possible without Intelligence, (*namely*) that all things should have their measure: winter and summer and night and day and rains and winds and periods of fine weather; other things also, if one will study them closely, will be found to have the best possible arrangement.

(Frg.4) Further, in addition to these, there are also the following important indications: men and all other animals live by means of Air, which they breathe in, and this for them is both Soul (Life) and Intelligence, as had been clearly demonstrated in this treatise; and if this is taken from (*them*), Intelligence also leaves.

CONTRA PARMENIDES, AND THE DEVELOPMENT OF AN ONTOLOGY

In order to answer the inevitable Eleatic question of how it is possible for the many changing things of experience to be manifestations of one unchanging substance, Diogenes makes use of Leucippus' "Void" along with Anaximenes' "Condensation and Rarefaction." The following passage from Diogenes Laertius, which, incidentally, also ascribes to Diogenes of Apollonia belief in a plurality of worlds, mentions both:

T127   Diogenes Laertius 9. 57. [Loeb]
Air is the universal element. There are worlds unlimited in
number, and unlimited empty space. Air by condensation
and rarefaction generates the worlds. Nothing comes into
being from what is not or passes away into what is not.

Leucippus' answer to Parmenides was an infinity of Parmenidean Ones moving in the Void according to Necessity. Diogenes' answer is a Parmenidean One interspersed with Void capable of taking on varying densities and degrees of heat at different locations through the process of Condensation and Rarefaction. Instead of necessity, the living intelligence of the Parmenidean One (for Diogenes, Air) steers all. Reference to degree of heat as well as "steering" or "guiding" remind one of the nature and function of Heraclitus' *Logos*-Fire. Heraclitus also thought that his *Logos*-Fire, through breathing, was the source of life and intelligence.

(Frg.5) And it seems to me that that which has Intelligence is that which is called Air by mankind; and further, that by this, all creatures are guided, and that it rules everything; for this in itself seems to me to be God and to reach everywhere and to arrange everything and to be in everything. And there is nothing which has no share of it; but the share of each thing is not the same as that of any other, but on the contrary there are many forms both of the Air itself and of Intelligence; for it is manifold in form: hotter and colder and dryer and wetter and more stationary or having a swifter motion; and there are many other differences inherent in it and infinite (*forms*) of savour and colour. Also in all animals the

Soul is the same thing, (*namely*) Air, warmer than that outside in which we are, but much colder than that nearer the sun. This degree of warmth is not the same in any of the animals (and indeed, it is not the same among different human beings), but it differs, not greatly, but so as to be similar. But in fact, no one thing among things subject to change can possibly be exactly like any other thing, without becoming the same thing. Since therefore change is manifold, animals also are manifold and many, and not like one another either in form or in way of life or intelligence, because of the large number of (*the results of*) changes. Nevertheless, all things live, see and hear by the same thing (*Air*), and all have the rest of Intelligence also from the same.

Points worth noting in this fragment are:
1. That Diogenes explicitly refers to air by the term "God" and that this God is immanent in everything.
2. That, though degree of warmth is singled out for special attention, the opposties as well as all other sensed characteristics really qualify Air as it is in itself and are not mere subjective manifestations. (In this respect Diogenes' position is a qualitative monism parallelling the qualitative pluralism of Empedocles and Anaxagoras and differing from the "geometrical pluralism" of the Atomists.)
3. That differences among animals and man with respect to form, way of life, and degree of intelligence are due to differences in degree of warmth.
4. That Air is not only the principle of life but also that which makes sensation possible.

SENSATION AND THOUGHT

T128 Theophrastus *De Sensu* 39ff. [K&R440]
Diogenes attributes thinking and the senses, as also life, to air. Therefore he would seem to do so by the action of similars (for he says that there would be no action or being acted upon, unless all things were from one). The sense of smell is produced by the air round the brain. . . . (40) Hearing is produced whenever the air within the ears, being moved by the air outside, spreads toward the brain. Vision occurs when things are reflected on the pupil, and it, being mixed with the air within, produces a sensation. A proof of this is that, if there is an inflamation of the veins (i.e. those in the eye), there is no mixture with the air within, nor vision, although the reflection exists exactly as before. Taste occurs

to the tongue by what is rare and gentle. About touch he
gave no definition, either about its nature or its objects. But
after this he attempts to say what is the cause of more
accurate sensations, and what sort of objects they have. (41)
Smell is keenest for those who have least air in their heads,
for it is mixed most quickly; and, in addition, if a man draws
it through a longer and narrower channel; for in this way it is
more swiftly addressed. Therefore some living creatures are
more perceptive of smell than are men; yet nevertheless, if
the smell were symmetrical with the air, with regard to
mixture, man would smell perfectly....That the air within
perceives, being a small portion of the god, is indicated by
the fact that often when we have our mind on other things,
we neither see nor hear. (43) Pleasure and pain come about
in this way: whenever air mixes in quantity with the blood
and lightens it, being in accordance with nature, and pene-
trates through the whole body, pleasure is produced; but
whenever the air is present contrary to nature and does not
mix, then the blood coagulates and becomes weaker and
thicker, and pain is produced. Similarly confidence and
health and their opposites....(44) Thought, as has been
said, is caused by pure and dry air; for a moist emanation
inhibits the intelligence; for this reason thought is dimin-
ished in sleep, drunkenness and surfeit. That moisture
removes intelligence is indicated by the fact that other living
creatures are inferior in intellect, for they breathe the air
from the earth and take to themselves moister sustenance.
Birds breathe pure air, but have a constitution similar to that
of fishes; for their flesh is solid, and the breath does not
penetrate all through but stays around the abdomen....
Plants, through not being hollow and not receiving air
within them, are completely devoid of intelligence.

NATURAL PHILOSOPHY AND SCIENCE

Though Diogenes wrote on cosmogony, cosmology, meteorology,
and magnetism, no fragments and little other information remain. It
seems that he showed little originality in these areas. The following two
passages from commentators bear on Diogenes' cosmogony:

T129 [Plutarch] *Strom.* 12 [K&R438]
He gives this account of cosmogony: the whole was in
motion, and became rare in some places and dense in others;

where the dense ran together centripetally it made the earth, and so the rest by the same method, while the lightest parts took the upper position and produced the sun.

T130 Diogenes Laertius 9. 57. [Loeb]

The earth is spherical, firmly supported in the centre, having its construction determined by the revolution which comes from heat and by the congealment caused by cold.

Diogenes obviously had strong biological interests and there are two fragments on physiology, the second of which, remarkable for its detail, must have been based on careful empirical investigation.

(Frg.9) (Galen *quoting* Rufus of Ephesus: *All medical men agree that the male foetus is formed sooner and moves sooner than the female; Diogenes alone says the contrary*).

(Frg.6) The blood-vessels in man are as follows: there are two main blood-vessels; these extend from the abdomen along the spinal column, one to the right, one to the left, going (*down*) to each of the legs correspondingly, and up to the head past the collar-bone through the throat. From these, blood-vessels extend throughout the whole body: from the right-hand one to the right side, from the left-hand one to the left side; the two biggest to the heart along the spine, and others a little higher through the chest below the armpit to each of the corresponding arms. And the one is called splenetic (*after the spleen*), and other (*after the liver*) hepatic. The extreme end of each of them divides, one branch going to the thumb, the other to the wrist, and from these go fine and many-branched veins to the rest of the hand and the fingers. (*Two*) other finer blood-vessels lead from the original (*main*) blood-vessels on the right to the liver, and on the left to the spleen and the kidneys. Those extending to the legs divide at the point of attachment (*to the body*) and extend throughout the thigh; the largest of them goes behind the thigh and is thick where it emerges; a second goes inside the thigh and is a little less thick. Then they travel past the knee to the shin and the foot, as in the hands; and they descend into the ankle and thence to the toes.

From the chief blood-vessels, many fine veins divide off also to the abdomen and the sides. Those which extend to the head through the throat come into view as large blood-vessels in the neck; and from each of these, at its extremity, many divide off to the head, those on the right going to the left, those on the left going to the right; and they each end at the ear.

There is another blood-vessel on each side of the neck parallel to the large one, a little smaller than the latter; into this the majority of those from the head itself unite. These extend through the throat inside, and from each of them (*blood-vessels*) travel below the shoulder-blade and to the arms. And beside the splenetic and hepatic blood-vessels others a little smaller appear: these are opened when there is any pain under the skin, but if the pain is in the abdomen, the hepatic and splenetic vessels are bled. There are others also leading from these below the breasts. There are other fine ones again which lead from each (*of the main vessels*) through the spinal marrow to the testicles in men, and in women to the womb. (The main blood-vessels, which come from the abdomen, are broader, and then become finer, until they change over from right to left and from left to right). These are called after the semen. The thickest blood is swallowed up by the fleshy parts; but if any is left over after passing through these parts, it becomes fine and warm and foamlike.

ONE REMAINING FRAGMENT

The following fragment is included for the sake of completeness: (Frg. 10) (*Contracted form of the word 'full'*).

NOTES

1. Theophrastus *Phys. Op.* Frag. 2 *ap.* Simplicium *Phys.* 25. 1; Kirk & Raven, p. 429.
2. Jaeger, *Theology of the Early Greek Philosophers*, p. 165, and p. 243, n53.
3. Theophrastus *Phys. Op.* Frag. 2 *ap* Simplicium *Phys.* 25. 1; Kirk & Raven, p. 429.
4. *Ibid.*
5. Guthrie, vol. 2, p. 367.

PART IV
THE MEDICAL TRADITION
AND THE SOPHISTS

The Medical Tradition

The Sophists

CHAPTER 11

The Medical Tradition

The rational method of the nature philosophers is thrown into sharper relief by comparison with the more empirical approach of the Greek medical tradition.

Greek medical science was still in a nascent state at the time of Alcmaeon of Croton, whose life probably overlapped that of Pythagoras and who, though thought by some later commentators to be a Pythagorean, was distinguished from them by Aristotle on the basis of his treatment of opposites. Including Alcmaeon among those Pythagoreans for whom there are ten pairs of opposites, he says:

> **T131**   Aristotle *Meta.* 986a27-986b1.
> In this way Alcmaeon of Croton seems also to have conceived the matter, and either he got this view from them or they got it from him; for he expressed himself similarly to them. For he says most human affairs go in pairs, meaning not definite contrarieties, e.g. white and black, sweet and bitter, good and bad, great and small. He threw out indefinite suggestions about the other contrarieties, but the Pythagoreans declared both how many and which their contrarieties are.†

By the time of the writing of the Hippocratic treatise *On Medicine* between 450 and 420 B.C., medicine had become more clearly inde-

---

†See T31, pp. 85-6 for the whole context.

pendent of natural philosophy.[1] Natural philosophers contemporary with or after Alcmeon, such as Empedocles, Anaxagoras and Democritus, took an interest in medical questions, but their interest was from a vantage point different from that of Hippocrates. While the medical doctrines of the natural philosophers and physicians under their influence are determined by one or another theory of the universe as a whole, Hippocrates approaches medicine from a purely empirical point of view—an approach that in its origin can be traced back to Alcmaeon.

With the exception of the Eleatics, the natural philosophers took it as their function to explain phenomena as observed. But as should by now be clear, the explanations they gave, though rational in character, yet originated in the "collective representations" or "convictions" of their culture.† This in itself is not to be criticized except insofar as adherence to such presuppositions blinds a thinker to workable alternatives. That such was the result, however, is suggested by the generally dogmatic tone of the natural philosophers. In this respect as well as in their primarily theoretical rather than practical interest, the natural philosophers were, as Cornford argues, closer in spirit to seer-poets than to scientists in the contemporary sense.[2] This is further borne out by the fact that, with the possible exception of the Pythagoreans and Empedocles, there is practically no evidence that any of the natural philosophers performed experiments. In contrast, while Alcmaeon and Hippocrates had not yet developed explicit experimental method in the modern sense, their emphasis on the epistemological primacy of sense experience, when combined with the practical concern of the medical doctor to cure his patient, certainly suggests at least an implicit experimentation.

But then, the differing levels of development of relevant experimentation in natural philosophy and in medicine, and recognition of the kinship between natural philosopher and seer-poet do not necessarily conflict with the notion that the original impetus to the differentiation of philosopher from poet was due to the stimulus given rational thought by technological developments in Ionia. Further, one can truthfully say that natural science without paradigm, model, assumption, or hypothesis would be but a very pale shadow of its real self. Perhaps in the end it is as legitimate to observe that the physicians would have been well served by some judicious *a priori* theorizing as it is to say that the theories of the natural philosophers suffered because of insufficient experimental grounding. So viewed, the empirical method of Alcmaeon and Hippocrates, if not so much in opposition to the "dogmatic method" of the natural philosophers, as Cornford would have it, surely appears as a very necessary corrective.

---

†See pp. 9-12.

ALCMAEON OF CROTON

Nothing is known of Alcmaeon's life beyond the fact that he flour-ished early in the fifth century B.C.,[3] that he was from Croton, that he at one time studied with Pythagoras, and that he probably wrote a book which was the source of his remaining fragments.[4]

Physiology and medicine were Alcmaeon's prime interest, which accounts for his concern with cognition and the nature of the soul. Because medicine had not yet emerged as a distinct discipline, however, Alcmaeon also expressed opinions on the immortality of the soul as well as on astronomy and cosmology—thus going beyond the limitations of his own medical empiricism. There are no fragments and little other information concerning his views on these last two subjects, but in any case it would seem that Alcmaeon's contributions are his ideas concern-ing knowledge and the soul.

EMPIRICAL THEORY OF KNOWLEDGE

Alcmaeon is reported to have begun his book on natural science on a nondogmatic theme:

> (Frg.1) Alcmaeon of Croton, son of Peirithous, said the following to Brotinus and Leon and Bathyllus: concerning things unseen, (as) concerning things mortal, the gods have certainty, whereas to us as men conjecture (*only is possible*).

Frg.4, which follows, bears out Aristotle's separation of Alcmaeon from the Pythagoreans and also introduces his influential conception of the role of harmony (translated more literally in the fragment as "equal-ity of rights"). This influence probably extended even to the Pyth-agoreans.[5]

> (Frg.4) *Health is the* equality of rights *of the functions, wet-dry, cold-hot, bitter-sweet and the rest; but* single rule *among them causes disease; the single rule of either pair is deleterious. Disease occurs sometimes from an internal cause such as excess of heat or cold, sometimes from an external cause such as excess or deficiency of food, some-times in a certain part, such as blood, marrow or brain; but these parts also are sometimes affected by external causes, such as certain waters or a particular site or fatigue or constraint or similar reasons. But* health is the harmonious mixture of the qualities.

What is of interest with respect to Alcmaeon's theory of knowledge is that in contrast with the Pythagorean table of opposites, the opposites mentioned by Alcmaeon consist exclusively of sensed characteristics. In addition, no definite number of them is singled out as more important than the others. Both assumptions tie in with Alcmaeon's concern with staying close to the plane of experience and his refusal to dogmatize.

An account of Alcmaeon's physiological approach to sensation contained in Frg. 1a exhibits not only his empiricism but two other original contributions as well, viz., his distinction of sensation from understanding and his fixing on the brain as the center of mental activity. Contrast this, for example with his contemporary, Empedocles, for whom sensation and thought were regarded as to some extent analogous, and for whom the heart was the physical center:

T132   Theophrastus *De Sensu* 25f [Guthrie 1. 347]
Among those who explain sensation by dissimilars, Alcmaeon begins by clarifying the difference between men and lower animals. Man, he says, differs from the others in that he alone has understanding, whereas they have sensation but do not understand:* (Frg. 1a)† Thought is distinct from sensation, not, as it is for Empedocles, the same.

He then proceeds to each sense separately. Hearing is through the ears because they contain void, which resounds. Sound is produced in the cavity (*sc.* of the outer ear—Beare), and the air (of the intra-tympanic ear—*id.*) echoes it. A man smells with his nostrils, as he draws the breath up to the brain in the act of breathing. Tastes are distinguished by the tongue, which being warm and soft melts the object by its heat and owing to its porous and delicate structure receives and transmits the flavour. The eyes see through the water surrounding them. That the eye contains fire is evident, for the fire flashes forth when it is struck, and it sees by means of the bright element and the transparent when the latter gives back a reflection, and the purer this element is, the better it sees.

All the senses are in some way connected to the brain, and for this reason they are incapacitated if it is disturbed or shifted, for it obstructs the passages through which the sensations take place.

Concerning the mode or the organs of touch he has nothing to say. This then is the extent of his explanations.

---

*The word used, ξυνίεναι, means literally 'to put together', and traces of this basic meaning probably survived in the mind of a Greek writer of the fifth century. All animals have sensation, but only man can make a synthesis of his sensations.
†Freeman's version of Fragment 1a: "Man differs from the other (*creatures*) in that he alone understands; the others perceive, but do not understand."

DOCTRINE OF THE SOUL

Although in a general way the ideas were part and parcel of Greek culture, Aristotle tells us that Alcmaeon explicitly reasoned that the soul, as the cause of life activity, must be immortal because of the resemblance of this life activity to the motion of the heavenly bodies, also assumed to be divine and immortal.

> **T133**   Aristotle *De Anima* 405a29–33
> ...he says that it (i.e. the soul) is immortal because it resembles 'the immortals', and that this immortality belongs to it in virtue of its ceaseless movement; for all the 'things divine', moon, sun, and planets, and the whole heavens, are in perpetual movement.

The parallel between macrocosm and microcosm is carried a step further in the next fragment:

> (Frg.2) Men perish because they cannot join the beginning to the end.

Since the motion of the heavenly bodies is circular, so in some sense must be the motion attributed to the divine soul. The beginning and end referred to, then, are the beginning and end of a circle, and death occurs when the circle is incomplete. One is led to think here of Alcmaeon's definition of health as a harmony of sensible opposites— perhaps the empirical equivalent of "joining the beginning to the end."

REMAINING FRAGMENTS

The only two remaining fragments require no discussion:

> (Frg.3) (*In mules, the males are sterile because of the fineness and coldness of the seed, and the females because their wombs do not open*).
> (Frg.5) It is easier to guard against an enemy than against a friend.

HIPPOCRATES OF COS

The earliest Greek medical writings are the Hippocratic collection. Some of them are ascribed to Hippocrates himself; the authorship of others is unknown; some are undoubtedly apocryphal. The corpus is extensive, the number of works varying from edition to edition. How they came to be gathered together and ascribed to Hippocrates is uncertain.

Of Hippocrates himself, it is believed he was born on the island of Cos off the Ionian coast and flourished during the latter half of the fifth century B.C. He belonged to a family of physicians and traveled extensively in Greece. Little else is known of the externals of his life.

The ideas of the Hippocratic Corpus chosen for presentation here are not intended as representative of its overall content. Rather the principle of selection has been their relevance to the work of the natural philosophers and, even more particularly, to their theory of knowledge.

CONTRA THE NATURAL PHILOSOPHERS AND THE PHYSICIANS INFLUENCED BY THEM

Empedocles is taken as an example of those who would base medicine on an a priori view of the nature of man. All medical knowledge, insists the writer of *Ancient Medicine*, can come *only* from medical practice.

> **S1** Hippocrates *Ancient Medicine* 20. [Loeb]
> Certain physicians and philosophers assert that nobody can know medicine who is ignorant what man is; he who would treat patients properly must, they say, learn this. But the question they raise is one for philosophy; it is the province of those who, like Empedocles, have written on natural science, what man is from the beginning, how he came into being at the first, and from what elements he was originally constructed. But my view is, first, that all that philosophers or physicians have said or written on natural science no more pertains to medicine than to painting.* I also hold that clear knowledge about natural science can be acquired from medicine and from no other source.[6]

The following selection makes clear the opposition of the Hippocratic writer to "hypotheses" or "postulates," terms which in their time had the connotation of prejudiced assumptions. The sarcastic point is also made that, though proceeding in dogmatic fashion may be acceptable when one is talking about "what is in the sky and below the earth," because no one can tell whether the claims made are true or false, dogmatism is not appropriate in medicine, which is an art of intimate importance to all men.

> **S2** Hippocrates *Ancient Medicine* 1. [Loeb]
> All who, on attempting to speak or to write on medicine, have assumed for themselves a postulate as a basis for their discussion—heat, cold, moisture, dryness, or anything else that they may fancy—who narrow down the causal principle

---

*Or perhaps, "pertains less to medicine than to literature."

of diseases and of death among men, and make it the same in all cases, postulating one thing or two, all these obviously blunder in many points even of their statements, but they are most open to censure because they blunder in what is an art, and one which all men use on the most important occasions, and give the greatest honours to the good craftsmen and practitioners in it .... Wherefore I have deemed that it has no need of an empty postulate,* as do insoluble mysteries, about which any exponent must use a postulate, for example, things in the sky or below the earth. If a man were to learn and declare the state of these, neither to the speaker himself nor to his audience would it be clear whether his statements were true or not. For there is no test the application of which would give certainty.

Disagreement among natural philosophers who attempt to explain man on the basis of explanatory principles "not clearly descriptive of him" is an indication that they do not know what they are talking about. Physicians who say that man is made from an arbitrarily chosen single element are also to be criticized because illnesses as well as cures are of many kinds.

S3   Hippocrates *Nature of Man* 1, 2. [Loeb]
He who is accustomed to hear speakers discuss the nature of man beyond its relations to medicine will not find the present account of any interest. For I do not say at all that a man is air, or fire, or water, or earth, or anything else that is not an obvious constituent of a man; such accounts I leave to those that care to give them. Those, however, who give them have not in my opinion correct knowledge. For while adopting the same idea they do not give the same account. Though they add the same appendix to their idea—saying that "what is" is a unity, and that this is both unity and the all—yet they are not agreed as to its name. One of them asserts that this one and the all is air, another calls it fire, another, water, and another, earth; while each appends to his own account evidence and proofs that amount to nothing. The fact that, while adopting the same idea, they do not give the same account, shows that their knowledge too is at fault....

Now about these men I have said enough, and I will turn to physicians. Some of them say that man is blood, others

---

*Or, reading καινῆς, "a novel postulate." But the writer's objection is not that the postulate is novel, but that it is a postulate. A postulate, he says, is "empty" in a sphere where accurate and verifiable knowledge is possible. Only in regions where science cannot penetrate are ὑποθεσεις legitimate. For this reason I read κενῆς.

that he is bile, a few that he is phlegm. Physicians, like metaphysicians, all add the same appendix. For they say that a man is a unity, giving it the name that severally they wish to give it; this changes its form and its power,* being constrained by the hot and the cold, and becomes sweet, bitter, white, black and so on. But in my opinion these views also are incorrect. Most physicians then maintain views like these, if not identical with them; but I hold that if man were a unity he would never feel pain, as there would be nothing from which a unity could suffer pain. And even if he were to suffer, the cure too would have to be one. But as a matter of fact cures are many. For in the body are many constituents, which, by heating, by cooling, by drying or by wetting one another contrary to nature, engender diseases; so that both the forms** of diseases are many and the healing of them is manifold.

A most telling point is that the practitioner who adheres to some prejudiced assumption experiences a gap between his theory and practice due to the fact that supposed crucial factors such as heat always occur concomitantly with other characteristics equally influential on the course of the disease. If such a practitioner upon being asked "What sort of food?" after having prescribed something hot, specified some special sort of hot food, his practice belies this theory.

S4   Hippocrates *Ancient Medicine* 15. [Loeb]
I am at a loss to understand how those who maintain the other view, and abandon the old method to rest the art on a postulate, treat their patients on the lines of their postulate. For they have not discovered, I think, an absolute hot or cold, dry or moist, that participates in no other form. But I think that they have at their disposal the same foods and the same drinks as we all use, and to one they add the attribute of being hot, to another, cold, to another, dry, to another, moist, since it would be futile to order a patient to take something hot, as he would at once ask, "What hot thing?" So that they must either talk nonsense or have recourse to one of these known substances. And if one hot thing happens to be astringent, and another hot thing insipid, and a third hot thing causes flatulence (for there are many var-

---

*By "power" (δύναμις) is probably meant the sum total of a thing's characteristics or qualities. Recent research, however, makes it likely that in the medical writers δύναμις is often used with ἰδέη or φύσις to form a tautological phrase meaning "real essence."
**A. E. Taylor thinks that this phrase must mean, "there are many substances in which disease arises," i.e., disease is not necessarily "diseased state of the *blood*."

ious kinds of hot things, possessing many opposite powers), surely it will make a difference whether he administers the hot astringent thing, or the hot insipid thing, or that which is cold and astringent at the same time (for there is such a thing), or the cold insipid thing. For I am sure that each of these pairs produces exactly the opposite of that produced by the other, not only in a man, but in a leathern or wooden vessel, and in many other things less sensitive than man. For it is not the heat which possesses the great power, but the astringent and the insipid, and the other qualities I have mentioned, both in man and out of man, whether eaten or drunk, whether applied externally as ointment or as plaster.

POSITIVE HIPPOCRATIC IDEAS

A selection of quotations from Hippocratic precepts evidences a conception of the proper epistemological relation between sense perception and reason which is sharply different from that of the natural philosophers. In general, the natural philosophers disparage sense perception in preference to the greater discriminative power of thought, while at the same time presupposing something non-sensible which is perceptible by thought and analogous to, though independent of, the qualities which are objects of sensation. Alcmaeon had claimed that sensation and thought were basically different from one another. The selection which follows also presupposes that they are different, but in addition makes thought epistemologically dependent on sensation, which is in no way deceptive and must provide the data for all rational knowledge. Purely verbal conclusions without a solid basis in fact are fruitless.

S5   Hippocrates *Precepts* 1, 2. [Loeb]
....one must attend in medical practice not primarily to plausible theories but to experience combined with reason. For a theory is a composite memory of things apprehended with sense-perception. For the sense-perception, coming first in experience and conveying to the intellect the things subjected to it, is clearly imagined, and the intellect, receiving these things many times, noting the occasion, the time and the manner, stores them up in itself and remembers. Now I approve of theorising also if it lays its foundations in incident, and deduces its conclusions in accordance with phenomena. For if theorising lays its foundation in clear fact, it is found to exist in the domain of intellect, which itself receives from other sources each of its impressions. So we

must conceive of our nature as being stirred and instructed under compulsion by the great variety of things; and the intellect, as I have said, taking over from nature the impressions, leads us afterwards into truth. But if it begins, not from a clear impression, but from a plausible fiction,* it often induces a grievous and troublesome condition. All who so act are lost in a blind alley....

But conclusions which are merely verbal cannot bear fruit, only those do which are based on demonstrated fact. For affirmation and talk are deceptive and treacherous. Wherefore one must hold fast to facts in generalisations also,** and occupy oneself with facts persistently, if one is to acquire that ready and infallible habit which we call "the art of medicine." For so to do will bestow a very great advantage upon sick folk and medical practitioners. Do not hesitate to inquire of laymen, if thereby there seems likely to result any improvement in treatment. For so I think the whole art has been set forth, by observing some part of the final end in each of many particulars, and then combining all into a single whole. So one must pay attention to generalities in incidents, with help and quietness rather than with professions and the excuses that accompany ill-success.

In the interests of communication with those most vitally concerned i.e., "everyday people," the writer of *Ancient Medicine* also thought that medical language should never be far removed from what is intelligible to them. This is set forth as an added argument against basing medicine on hypotheses or prejudiced assumptions.

S6 Hippocrates *Ancient Medicine* 2. [Loeb]
But it is particularly necessary, in my opinion, for one who discusses this art to discuss things familiar to ordinary folk. For the subject of inquiry and discussion is simply and solely the sufferings of these same ordinary folk when they are sick or in pain. Now to learn by themselves how their own sufferings come about and cease, and the reasons why they get worse or better, is not an easy task for ordinary folk; but when these things have been discovered and are set forth by another, it is simple. For merely an effort of memory is required of each man when he listens to a statement of his experiences. But if you miss being understood by laymen, and fail to put your hearers in this condition, you will miss

---

*i.e., if the general statement from which we deduce conclusions be a plausible but untrue hypothesis. Conclusions drawn from such hypotheses lead nowhere.
**Or, possibly, "even from beginning to end."

reality. Therefore for this reason also medicine has no need of any postulate.

Finally we come to the conception of man and his health set forth in the Hippocratic work "The Nature of Man":

S7   Hippocrates *Nature of Man* 4, 5. [Loeb]

The body of man has in itself blood, phlegm, yellow bile and black bile; these make up the nature of the body, and through these he feels pain or enjoys health. Now he enjoys the most perfect health when these elements are duly proportioned to one another in respect of compounding, power and bulk, and when they are perfectly mingled. Pain is felt when one of these elements is in defect or excess, or is isolated in the body without being compounded with all the others. For when an element is isolated and stands by itself, not only must the place which it left become diseased, but the place where it stands in a flood must, because of the excess, cause pain and distress. In fact when more of an element flows out of the body than is necessary to get rid of superfluity, the emptiness causes pain....

Now I promised to show that what are according to me the constituents of man remain always the same, according to both convention and nature. These constituents are, I hold, blood, phlegm, yellow bile, and black bile. First I assert that the names of these according to convention are separated, and that none of them has the same name as the others; furthermore, that according to nature their essential forms are separated, phlegm being quite unlike blood, blood being quite unlike bile, bile being quite unlike phlegm. How could they be like one another, when their colours appear not alike to the sight nor does their touch seem alike to the hand? For they are not equally warm, nor cold, nor dry, nor moist. Since then they are so different from one another in essential form and in power, they cannot be one, if fire and water are not one.

It is clear that Alcmaeon's notion of health as a harmony of sensed factors has been preserved, though they are no longer opposites and have been reduced to four in number.

DISCUSSION OF A PARTICULAR ILLNESS: THE SACRED DISEASE

The following selections from *The Sacred Disease*, i.e., epilepsy, make clear Hippocratic opposition to charlatanism as well as Hippocratic support of the idea that diseases are purely natural phenomena.

All diseases have a natural explanation: all diseases are both equally sacred and human.

S8 Hippocrates *The Sacred Disease* 1, 2. [Loeb]
I am about to discuss the disease called "sacred." It is not, in my opinion, any more divine or more sacred than other diseases, but has a natural cause, and its supposed divine origin is due to men's inexperience, and to their wonder at its peculiar character. Now while men continue to believe in its divine origin because they are at a loss to understand it, they really disprove its divinity by the facile method of healing which they adopt, consisting as it does of purifications and incantations. But if it is to be considered divine just because it is wonderful, there will be not one sacred disease but many, for I will show that other diseases are no less wonderful and portentous, and yet nobody considers them sacred.

My own view is that those who first attributed a sacred character to this malady were like the magicians, purifiers, charlatans and quacks of our own day, men who claim great piety and superior knowledge. Being at a loss, and having no treatment which would help, they concealed and sheltered themselves behind superstition, and called this illness sacred, in order that their utter ignorance might not be manifest. They added a plausible story, and established a method of treatment that secured their own position. They used purifications and incantations; they forbade the use of baths, and of many foods that are unsuitable for sick folk....

These observances they impose because of the divine origin of the disease, claiming superior knowledge and alleging other causes, so that, should the patient recover, the reputation for cleverness may be theirs; but should he die, they may have a sure fund of excuses, with the defence that they are not at all to blame, but the gods.

S9 Hippocrates *The Sacred Disease* 21. [Loeb]
This disease styled sacred comes from the same causes as others, from the things that come and go from the body, from cold, sun, and from the changing restlessness of winds. These things are divine. So that there is no need to put the disease in a special class and to consider it more divine than the others; they are all divine and all human. Each has a nature and power of its own; none is hopeless or incapable of treatment. Most are cured by the same things as caused them. One thing is food for one thing, and another for

another, though occasionally each actually does harm. So the physician must know how, by distinguishing the seasons for individual things, he may assign to one thing nutriment and growth, and to another diminution and harm. For in this disease as in all others it is necessary, not to increase the illness, but to wear it down by applying to each what is most hostile to it, not that to which it is conformable. For what is [in] conformity gives vigour and increase; what is hostile causes weakness and decay. Whoever knows how to cause in men by regimen moist or dry, hot or cold, he can cure this disease also, if he distinguish the seasons for useful treatment, without having recourse to purifications and magic.

DIFFERING ATTITUDES OF THE NATURAL PHILOSOPHERS, MEDICAL TRADITION, AND SHOPHISTS TOWARD EXPERIENCE

The matter of fact attitude of Alcmaeon and Hippocrates toward experience, reason, and their relation contrasts both with that of the natural philosophers and that of the Sophists—though in differing ways. In general, with the exception of the Eleatics, the natural philosophers took experience as their starting point, and regarded it as their responsibility to explain it; so far there is a coincidence with the Medical Tradition. But the natural philosophers also think of reason as apprehending a reality beyond appearances in a manner analogous to the way objects are perceived—a view which for them also entails the deceptiveness of perception. Where Alcmaeon and Hippocrates differ from the natural philosophers is in their notion that reason is limited to the formal function of interpreting experience: Reason deals with experience as manifest in practice rather than with some reality beyond experience. And the reality dealt with is always the particular case rather than (in their view) a general abstraction unrelated to the particular case.

The emphasis of Alcmaeon and Hippocrates on the particularity of the real as revealed in medical practice parallels what will be the emphasis of the Sophists on the particularity of values as revealed in moral and political practice. But while the practice of the medical doctor is dominated by the ideal of scientific objectivity, the moral and political practice of fifth century Athens worked in precisely the opposite direction. Many of the Sophists will deny any standard of value or truth beyond the particularity of experience, and the general impact of the Sophists in the context of Fifth Century Athenian culture will be in the direction of subjective relativism.

NOTES

1. Guthrie, vol. 1, p. 358.

2. Cornford, *Principium Sapientiae*, pp. 107-8.

3. Aristotle *Meta.* 986a29; Kirk & Raven, pp. 232-3, based on the possible claim of Aristotle that "Alcmaeon was a young man in Pythagoras' old age..."

4. Diogenes Laertius 8. 83.

5. Kirk & Raven, p. 234.

6. All "S" selections in this chapter are from the Loeb Classical Library as listed under "Sources Cited."

CHAPTER 12
The Sophists

Originally the term *Sophist* was used to denote a "skilled craftsman" or a "wise man." Not until the fifth century B.C. was it applied to the group of travelling professional teachers that arose at that time. The derogatory use of it to mark the use of fallacious arguments (sophistry) dates from that era also. In a dialogue devoted to discovering the nature of the Sophist, Plato characterizes him as "a paid hunter after wealth," "a merchant in the goods of the soul," "a manufacturer of the learned wares he sells," and "a disputer" who knowingly teaches falsehood. This is a powerful charge, not devoid of some basis in fact, but strongly colored by Plato's own views of what the Sophists were up to.

On the other hand, if Plato's view of the Sophists is biased and therefore not adequate by itself, a look at their remaining fragments is not adequate either. For any proper appreciation, we must consider the unique contribution which the Sophists made to the development of Greek culture, and the first part of this chapter will be devoted to that task. The second part consists of selected facts, fragments, and commentary on some important Sophists. Only a few important fragments are included here because of limitations of space.

THE GREEK ENLIGHTENMENT

With the Sophists, we reach a turning point in early Greek thought. This is true in at least two closely related respects. First, the Sophists were no longer very greatly interested in natural science. Rather, political conflict had stimulated a preoccupation with political and ethical problems. Second, though general political factors and not just the Sophists themselves are largely responsible for the emergence of the Individualist-Intellectual stage in the evolution of Greek moral convictions,† this emergence coincided with the arrival of the Sophists on the scene of Greek intellectual life. In the Archaic stage, *Themis* or established right was the dominant moral concept—in other words, an unquestioning acceptance of the rules of a tribal society as handed down by the ruler. Xenophanes was one of the first to question *Themis* and to suggest that the rule of reason should be paramount in such matters; but it was Heraclitus who brought the Classical stage to fruition by envisioning man as part of the cosmos and subject to its laws as they are discoverable through reason. Development from the Archaic to the Classical stage parallels the substitution of the *Polis* or city-state for tribal and familial ties as symbols of social loyalty. A rationally discoverable *Diké*, or just law, is the foundation of the *Polis*‡ and education in *Areté*, or virtue, rather than blood line the means whereby loyalty to society is insured.§

Whereas Parmenides' denial of the applicability of rational law to the world of change, whether cosmic or human, had challenged the very foundation of the Classical synthesis, the Classical position now came to be attacked at a no less vital point, viz., its assumption of the applicability of *one* law to both the cosmic and human domains. By the time of Pericles, from the defeat of the Persians until the onset of the Peloponnesian War, roughly 475-430 B.C., the idea that human affairs stand under the governance of cosmic law becomes increasingly untenable. The common observations acquired in travel alone were enough to call such a view into question. How could the human and the cosmic be one under the same laws when everywhere the human structures varied so greatly? This certainly would have been most obvious to the wandering teachers we know as the Sophists.

Gradually, under the pressure of such questioning, the distinction between *Physis*--meaning that which comes about through nature—and *Nomos*—that which comes about through the customs of mankind—came into use. And with it the traditional morality grounded in the old religion and its customs came under a withering fire. Relativism in conduct and skepticism in knowledge carried the field. It is on these grounds and in reaction to this development that Socrates and Plato try

---

†See pp. 9ff.

‡See the quoted passage from Aeschylus' *Eumenides* on pp. 60-1.

§See pp. 10ff for an explanation of the Greek terms appearing in this paragraph as well as elsewhere in this chapter.

to combat the teachings of the Sophists. The Socratic method of inquiry was based upon the assumption that a natural foundation for virtue can be discovered through rational inquiry. But this breaking down of traditional ways of thinking and acting was a result of something more important, something that went beyond the opening up of the world through travel, and the threat of a common enemy.

The defeat of the Persians by the Greeks had left Athens as the dominant city throughout the Greek world. Without any doubt, it was Athenian money, energy, and leadership which turned the trick. Under the protection of their navy and with the weight of their prestige, Athens rapidly became the mercantile center of the whole Mediterranean world. This completely changed the character of the city from a seat of agrarian and aristocratic power ruled by customs and laws grounded in the religious tradition, to a cosmopolitan city of merchants and businessmen ruled chiefly by self-interest. And it wasn't long before what had been a sphere of influence justly acquired in the defeat of a common enemy turned into the Athenian Empire. The gradual enfranchisement of the new merchant class in Athens, culminating in its extension to the sailors who maintained the conditions of prosperity by force, created the participatory type of democracy, which, in effect, turned the government of the city into a popularity contest. To succeed in this atmosphere required a particular kind of *Areté* or virtue—the ability to persuade others. A great deal of the competition, both economic and political, took the form of litigation in the courts, and there being no lawyers, each citizen had to be able to defend himself before his peers and in the face of his accusers. The need for rhetorical ability was pressing, and, more than any other, it was this virtue that the Sophists professed to teach.

The great age of speculation with which we have been primarily concerned in this book brought along with it all kinds of new knowledge. It was accompanied by the founding and separate establishment of many disciplines, trades, and sciences, for this speculation was rooted in observation and curiosity about nature. Recall the list of subjects Democritus occupied himself with—Hades, Ethics, Astronomy, colours, causes of Seeds, Plants and Fruit, Geometry, the Calendar, Rhythm and Harmony, Poetry, Song, Diet, Farming, Medical Method—it runs the gamut of human concern, from the theoretical to the practical. Such breadth of knowledge and concern is typical of the Greek Enlightenment, and the Sophists played a large part in the development and spread of this new knowledge throughout Greece. Some forty years after the turn of the fifth century B.C., Aristophanes tells us that people who could not read and write were difficult to find in Athens. Gilbert Murray gives an insight into the role of the Sophists in bringing about this transformation:

Across the mind of our stupid peasant the great national struggle against Persia brought first the idea that perhaps really it was better to die than to be a slave; that it was well to face death not merely for his own home but actually—incredible as it seemed—for other people's homes, for the homes of those wretched people in the next village. Our own special customs and taboos, he would reflect with a shiver, do not really matter when they are brought into conflict with a common Hellenism or a common humanity. There are greater things about us than we know. There are also greater men. These men who are in everybody's mouth: Themistocles above all, who has defeated the Persian and saved Greece: but crowds of others besides, Aristides the Just and Miltiades, the hero of Marathon; Demokedes, the learned physician, who was sought out by people in need of help from Italy to Susa; Hecataeus, who made a picture of the whole earth, showing all the countries and cities and rivers and how far each is from the next, and who could have saved the Ionians if they had only listened to him; Pythagoras, who had discovered all about numbers and knew the wickedness of the world and founded a society, bound by strict rules, to combat it. What is it about these men that has made them so different from you and me and the other farmers who meet in the agora on market-day? It is *sophia*, wisdom; it is *arete*, virtue. They are not a bit stronger in the arm, not bigger, not richer, or more high born: They are just wiser and thus better men. Cannot we be made wise?... it was in answer to this call for *sophia* that the Sophists arose. Doubtless they were of all kinds; great men and small, honest and dishonest; teachers of real wisdom and pretense. Our tradition is rather bitter against them, because it dates from the bitter time of reaction and disappointment, when the hopes of the fifth century and the men who guided it seemed to have led Athens only to her fall. Plato in particular is against them as he is against Athens herself. In the main, the judgment of the afterworld upon them will depend on the side we take in the never-ending battle; they fought for light and knowledge and freedom and the development of all man's powers.[1]

It may well be that the choice Murray speaks of is not quite so clear-cut; but he is right in his claim that it was to meet the felt need for knowledge that the Sophists came into existence. Jaeger likens them to the *literati* of the Renaissance who confounded their listeners with their knowledge and abilities.[2] They were walking encyclopedias of the arts, crafts, and fields of science, selling their wares to all who would pay. The most accomplished were able to amass a fortune.

Jaeger distinguishes three sorts of educational methods used by the Sophists.[3] He refers to them as the Encyclopedic, the Formal, and the Political and Ethical. The first involved acquainting the intellect with a wide variety of facts, the second entailed the formal training of the intellect, and the third treated the intellect as operating in a social context and educated the individual as belonging to a community. It should be noted that this third method is not far removed from the Classical tradition. Jaeger mentions Hippias of Elis as exemplifying the first, and Protagoras as illustrating the third. Perhaps Gorgias, who is reputed to have taught nothing but rhetoric, would be an example of the second, and Jaeger mentions Prodicus of Ceos also. They were educating the future leaders of Athens.

At their best, the Sophists did not claim that their training would turn a bad man into a moral one in our sense of the word "moral": they were only improving the skills essential to Athenian political life. Unfortunately for the Sophists' good name, however, so successful were they that the major standard of individual and civic virtue became the generally cheap success of the market-place.

SOME IMPORTANT SOPHISTS

A. *Protagoras of Abdera*

Protagoras, chief among the older generation of Sophists, who lived during the latter half of the fifth century B.C., is said to have flourished in the 84th Olympiad (444–441 B.C.) and to have died at the age of seventy. Although nothing reliable is known of his early life, Diogenes Laertius has this to say of him:

> **T134** Diogenes Laertius 9. 50–56. [Loeb]
> Protagoras, son of Artermon...was born at Abdera....He and Prodicus of Ceos gave public reading for which fees were charged....Protagoras studied under Democritus... was the first to maintain that there are two sides to every question, opposed to each other, and he even argued in this fashion, being the first to do so. Furthermore he began a work thus: [Frg. 1] "Man is the measure of all things, of things that are that they are, and of things that are not that they are not."† He used to say that soul was nothing apart

---

†Freeman's version of Fragment 1: "(*From 'Truth' or 'Refutatory Arguments'*). Of all things the measure is Man, of the things that are, that they are, and of the things that are not, that they are not."

from the senses...and that everything is true. In another
work he began thus: [Frg. 4.] "As to the gods, I have no
means of knowing either that they exist or that they do not
exist. For many are the obstacles that impede knowledge,
both the obscurity of the question and the shortness of
human life."† For this introduction to his book the Athenians expelled him; and they burnt his works in the market
place, after sending round a herald to collect them from all
who had copies in their possession.

He was the first to exact a fee of a hundred minae and the
first to distinguish the tenses of verbs, to emphasize the
importance of seizing the right moment, to institute contests
in debating, and to teach rival pleaders the tricks of their
trade. Furthermore, in his dialectic he neglected the meaning in favour of verbal quibbling, and he was the father of
the whole tribe of eristical disputants now so much in evidence. He too first introduced the method of discussion
which is called Socratic. Again, as we learn from Plato in the
Euthydemus, he was the first to use in discussion the argument of Antisthenes which strives to prove that contradiction is impossible, and the first to point out how to attack
and refute any proposition laid down....He too invented
the shoulder-pad on which porters carry their burdens, so
we are told by Aristotle in his treatise *On Education*; for he
himself had been a porter, says Epicurus somewhere. This
was how he was taken up by Democritus, who saw how
skilfully his bundles of wood were tied. He was the first to
mark off the parts of discourse into four, namely, wish,
question, answer, command....

The works of his which survive are these: *The Art of
Controversy. Of Wrestling. On Mathematics. Of the State.
Of Ambition. Of Virtues. Of the Ancient Order of Things.
On the Dwellers in Hades. Of the Misdeeds of Mankind. A
Book of Precepts.* Of Forensic Speech for a Fee, two books
of opposing arguments...‡

The story is told that once, when he asked Euathlus his
disciple [who had studied with him and agreed to pay if and
only if he won his first case at law] for his fee, the latter

---

† Freeman's translation of Fragment 4 is: "*(From 'On the Gods').* About the gods, I am not
able to know whether they exist or do not exist, nor what they are like in form; for the
factors preventing knowledge are many: the obscurity of the subject, and the shortness of
human life."

‡ Though some are doubtful, most of the titles mentioned in this testimonium are included
among Protagoras' fragments. Some of the ideas are included as well.

replied, "But I have not won a case yet." "Nay," said Protagoras, "if I win this case against you I must have the fee, for
winning it; if you win, I must have it, because you win it."

It is reported that Euathlus turned the tables on Protagoras by pointing
out that, on the contrary, he owed nothing either way: if he wins the suit
he is cleared by the court, if not then he is cleared by the agreement.[4]

The best picture we have of Protagorean doctrine is from Plato in the
dialogues *Protagoras* and *Theaetetus*. Protagoras speaks:

T135   Plato *Protagoras* 316d, 318d[5]

Personally I hold that the Sophists' art is an ancient one, but
that those who put their hand to it in former times, fearing
the odium which it brings, adopted a disguise and worked
under cover. Some used poetry as a screen, for instance
Homer and Hesiod and Simonides, others religious rites and
prophecy, like Orpheus and Musaeus and their school; some
even—so I have noticed—physical training, like Iccus of
Tarentum and in our own day Herodicus of Selymbria, the
former Megarian, as great a Sophist as any. Music was used
as cover by your own Agathocles, a great Sophist, and
Pythoclides of Ceos and many others. All of them, as I say,
used these arts as a screen to escape malice. I myself, however, am not of their mind in this. I don't believe they
accomplished their purpose, for they did not pass unob-
served by the men who held the reins of power in their cities,
though it is on their account that these disguises are adopted;...I therefore have always gone the opposite way to my
predecessors'. I admit to being a Sophist and an educator,
and I consider this a better precaution than the other—
admission rather than denial....

When he comes to me, Hippocrates† will not be put
through the same things that another Sophist would inflict
on him. The others treat their pupils badly. These young
men, who have deliberatly turned their backs on specializa-
tion, they take and plunge into special studies again, teaching them arithmetic and astronomy and geometry and
music—here he glanced at Hippias—but from me he will
learn only what he has come to learn. What is that subject?
The proper care of his personal affairs, so that ne may best
manage his own household, and also of the state's affairs, so
as to become a real power in the city, both as speaker and
man of action.

Do I follow you? said I [Socrates]. I take you to be
describing the art of politics, and promising to make men

---

†Not the physician, but a pupil of Protagoras.

good citizens. That, said he [Protagoras], is exactly what I
profess to do.

Freeman summarizes Protagoras' general views on education very
neatly:

> The civic virtues can be taught, and are taught by constant
> correction from childhood upward; the punishment inflic-
> ted by the laws had education, not revenge, as its object.
> Men all are endowed with the qualities which make life in a
> community possible—a sense of reverence and a sense of
> right—and it is to these that the educator appeals.[6]

In the following selection from the *Theaetetus* Socrates gives an
account of the "man is the measure" doctrine:

T136   Plato *Theaetetus* 152a[7]

Socrates:... It is the same that was given by Protagoras,
though he stated it in a somewhat different way. He says,
you will remember that man is the measure of all things—
alike of the being of things that are and of the not-being of
things that are not. No doubt you have read that.

Theaetetus: Yes, often.

Socrates: He puts it in this sort of way, doesn't he, that any
given thing is to me such as it appears to me, and is to you
such as it appears to you, you and I being men?

Theaetetus: Yes, that is how he puts it.

Socrates: Well, what a wise man says is not likely to be
nonsense. So let us follow up his meaning. Sometimes when
the wind is blowing, one of us feels chilly, the other does not,
or one may feel slightly chilly, the other quite cold.

Theaetetus: Certainly.

Socrates: Well, in that case are we to say that the wind in
itself is cold or not cold? Or shall we agree with Protagoras
that it is cold to the one who feels chilly, and not to the other?

Theaetetus: That seems reasonable.

Socrates: And further that it so "appears" to each of us.

Theaetetus: Yes.

Socrates: And "appears" means that he "perceives" it so?

Theaetetus: True.

Socrates: "Appearing," then, is the same thing as "per-
ceiving," in the case of what is hot or anything of that kind.
They are to each man such as he *perceives* them.

Theaetetus: So it seems.

Socrates: Perception, then, is always of something that is,
and, as being knowledge, it is infallible.

Theaetetus: That is clear.

Along with the view that the perception of the individual is true for the individual, Protagoras seems to have held that the perceptions of mankind are the measure of what exists and what does not exist. But while denying any applicable sense of truth, Protagoras also held some perceptions to be better than others and directed his persuasive techniques to bringing about the better. It would seem that his sense of "better" rested on social considerations grounded in the sensibilities of man as man. His views are not far removed from the classical position of Heraclitus, but the differences are worthy of consideration as we find them expressed in the following passage.

T137 Plato *Theaetetus* 166c[8]

For I do indeed assert that the truth is as I have written. Each one of us is a measure of what is and of what is not, but there is all the difference in the world between one man and another just in the very fact that what is and appears to one is different from what is and appears to the other. And as for wisdom and the wise man, I am very far from saying they do not exist. By a wise man I mean precisely a man who can change any one of us, when what is bad appears and is to him, and make what is good appear and be to him. In this statement, again, don't set off in chase of words, but let me explain still more clearly what I mean. Remember how it was put earlier in the conversation. To the sick man his food appears sour and is so, to the healthy man it is and appears the opposite. Now there is no call to represent either of the two as wiser—that cannot be—nor is the sick man to be pronounced unwise because he thinks as he does, or the healthy man wise because he thinks differently. What is wanted is a change to the opposite condition, because the other state is better.

And so too in education a change has to be effected from the worse condition to the better; only, whereas the physician produces a change by means of drugs, the Sophist does it by discourse. It is not that a man makes someone who previously thought what is false think what is true, for it is not possible either to think the thing that is not or to think anything but what one experiences, and all experiences are true. Rather, I should say, when someone by reason of a depraved condition of mind has thoughts of a like character, one makes him, by reason of a sound condition, think other and sound thoughts, which some people ignorantly call true, whereas I should say that one set of thoughts is better than the other, but not in any way truer. And as for wise, my dear Socrates, so far from calling them frogs, I call them, when they have to do with the body, physicians, and when they have to do with plants, husbandmen. For I assert that husbandmen too, when plants are sickly and have depraved sensations, substitute for these sensations that are sound and healthy, and moreover that wise and honest public speakers substitute in the community sound for unsound views of what is right. For I hold that whatever practices seem right and laudable to any particular state are so, for that state, so long as it holds by them. Only, when the practices are, in any particular case, unsound for them, the wise man substitutes others that are and appear sound. On the same principle the Sophist, since he can in the same manner guide his pupils in the way they should go, is wise and worth a considerable fee to them when their education is completed. In this way it is true both that some men are wiser than others and that no one thinks falsely, and you, whether you like it or not, must put up with being a measure, since by these considerations my doctine is saved from shipwreck.

B.   *Gorgias of Leontini*

Gorgias was born about 480 B.C. and lived well into the fourth century. He is said to have studied with Empedocles, and among his pupils was the Meno of Plato's dialogue, Proxenus, a friend of Xenophon and, most famous of all, Isocrates.† He first came to Athens as chief of an embassy from his native city in 427 B.C.

T138   Diodorus Siculus 12. 53. [Loeb]
This year in Sicily the Leontines, who were colonists from Chalcis but also kinsmen of the Athenians, were attacked, as it happened, by the Syracusans. And being hardpressed in the war and in danger of having their city taken by storm because of the superior power of the Syracusans, they dispatched ambassadors to Athens asking the Athenian people to send them immediate aid and save their city from the perils threatening it. The leader of the embassy was Gorgias the rhetorician, who in eloquence far surpassed all his contemporaries. He was the first man to devise rules of rhetoric and so far excelled all other men in the instruction offered by the sophists that he received from his pupils a fee of one hundred minas!...[a large sum] Now when Gorgias had arrived in Athens and been introduced to the people in assembly, he discoursed to them upon the subject of the alliance, and by the novelty of his speech he filled the Athen-

---

†Attic orator and writer.

ians, who are by nature clever and fond of dialectic, with
wonder. For he was the first to use the rather unusual and
carefully devised structures of speech, such as antithesis,
sentences with equal members or balanced clauses or similar
endings, and the like, all of which at that time was enthusias-
tically received because the device was exotic, but is now
looked upon as laboured and to be ridiculed when employed
too frequently and tediously. In the end he won the Athenians over to an alliance with the Leontines, and after having
been admired in Athens for his rhetorical skill he made his
return to Leontini.

Certainly Plato knew Gorgias, and in the dialogue named for him we
have Gorgias' views on his own profession.

T139 Plato *Gorgias* 456a[9]

Gorgias: And when any of the choices you mentioned just
now is in question, Socrates, you see that it is the orators
who give advice and carry their motions.

Socrates: That is what surprises me, Gorgias, and that is
why I asked you long since what is the scope of rhetoric.
When so looked at, it seems to me to possess almost super-
human importance.

Gorgias: Ah, if only you knew all, Socrates, and realized
that rhetoric includes practically all other faculties under her
control. And I will give you good proof of this. I have often,
along with my brother and with other physicians, visited one
of their patients who refused to drink his medicine or submit
to the surgeon's knife or cautery: and when the doctor was
unable to persuade them, I did so, by no other art but
rhetoric. And I claim too that, if a rhetorician and a doctor
visited any city you like to name and they had to contend in
argument before the Assembly or any other gathering as to
which of the two should be chosen as doctor, the doctor
would be nowhere, but the man who could speak would be
chosen, if he so wished. And if he should compete against
any other craftsman whatever, the rhetorician rather then
any other would persuade the people to choose him: for
there is no subject on which a rhetorician would not speak
more persuasively than any other craftsman, before a
crowd. Such then is the scope and character of rhetoric: but
it should be used, Socrates, like every other competitive art.
We must not employ other competitive arts against one and
all merely because we have learned boxing or mixed fighting
or weapon combat, so that we are stronger than our friends

and foes: we must not, I say, for this reason strike our friends or wound or kill them. No indeed, and if a man who is physically sound has attended the wrestling school and has become a good boxer, and then strikes his father or mother or any others of his kinsmen or friends, we must not for this reason detest or banish from our cities the physical trainers or drill instructors. For they imparted this instruction for just employment against enemies or wrongdoers, in self-defense not aggression: but such people perversely employ their strength and skill in the wrong way. And so the teachers are not guilty, and the craft is not for this reason evil or to blame, but rather, in my opinion, those who make improper use of it. And the same argument applies also to rhetoric. The rhetorician is competent to speak against anybody or any subject, and to prove himself more convincing before a crowd on practically every topic he wishes: but he should not any the more rob doctors—or any other craftsmen either—of their reputation, merely because he has the power: one should make proper use of rhetoric as of athletic gifts.

Plato's treatment of Gorgias is never as anything but a rhetorician, although in the *Meno* he assigns the effluence theory of perception to him.† There is no doubt that Gorgias was the father of rhetoric and laid down basic principles for that art. He considered it the most powerful art and, like Protagoras, believed it could be taught and should be used only for the good.

Gorgias was personally acquainted with, and respected and admired by the first men of Athens during its Golden Age. So widely was his style of speaking imitated that a new verb "gorgiazein" came into use.[10] He was invited to speak at the funeral for the Athenian war dead, a great tribute to someone not from Athens. The following passage from it survives and exhibits his use of antitheses.

(Frg.6) For what did these men lack that men should have? What did they have that men should not have? Would that I could express what I wish, and may I wish what I ought, avoiding divine wrath, shunning human envy! For the courage these men possessed was divine, and the mortal part (*alone*) was human. Often, indeed, they preferred mild reasonableness to harsh justice, often also correctness of speech to exactitude of law, holding that the most divine and most generally applicable law was to say or keep silent, do or not

†For the meaning of this effluence theory of perception see Empedocles pp. 157ff.

do, the necessary thing at the necessary moment. They doubly exercised, above all, as was right, mind and body, the one in counsel, the other in action; helpers of those in undeserved adversity, chastisers of those in undeserved prosperity; bold for the common good, quick to feel for the right cause, checking with the prudence of the mind the imprudence of the body; violent towards the violent, restrained towards the restrained, fearless towards the fearless, terrifying among the terrifying. As evidence of these things, they have set up trophies over the enemy, an honour to Zeus, a dedication of themselves: men not unacquainted with the inborn spirit of the warrior, with love such as the law allows, with rivalry under arms, with peace, friend of the arts; men showing reverence towards the gods by their justice, piety towards their parents by their care, justice towards their fellow-citizens by their fair dealing, respect towards their friends by keeping faith with them. Therefore, although they are dead, the longing for them has not died with them, but immortal though in mortal bodies, it lives on for those who live no more.

Aristotle makes the following comment upon the teachings of the Sophists in general and Gorgias in particular.

T140 Aristotle *Soph. El.* 183b36-184a4

For the training given by the paid professors of contentious arguments was like the treatment of the matter by Gorgias. For they used to hand out speeches to be learned by heart, some rhetorical, others in the form of question and answer, each side supposing that their arguments on either side generally fall among them. And therefore the teaching they gave their pupils was ready but rough. For they used to suppose that they trained people by imparting to them not the art but its products.

The only apparently philosophical writing by Gorgias is his three-pronged argument against knowing, being, and communicating, reproduced below. It represents an extension of the Protagorean relativity of knowledge to the notion of being and talk about it. There is no clue whether this was written for philosophical purposes or as an exercise in argument for his pupils. Read as a parody of Parmenides, however, as Guthrie suggests[11], it would be at once both humorous and serious in intent from the point of view of one interested in ridiculing the Eleatic affirmation of *Physis* as Being.

(Frg.3) (Sextus, *from 'On Being' or 'On Nature'*):

I.   Nothing exists.
     (*a*) Not-Being does not exist.
     (*b*) Being does not exist.
            i.   as everlasting.
            ii.   as created.
            iii. as both.
            iv.   as One.
            v.   as Many.
     (*c*) A mixture of Being and Not-Being does not exist.
II. If anything exists, it is incomprehensible.
III. If it is comprehensible, it is incommunicable.

I.   Nothing exists.
     If anything exists, it must be either Being or Not-Being, or both
     Being and Not-Being.
     (*a*) It cannot be Not-Being, for Not-Being does not exist; if it
            did, it would be at the same time Being and Not-Being,
            which is impossible.
     (*b*) It cannot be Being, for Being does not exist. If Being
     exists, it must be either everlasting, or created, or both.
            i.   It cannot be everlasting; if it were, it would have no
                  beginning, and therefore would be boundless; if it is
                  boundless, then it has no position, for if it had position
                  it would be contained in something, and so it would no
                  longer be boundless; for that which contains is greater
                  than that which is contained, and nothing is greater
                  than the boundless. It cannot be contained by itself,
                  for then the thing containing and the thing contained
                  would be the same, and Being would become two
                  things—both position and body—which is absurd.
                  Hence if Being is everlasting it is boundless; if
                  boundless, it has no position ('is nowhere'); if without
                  position, it does not exist.
            ii.   Similarly, Being cannot be created; if it were, it must
                  come from something, either Being or Not-Being, both
                  of which are impossible.
            iii. Similarly, Being cannot be both everlasting and
                  created, since they are opposite. Therefore Being does
                  not exist.
            iv.   Being cannot be One, because if it exists it has size, and
                  is therefore infinitely divisible; at least it has threefold,
                  having length, breadth and depth.

    v.   It cannot be Many, because the Many is made up of an addition of Ones, so that since the One does not exist, the Many do not exist either.

   (c) A mixture of Being and Not-Being is impossible. Therefore since Being does not exist, nothing exists.

II. If anything exists, it is incomprehensible.

If the concepts of the mind are not realities, reality cannot be thought: if the thing thought is white, then white is thought about; if the thing thought is non-existent, then non-existence is thought about; this is equivalent to saying that 'existence, reality, is not thought about, cannot be thought'. Many things thought about are not realities: we can conceive of a chariot running on the sea, or a winged man. Also, since things seen are the objects of sight, and things heard are the objects of hearing, and we accept as real things seen without their being heard, and vice versa; so we would have to accept things thought without their being seen or heard; but this would mean believing in things like the chariot racing on the sea.

Therefore reality is not the object of thought, and cannot be comprehended by it. Pure mind, as opposed to sense-perception, or even as an equality valid criterion, is a myth.

III. If anything is comprehensible, it is incommunicable.

The things which exist are perceptibles; the objects of sight are appre- hended by sight, the objects of hearing by hearing, and there is no interchange; so that these sense-perceptions cannot com- municate with one another. Further, that with which we communicate is speech, and speech is not the same thing as the things that exist, the perceptibles; so that we communicate not the things which exist, but only speech; just as that which is seen, cannot become that which is heard, so our speech cannot be equated with that which exists, since it is outside us. Further, speech is composed from the percepts which we receive from without, that is, from perceptibles; so that it is not speech which communicates perceptibles, but perceptibles which create speech. Further, speech can never exactly represent perceptibles, since it is different from them, and perceptibles are apprehended each by the one kind of organ, speech by another. Hence, since the objects of sight cannot be presented to any other organ but sight, and the different sense-organs cannot give their information to one another, similarly speech cannot give any information about perceptibles.

Therefore, it anything exists and is comprehended, it is incommunicable.

C.   *Contributors to the Controversy Over Physis and Nomos*

Returning to the themes of the Sophists' distinction of *Nomos* from *Physis* and the onset of the Individualist-Intellectual state of the development of moral convictions, it is to be remarked once again that the terminal point of this stage was a subjective relativism regarding both fact and value. Though the Sophists were not as a group subjective relativists (perhaps neither Protagoras nor Gorgias was, for example), their ideas lent strength to the cultural movement in that direction. For Heraclitus, foremost representative of the Classical stage, *Nomos* had been the expression of *Physis* in human affairs. For the majority of Sophists however, not only were *Nomos* and *Physis* separated, but at the same time that the realities of political conflict in Athens led to conceiving of *Nomos* as only man-made, *Physis* lost its divinity and tended to be conceived in the political image of its interpreters.

While the view of the Sophist Thrasymachus of Chalcedon (active in the latter half of the fifth century) that *Diké* or Justice is the interest of the stronger, as it appears in Plato's *Republic*, is in itself politically neutral, social change in Athens had proceeded too far for the Classical alternative to be viable, and the Sophists' arguments are used by progressives and conservatives alike.

> **T141**   Plato *Republic* 343b. [Loeb]
> ...you think that the shepherds and the neatherds are considering the good of the sheep and the cattle and fatten and tend them with anything else in view than the good of their masters and themselves. And by the same token you seem to suppose that the rulers in our cities, I mean the real rulers, differ at all in their thoughts of the governed from a man's attitude toward his sheep or that they think of anything else night and day than the sources of their own profit. And you are so far out concerning the just and justice and the unjust and injustice that you don't know that justice and the just are literally the other fellow's good—the advantage of the stronger and the ruler, but a detriment that is all his own of the subject who obeys and serves—while injustice is the contrary and rules those who are simple in every sense of the word and just, and they being thus ruled do what is for his advantage who is the stronger and make him happy by serving him, but themselves by no manner of means. And you must look at the matter, my simple-minded Socrates, in this way, that the just man always comes out at a disadvantage in his relation with the unjust. To begin with, in their business dealings in any joint undertaking of the two you

will never find that the just man has the advantage over the unjust at the dissolution of the partnership but that he always has the worst of it. Then again, in their relations with the state, if there are direct taxes or contributions to be paid, the just man contributes more from an equal estate and the other less, and when there is a distribution the one gains much and the other nothing. And so when each holds office, apart from any other loss the just man must count on his own affairs' falling into disorder through neglect, while because of his justice he makes no profit from the state, and thereto he will displease his friends and his acquaintances by his unwillingness to serve them unjustly. But to the unjust man all the opposite advantages accrue. I mean, of course, the one I was just speaking of, the man who has the ability to overreach on a large scale. Consider this type of man, then, if you wish to judge how much more profitable it is to him personally to be unjust than to be just. And the easiest way of all to understand this matter will be to turn to the most consummate form of injustice which makes the man who has done the wrong most happy and those who are wronged and who would not themselves willingly do wrong most miserable. And this is tyranny, which both by stealth and by force takes away what belongs to others, both sacred and profane, both private and public, not little by little but at one swoop. For each several part of such wrongdoing the male- factor who fails to escape detection is fined and incurs the extreme of contumely, for temple robbers, kidnappers, bur- glars, swindlers, and thieves are the appellations of those who commit these several forms of injustice. But when in addition to the property of the citizens men kidnap and enslave the citizens themselves instead of these opprobrious names they are pronounced happy and blessed not only by their fellow citizens but by all who hear the story of the man who has committed complete and entire injustice. For it is not the fear of doing but of suffering wrong that calls forth the reproaches of those who revile injustice. Thus, Socrates, injustice on a sufficiently large scale is a stronger, freer, and more masterful thing than justice, and, as I said in the beginning, it is the advantage of the stronger that is the just, while the unjust is what profits a man's self and is for his advantage.

Critias of Athens (ca. 480–403 B.C.), an elder relative of Plato, a student of the Sophists and conservative in political action (he was one of the Thirty Tyrants),† offers the following also politically neutral account not only of the origin of *Nomos* but also of what the Classical sythesis had regarded as its cosmic divine sanction. While *Nomos* is regarded by him as a human invention to curb open crimes of violence, the gods are but another human invention designed to combat secret crimes of violence.

(Frg.25) (*From "Sisyphus", satyric play*)

There was a time when the life of men was unordered, bestial and the slave of force, when there was no reward for the virtuous and no punishment for the wicked. Then, I think, men devised retributory laws, in order that Justice might be dictator and have arrogance as its slave, and if anyone sinned, he was punished. Then, when the laws forbade them to commit open crimes of violence, and they began to do them in secret, a wise and clever man invented fear (*of the gods*) for mortals, that there might be some means of frightening the wicked, even if they do anything or say or think it in secret. Hence he introduced the Divine (*religion*), saying that there is a God flourishing with immortal life, hearing and seeing with his mind, and thinking of everything and caring about these things, and having divine nature, who will hear everything said among mortals, and will be able to see all that is done. And even if you plan anything evil in secret, you will not escape the gods in this; for they have surpassing intelligence. In saying these words, he introduced the pleasantest of teachings, covering up the truth with a false theory; and he said that the gods dwelt there where he could most frighten men by saying it, whence he knew that fears exist for mortals and rewards for the hard life: in the upper periphery, where they saw lightenings and heard the dread rumblings of thunder, and the starry-faced body of heaven, the beautiful embroidery of Time the skilled craftsman, whence come forth the bright mass of the sun, and the wet shower upon the earth. With such fears did he surround mankind, through which he well established the deity with his argument, and in a fitting place, and quenched lawlessness among men. . . .Thus, I think, for the first time did someone persuade mortals to believe in a race of deities.

---

†The Thirty Tyrants constituted a quisling government of Athens after its conquest by Sparta in the Peloponnesian War. They were of conservative political persuasion, and got their name from the repressive measures to which they resorted during their short one-year rule.

Callicles, a character in Plato's *Gorgias*, supposed by Plato to be an ardent student of the Sophists, argues for the conservative position and against the Athenian ideal of equality. Appealing to the waning Greek belief in *Physis* as a standard, he argues that the democratically oriented law of Athens conflicts with what is natural, namely, that the strong should rule. The contrast with Thrasymachus' view† should be noted: for him the strong rule only by *Nomos*.

T142   Plato *Gorgias* 483b[12]

For to suffer wrong is not even fit for a man but only for a slave, for whom it is better to be dead than alive: since when wronged and outraged he is unable to help himself or any other for whom he cares. But in my opinion those who framed the laws are the weaker folk, the majority. And accordingly they frame the laws for themselves and their own advantage, and so too with their approval and censure: and to prevent the stronger who are able to overreach them from gaining the advantage over them, they frighten them by saying that to overreach others is shameful and evil, and injustice consists in seeking the advantage over others: for they are satisfied, I suppose, if being inferior they enjoy equality of status. That is the reason why seeking an advantage over the many is by convention said to be wrong and shameful, and they call it injustice. But in my view nature herself makes it plain that it is right for the better to have the advantage over the worse, the more able over the less. And both among all animals and in entire states and races of mankind it is plain that this is the case—that right is recognized to be the sovereignty and advantage of the stronger over the weaker. For what justification had Xerxes in invading Greece or his father in invading Scythia? And there are countless other similar instances one might mention. But I imagine that these men act in accordance with the true nature of right, yes and, by heaven, according to nature's own law, though not perhaps by the law we frame: we mold the best and strongest among ourselves, catching them young like lion cubs, and by spells and incantations we make slaves of them, saying that they must be content with equality and that this is what is right and fair. But if a man arises endowed with a nature sufficiently strong, he will, I believe, shake off all these controls, burst his fetters, and break loose; and trampling upon our scraps of paper, our spells and incantations, and all our unnatural conventions, he rises

†See p. 256.

up and reveals himself our master who was once our slave,
and there shines forth nature's true justice.

Some sympathizers with the Athenian democracy such as Protagoras
deny *Physis* as a standard, as does Thrasymachus, and associate the
egalitarian law of Athens with both *Nomos* and *Dikè*. But other democratic sympathizers along with Callicles see the conventional law of
Athens as in conflict with the natural. Such were the Sophists, Hippias
of Elis (active in the latter half of the fifth century), and Antiphon (who
lived during the latter half of the fifth century). For them, however, in
contrast with Callicles, the objection is that Athenian law is too paroch-
ial. By nature, they argue, all men are equal—not just Athenians. In the
Protagoras Plato has Hippias say:

T143 Plato *Protagoras* 337c[13]
I count you all my kinsmen and family and fellow citizens—
by nature, not by convention. By nature like is kin to like,
but custom, the tyrant of mankind, does much violence to
nature.

The same two themes, the divergence between *Nomos* and *Physis* and
the appeal to *Physis* as a standard, appear in Antiphon's fragments:

(Frg.44 [in part]) (Oxyrhynchus papyrus. From 'Truth').
Justice, then, is not to transgress that which is the law of the
city in which one is a citizen. A man therefore can best
conduct himself in harmony with justice, if when in the
company of witnesses he upholds the laws, and when alone
without witnesses he upholds the edicts of nature. For the
edicts of the laws are imposed artificially, but those of nature
are compulsory. And the edicts of the laws are arrived at by
consent, not by natural growth, whereas those of nature are
not a matter of consent.

So, if the man who transgresses the legal code evades
those who have agreed to these edicts, he avoids both dis-
grace and penalty; otherwise not. But if a man violates
against possibility any of the laws which are implanted in
nature, even if he evades all men's detection, the ill is no less,
and even if all see, it is no greater. For he is not hurt on
account of an opinion, but because of truth. The examination of these things is in general for this reason, that the
majority of just acts according to law are prescribed contrary to nature....

We revere and honour those born of noble fathers, but
those who are not born of noble houses we neither revere nor
honour. In this we are, in our relations with one another, like
barbarians, since we are all by nature born the same in every

way, both barbarians and Hellenes. And it is open to all men to observe the laws of nature, which are compulsory. Similarly all of these things can be acquired by all, and in none of these things is any of us distinguished as barbarian or Hellene. We all breathe into the air through mouth and nostrils, and we all eat with hands. . . .

Such Sophists as Hippias and Antiphon were the first cosmopolitans.

When we reflect upon the downfall of Athens and the Greek vision generally, it is difficult not to share in some measure Plato's opinion of the Sophists. But while Plato's position can be appreciated, the more balanced view must emphasize the liberating influence of the Sophists and see them as major instruments of and contributors to the Greek Enlightenment and that Greek vision of man which has informed, inspired and, to some degree, bedeviled Western Civilization.

NOTES

1. Gilbert Murray, *Euripides and His Age* (New York: Henry Holt & Co., 1913) p. 48ff.

2. Jaeger, *Paideia*, p. 297.

3. *Ibid.*, pp. 292-3.

4. Apulêius *Florida* 18; *The Apologia and Florida of Apulêius of Madaura*, reprint. trans. H. E. Butler (Clarendon Press, 1909; Westport, Conn. Greenwood Press, 1970).

5. Plato, *Plato: Protagoras and Meno*, trans. W. K. C. Guthrie (London: Penguin Classics, 1956) pp. 47-48, 49-50.

6. Freeman, *Companion*, p. 348.

7. Plato, *Plato: The Collected Dialogues*, pp. 856-857.

8. *Ibid.*, pp. 872-873.

9. Plato, *Plato: Socratic Dialogues*, trans. W. D. Woodhead (Edinburgh & New York: Thomas Nelson and Sons, 1959) p. 198ff.

10. Philostratus *V.S.* 1. 9. 3; Freeman, *Companion* p. 356n.g[1]

11. Guthrie, vol. 3, pp. 193-194.

12. Plato, *Plato: Socratic Dialogues*, p. 241ff.

13. Plato, *Plato: Protagoras and Meno*, p. 71.

Sources Cited

Aeschylus. *The Oresteia of Aeschylus*, ed. Edited by Robert W. Corrigan.
 Translated by George Thomson. New York: Dell Publishing Co., 1965.
Apulêius. *Florida* 18; *The Apologia and Florida of Apulêius of Madaura.*
 Translated by H. E. Butler. Reprint. Clarendon Press, 1909; Westport, Conn.:
 Greenwood Press, 1970.
Aristotle. *Oxford Translation of Aristotle*. Edited by W. D. Ross. London: Oxford
 University Press, 1931.
Bowra, C. M. *The Greek Experience*. New York: The World Publishing Co., 1959.
Burke, Kenneth. *Permanence and Change*. Library of the Liberal Arts, 2nd rev. ed.,
 Indianapolis, Ind. & New York: Bobbs-Merrill Co., 1965.
Burnet, John. *Early Greek Philosophy*. Reprint of 4th ed., 1930; New York: Meridian
 Books, 1957.
Cleve, Felix M. *The Giants of Pre-Socratic Greek Philosophy*. vols. 1 and 2. The Hague:
 Martinus Nijoff.
Cornford, F. M. "Mysticism and Science in the Pythagorean Tradition," *Classical
 Quarterly* 16, 1922.
———. *Principium Sapientiae*. New York: Harper & Row Torchbooks,1965.
———. *Plato and Parmenides*. Indianapolis & New York: Bobbs-Merrill Co., (no date).
———. *From Religion to Philosophy*. New York: Harper & Row Torchbooks, 1957.
———. *Before and After Socrates*. Cambridge: Cambridge University Press, 1965.
Diodorus Siculus, *Library of History*. Translated by C. H. Oldfather. Cambridge:
 Harvard University Press, Loeb Classical Library, 1942.
Diogenes Laertius, *Lives of the Philosophers.* Translated by R.D. Hicks. Cambridge:
 Harvard University Press, Loeb Classical Library, 1942.
Dodds, E. R. *The Greeks and the Irrational*. Boston: Beacon Press, 1957.
Fairbanks, Arthur. *The First Philosophers of Greece*. London: Routledge and Kegan
 Paul, 1917.
Farrington, Benjamin. *Greek Science*. New York: Penguin Books, 1953.

Freeman, Kathleen. *Ancilla to the Pre-Socratic Philosophers*. Oxford: Basil Blackwell & Mott, 1962.

——. *Companion to the Pre-Socratic Philosophers*. 2nd ed. Cambridge: Harvard
University Press, 1966.

Frankfort, H. & H. A., Wilson, John A., Jacobsen, Thorkild. *Before Philosophy*. Reprint. New York: Penguin Books, 1954.

Guthrie, W. K. C. *A History of Greek Philosophy*. vols. 1, 2, 3. Cambridge: Cambridge
University Press, vol. 1, 1962, vol. 2, 1965, vol. 3, 1969.

Hamilton, Edith. *The Greek Way*. New York: W. W. Norton & Co., 1942.

Heath, Thomas L. *A History of Greek Mathematics I*. Oxford: The Clarendon, Press,
1965 [1921].

Heidegger, Martin. *An Introduction to Metaphysics*. Translated by Ralph Manheim.
New York: Doubleday Anchor Books, 1961.

Herodotus, *The Persian Wars*. Translated by A. D. Godley. Cambridge: Harvard
University Press, Loeb Classical Library, 1924.

Hesiod, *Theogony*. Translated by H. G. Evelyn White. Cambridge: Harvard University
Press, Loeb Classical Library, 1914.

Hippocrates, *Ancient Medicine, Precepts, The Sacred Disease* and *The Nature of Man*.
Translated by W. H. S. Jones and E. T. Withington. Cambridge: Harvard
University Press, Loeb Classical Library, 1962.

Huntington, Ellsworth. *Mainsprings of Civilization*. 1945. New York: Mentor Books,
1959.

Jaeger, W. W. *Paideia: The Ideals of Greek Culture*. 3 vols. 2nd ed. Oxford: University
Press, Galaxy Books, 1965.

——. *Theology of the Early Greek Philosopohers*. Oxford: Clarendon Press, 1947.

Kahn, C. H. *Anaximander and the Origins of Greek Cosmology*. New York & London:
Columbia University Press, 1960.

Kirk, G. S. & J. E. Raven. *The Presocratic Philosophers*. Cambridge: Cambridge
University Press, 1957.

Loew, Cornelius. *Myth, Sacred History and Philosophy*. Harcourt, Brace and World,
Inc., 1967.

Malinowski, Bronislaw. *Magic, Science and Religion and Other Essays*. New York:
Doubleday Anchor Books. 1955.

Mourelatos, Alexander P. D. *The Pre-Socratics*. New York: Doubleday Anchor Books,
1974.

Murray, Gilbert. *Euripides and His Age*. New York: Henry Holt & Co., 1913.

Nahm, Milton C. *Selections from Early Greek Philosophy*, 4th ed. New York: Appleton-
Century-Crofts, 1964.

Pepper, Stephen C. *World Hypotheses*. Berkeley: University of California Press, 1966.

Plato. *Plato: The Collected Dialogues*. Edited by Edith Hamilton and Huntington
Cairns. Princeton: Princeton University Press, Bollingen series LXXI, 1961.

——. *Plato: The Last Days of Socrates*. Translated by Hugh Tredennick. Rev. ed.
London: Penguin Classics. 1969.

——. *Plato's Phaedrus*. Translated by R. Hackforth. Cambridge: Cambridge
University Press, 1942.

——. *Plato: Protagoras and Meno*. Translated by W. K. C. Guthrie. London:
Penguin Classics, 1956.

——. *Republic*. Translated by Paul Shorey. Cambridge: Harvard University Press,
Loeb Classical Library, 1960.

——. *Plato: Socratic Dialogues*. Translated by W. D. Woodhead. Edinburgh
and New York: Thomas Nelson and Sons, 1959.

Ross, W. D., ed. *Oxford Translation of Aristotle*. London: Oxford University Press,
1931.

Russell, Bertrand. *Our Knowledge of the External World.* New York: Mentor Books, New American Library, 1960.

de Santillana, Giorgio. *The Origins of Scientific Thought.* New York: Mentor Books, New American Library, 1961.

Sarton, George. *A History of Science: Ancient Science Through the Golden Age of Greece.* New York: John Wiley & Sons, 1964.

Strabo. *Geography.* Translated by Horace L. Jones. Cambridge: Harvard University Press, Loeb Classical Library, 1960.

Stratton, Malcolm. *Theophrastus and the Greek Physiological Psychology Before Aristotle.* London: George Allan and Unwin, Ltd., 1917.

Wheelwright, Philip. *Heraclitus.* New York: Atheneum, 1964.

Windelband, Wilhelm. *History of Ancient Philosophy.* New York: Dover Publications, 1956.

Winspear, Alban D. *The Genesis of Plato's Thought.* 2nd ed. rev. New York: Russell & Russell, 1956.

Ancient Commentators

Aetius the Doxographer: Later than fourth century B.C. Compiled a book of philosophic opinions.

Agathemerus: Probably third century A.D. Wrote an outline of geography.

Apollodorus of Athens: Born ca. 180 B.C. Chronicler of Greek history from the fall of Troy (1184 B.C.) to 119 B.C.

Apulêuis of Medaura in Africa: Born ca. A.D. 114.

Aristotle of Stagira: 384–322 B.C. Student of Plato, tutor to Alexander the Great, founder of the Lyceum. Wrote separate works on numerous subjects in philosophy. Bk. I of the *Metaphysics* is a commentary on the ideas of the Early Greek thinkers.

Augustine: A.D. 354–430 Christian saint. Wrote *City of God* and *Confessions*.

Cicero: 106–43 B.C. Roman statesman, orator and author.

Clement of Alexandria: Second and third century A.D. Philosopher converted to Christianity.

Diogenes Laertius: Third century A.D. Writer of a history of philosophy which is the only one of its kind in existence. He is one of our major secondary sources of much of what we know of the Early Greek thinkers.

Diodorus Siculus: First century B.C. and A.D. Wrote a history of the world in forty books (fifteen of which exist), that preserves important material.

Eratosthanes of Alexandria: ca. 276-194 B.C. Astronomer, geographer, mathematician, and librarian of Alexandria. He first calculated the circumference of the earth within fifty miles of current measurements.

Eudemus of Rhodes: Third century B.C. pupil and editor of Aristotle's works.

Eusebius: Christian bishop and general historian of ancient history.

Galen: A.D. 130. Next to Hippocrates, the most importnt ancient medical writer.

Hecataeus of Miletus: Sixth and fifth century B.C. Historian and traveler; a source for Herodotus.

Herodotus of Halicarnassus: A fifth century B.C. Greek author of a *History of the Persian Wars*, and noted traveler.

Hesiod: Eighth century B.C. Boetian poet and author of *Theogony*, a genealogy of the gods, and of *Works and Days,* an early farmers' almanac.

Hippolytus: A.D. 165-235. Christian saint, theologian and compiler.

Horace: Roman writer, 65 B.C.-8 B.C.

Iamblichus of Chalcis: Fourth century A.D. Neo-Platonic philosopher. Wrote ten volumes on Pythagoras, only five of which survive.

Philostratus of Athens: Second and third centureis A.D. Wrote *Lives of the Sophists.*

Plato: 428-347 B.C. Pupil of Socrates, founder of the Academy and author of numerous dialogues on all phases of philosophy.

Plutarch of Chaeronea: ca. A.D. 46-119. A Greek biographer and voluminous writer about the Greek and Roman world.

Porphyrius: A.D. 233-305. Pupil of Plotinus. We have his lives of Pythagoras and Plotinus, commentaries on Aristotole's *Categories* and Ptolemy's *Harmonica* and a 15-volume treatise against Christianity which was destroyed by order of the Emperor.

Proclus of Byzantium: Fifth century A.D. Neo-Platonic commentator on Plato's dialogues, Hesiod's *Works and Days* and Bk. 1 of Euclid.

Sextus Empiricus: Third century A.D. Greek physician and philosopher of the Skeptic school. His *Adversus Mathematicus* is an important source work.

Simplicius of Cilicia: Sixth century A.D. Neoplatonic commentator on Aristotle and Epictetus and the Stoics.

Speucippus: Fourth century B.C. kin to Plato, whom he succeeded at the Academy.

Strabo of Pontus: Born ca. 638 B.C. Greek geographer and historian whose *Geography* is the only surviving book on that subject from antiquity and whose *History* in 47 books gives us information about the early geographers.

Theophrastus of Lesbos: 371-288 B.C. Student of Aristotle, his successor at the Lyceum, and compiler of Aristotle's works. His *Doctrines of the Natural Philosophers* is the basic source of all history of ancient philosophy.

Thrasyllus of Alexandria: A.D. 14-27. Platonic scholar, mathematician and astrologer. Wrote on Platonic and Pythagorean philosophy and music.

INDEX OF FRAGMENTS AND TESTIMONIA

GENERAL INDEX

Alcmaeon of Croton: life, work and interests, 229; Pythagorean background, 227
health as harmony, 229-30, 231
epistemology, 229-30; and that of natural philosophers, 215; contrast with Pythagoreans, 229-30; contrast with Empedocles, 230
soul, 231

Anánke (necessity) *(See Moira, Necessity)*

Anaxagoras: life and work, 168-70, 184: relation to Pericles, 169; K&R on his books, 168; style of writing, 168
scientific bent contrasted with Empedocles' mysticism, 168, and movement toward atomism, 138, 142
ontology, 170ff; and the Eleatics, 170-1; and the Atomists 181, 189, 191; and Empedocles, 181
theory of matter, 170-5, 181; and Zeno's paradoxes of divisibility, 170-1
teleology, 181
homoeomerism, 171-3; Burnet on, 172; Cornford on, 172; Guthrie on, 172; K&R on, 172; Tannery on, 172
distinction between mind and matter, 172-3
theory of mind, 172-3, 176-81; and Heraclitus' *Logos*, 176-7; and Plato on Socrates' criticism, 178; its influence on Diogenes of Apollonia, 220
cosmogony and cosmology, 173-8, and the Ionians, 173; Democritus' criticisms, 187; vortices and their effect compared with Democritus, 191
seeds, 174-5; Guthrie on, 174-5; and Empedocles elements, 142
other worlds, 175-6; K&R on, 176
epistemology, 178-9; view of sensation, 178-9
physical science, 179-80; view of nature, 179

Anaximander: life and work, 35-6
Physis as *Apeiron*, 37-9; rendering of *Apeiron*, 38-9; as involving control or steering, (*kybernon*), 40; as divine, 41
best known fragment, 39 & n; and interpretation of, 39-41; Jaeger on, 39-40; and role of *Diké*, 39; and centrality of notion of cosmos, 39-40
change, 40-1; Wheelwright on, 40-1
scientific ideas, 41-4; on creation, 41; interest in number relations, 42; relation to Pythagoras, 42, 44, 92; position of earth, 42-3; de Santillana on principle of sufficient reason, 42-3; meteorology, 43; genesis of life, 43
cosmology, 43-4; its relation to Xenophanes, 44; and Pythagoreans, 44; and Heraclitus, 44

Anaximenes: writings, 44
Physis as Air, 44-5
change: role of condensation and rarefaction, 44; Wheelwright on relation to Heraclitus, 44; quality as quantity, 45; relation to Pythagoras and pluralists, 45
cosmology and meteorology, 44-5
influence: movement toward atomism, 138; Melissus' opposition, 123; on Diogenes, 216, 217

Antiphon the Sophist: view of *Physis* as equality of all men, 260-1

Apeiron (boundless stuff): in Anaximander, 37-9; in Xenophanes, 54

Areté (virtue): 10, 244; Tyrtaeus on, 11; its interrelation with *Polis* and *Diké*, 242; as ability to persuade others required in time of Sophists, 243

Argonauts, 12

Aristippus of Cyrene, 138n.

CRITIQUES OF THE PARANORMAL

____ESP & PARAPSYCHOLOGY: A CRITICAL RE-EVALUATION *C.E.M. Hansel* $7.95

____EXTRA-TERRESTRIAL INTELLIGENCE *James L. Christian, editor*   5.95

____OBJECTIONS TO ASTROLOGY *L. Jerome & B. Bok*   3.95

____THE PSYCHOLOGY OF THE PSYCHIC *David Marks & Richard Kammann*   7.95

____PHILOSOPHY & PARAPSYCHOLOGY *J. Ludwig, editor*   8.95

HUMANISM

____ETHICS WITHOUT GOD *K. Nielsen*   4.95

____HUMANIST ALTERNATIVE *Paul Kurtz, editor*   4.95

____HUMANIST ETHICS *Morris Storer, editor*   6.95

____HUMANIST FUNERAL SERVICE *Corliss Lamont*   1.95

____HUMANIST MANIFESTOS I & II   1.95

____HUMANIST WEDDING SERVICE *Corliss Lamont*   1.50

____HUMANISTIC PSYCHOLOGY *I. David Welch, George Tate, Fred Richards,*
    editors   8.95

____MORAL PROBLEMS IN CONTEMPORARY SOCIETY *Paul Kurtz, editor*   4.95

____VOICE IN THE WILDERNESS *Corliss Lamont*   4.95

PHILOSOPHY & ETHICS

____ART OF DECEPTION *Nicholas Capaldi*   4.95

____BENEFICENT EUTHANASIA *M. Kohl, editor*   7.95

____ESTHETICS CONTEMPORARY *Richard Kostelanetz, editor*   9.95

____EXUBERANCE: A PHILOSOPHY OF HAPPINESS *Paul Kurtz*   3.00

____FREEDOM OF CHOICE AFFIRMED *Corliss Lamont*   4.95

____HUMANHOOD: ESSAYS IN BIOMEDICAL ETHICS *Joseph Fletcher*   6.95

____JOURNEYS THROUGH PHILOSOPHY *N. Capaldi & L. Navia, editors*   9.95

____MORAL EDUCATION IN THEORY & PRACTICE *Robert Hall & John Davis*   7.95

____TEACH YOURSELF PHILOSOPHY *Antony Flew*   5.95

____THINKING STRAIGHT *Antony Flew*   4.95

____WORLDS OF PLATO & ARISTOTLE *J.B. Wilbur & H.J. Allen, editors*   5.95

____WORLDS OF THE EARLY GREEK PHILOSOPHERS *J.B. Wilbur & H.J. Allen,*
    editors   5.95

SEXOLOGY

____THE FRONTIERS OF SEX RESEARCH *Vern Bullough, editor*   6.95

____NEW BILL OF SEXUAL RIGHTS & RESPONSIBILITIES *Lester Kirkendall*   1.95

____NEW SEXUAL REVOLUTION *Lester Kirkendall, editor*   4.95

____PHILOSOPHY & SEX *Robert Baker & Fred Elliston, editors*   6.95

____SEX WITHOUT LOVE: A PHILOSOPHICAL EXPLORATION *Russell Vannoy* 6.95

SKEPTICS BOOKSHELF

____ANTHOLOGY OF ATHEISM & RATIONALISM *Gordon Stein, editor*   8.95

____ATHEISM: THE CASE AGAINST GOD *George H. Smith*   6.95

____CLASSICS OF FREE THOUGHT *Paul Blanshard, editor*   5.95

____CRITIQUES OF GOD *Peter Angeles, editor*   6.95

____WHAT ABOUT GODS? (for children) *Chris Brockman*   3.95

SOCIAL ISSUES

____AGE OF AGING: A READER IN SOCIAL GERONTOLOGY

Abraham Monk, editor   8.95

____REVERSE DISCRIMINATION *Barry Gross, editor*   7.95

The books listed above can be obtained from your book dealer
or directly from Prometheus Books.
Please check off the appropriate books.
Remittance must accompany all orders from individuals.
Please include 85¢ postage and handling for each book.
(N.Y. State residents add 7% sales tax)

Send to _____
                                       (Please type or print clearly)
Address _____

City _____ State_____ Zip_____

                                              Amount Enclosed_____

 **Prometheus Books**
1203 Kensington Avenue
Buffalo, New York 14215